Settler Colonial Governance in Nineteenth-Century Victoria

Aboriginal History Incorporated
Aboriginal History Inc. is a part of the Australian Centre for Indigenous History, Research School of Social Sciences, The Australian National University, and gratefully acknowledges the support of the School of History and the National Centre for Indigenous Studies, The Australian National University. Aboriginal History Inc. is administered by an Editorial Board which is responsible for all unsigned material. Views and opinions expressed by the author are not necessarily shared by Board members.

Contacting Aboriginal History
All correspondence should be addressed to the Editors, Aboriginal History Inc., ACIH, School of History, RSSS, 9 Fellows Road (Coombs Building), Acton, ANU, 2601, or aboriginal.history@anu.edu.au.

WARNING: Readers are notified that this publication may contain names or images of deceased persons.

Settler Colonial Governance in Nineteenth-Century Victoria

Edited by Leigh Boucher and Lynette Russell

PRESS

Published by ANU Press and Aboriginal History Inc.
The Australian National University
Acton ACT 2601, Australia
Email: anupress@anu.edu.au
This title is also available online at http://press.anu.edu.au

---

National Library of Australia Cataloguing-in-Publication entry

Title: Settler colonial governance in nineteenth century Victoria / Leigh Boucher and Lynette Russell (editors).

ISBN: 9781925022346 (paperback) 9781925022353 (ebook)

Subjects: Aboriginal Australians--Victoria--Government relations--History
Aboriginal Australians--Government policy--Victoria--History
Aboriginal Australians, Treatment of--Victoria--History.
Victoria--Politics and government--19th century.

Other Creators/Contributors:
Boucher, Leigh, 1979-, editor.
Russell, Lynette, editor.

Dewey Number: 994.0049915

All rights reserved. No part of this publication may be reproduced, stored in a retrieval system or transmitted in any form or by any means, electronic, mechanical, photocopying or otherwise, without the prior permission of the publisher.

Cover design by Ivo Lovric and layout by ANU Press

This edition © 2015 ANU Press and Aboriginal History Inc.

Contents

Maps and Illustrations vii
Acknowledgements ix

Introduction: Colonial history, postcolonial theory and the
   'Aboriginal problem' in colonial Victoria 1
   Leigh Boucher and Lynette Russell

1. 'Tickpen', 'Boro Boro': Aboriginal economic engagements
   in early Melbourne 27
   Lynette Russell

2. 'Thus have been preserved numerous interesting facts that
   would otherwise have been lost': Colonisation, protection and
   William Thomas's contribution to *The Aborigines of Victoria* . 47
   Rachel Standfield

3. The 1869 *Aborigines Protection Act*: Vernacular
   ethnography and the governance of Aboriginal subjects 63
   Leigh Boucher

4. 'They formed a little family as it were':
   The Board for the Protection of Aborigines (1875–1883) . . . 95
   Samuel Furphy

5. Managing mission life, 1869–1886 117
   Claire McLisky (with Lynette Russell and Leigh Boucher)

6. Photography, authenticity and Victoria's *Aborigines
   Protection Act* (1886) 139
   Jane Lydon

7. Women, authority and power on Ramahyuck Mission,
   Victoria, 1880–1910 165
   Joanna Cruickshank and Patricia Grimshaw

8. How different was Victoria? Aboriginal 'protection' in a
   comparative context 183
   Jessie Mitchell and Ann Curthoys

9. The 'Minutes of Evidence' project: Creating collaborative
   fields of engagement with the past, present and future. . . . 203
   *Jennifer Balint, Julie Evans, Nesam McMillan,
   Giordano Nanni and Melodie Reynolds-Diarra*

Maps and Illustrations

Maps

Introduction

Kara Rasmanis' 'Aboriginal Missions and Reserves in Victoria'.		25

Illustrations

Chapter 1

Figure 1	*Hut door*, 185?, ST Gill.	29
Figure 2	*Bushman's hut*, 1864, ST Gill.	30
Figure 3	*Stockman's hut*, 1856, ST Gill.	30
Figure 4	*Journal des Voyages* (The Travel Newspaper), 1881.	41
Figure 5	*Native Dignity,* 186?, ST Gill.	44

Chapter 6

Figure 1	'Skeletons of the Gibbon. Orang. Chimpanzee. Gorilla. Man.'	140
Figure 2	Enrico Hillyer Giglioli.	142
Figure 3	'Aborigines from the environs of Lake Moira, NSW.'	144
Figure 4	'Australians of the Moama and Echuca tribes, on the river Murray.'	145
Figure 5	'Australians of Victoria, of the Yarra-Yarra tribe.'	147
Figure 6	'Portraits of Aboriginal Natives Settled at Coranderrk, near Healesville; about 42 miles from Melbourne. Upper Yarra.'	148
Figure 7	'Badger's Creek at Coranderrk Aboriginal Station, c.1870–78.'	150
Figure 8	'The Hop Paddock, Coranderrk, Victoria, from Badger Creek.'	151
Figure 9	'Hop Gardens at Coranderrk Aboriginal Station, c.1870s.'	152

Figure 10	'Annie Rees and child at Coranderrk Aboriginal Station, c.1875–76.'	158
Figure 11	'Annie Rees with her children, Maryann and Charlotte, at Coranderrk Aboriginal Station, c.1876–77.'	159
Figure 12	'Sambo and Mooney at Coranderrk Aboriginal Station, c.1875.'	160
Figure 13	'Group of Aboriginal people from Different Tribes at Coranderrk Aboriginal Station, c.1870.'	163
Figure 14	'Group portrait outside a dwelling at Coranderrk Aboriginal Station, c.1870.'	163

Acknowledgements

The editors would like to thank the speakers and participants at the workshop that underpinned this collection. This workshop was supported by funding from the Australian Research Council. The publication of this collection would not have been possible without the generous support of the Faculty of Arts at Monash University.

Introduction: Colonial history, postcolonial theory and the 'Aboriginal problem' in colonial Victoria

Leigh Boucher and Lynette Russell[1]

In 1835, members of the Kulin confederacy of the Woiwurrung (Wurundjeri), Boonwurrung, Wathaurung, Taungurong and Dja Dja Wurrung noted the arrival of strangers with some trepidation. The European intrusion was probably not a complete surprise; from the moment they arrived, members of the settlement parties lead by John Batman and John Pascoe Fawkner thought they were watched 'warily' by people who lived on and around what would soon be (mis) named the Yarra River. Moreover, recent work by Robert Kenny suggests that the Kulin were far more knowledgeable about the white interlopers than historians previously thought, prompting a rethinking of the widely held assumption that Billibellary and his fellow Kulin negotiators were fooled by Batman into signing a treaty.[2] The actions of Aboriginal people in those early years of colonisation suggests that the failed 1803 settlement at Sorrento, the presence of the small-scale European outposts along the southern coast (including the Henty family in present-day Portland), and networks of information from the north provided the Kulin with important knowledge about the coming Europeans. They knew that a force was about to impinge on their lives; however, it is unlikely that either of the parties in that 1835 encounter could have predicted the pace and depth of the devastating transformation that would unfold in the coming years.

In the decades that followed, Victoria became an historically condensed example of the creative destructions of nineteenth-century British settler colonialism in which land-hungry Britons 'bred like rabbits and settled like bad weeds' to propel what James Belich describes as a 'settler revolution'.[3] Whilst Victoria seems to represent a straightforward intensification of the patterns Belich identifies, there were local idiosyncrasies and possibilities produced by this

---

1 We would like to thank the participants in the workshop that preceeded this publication, acknowledge the work of Jordy Silverstein who provided research assistance throughout the project and express our gratitude to Geoff Hunt for his careful editorial work on all the chapters.
2 Quoted in H Anderson, *Out of the Shadow: The Career of John Pascoe Fawkner*, FW Cheshire, Melbourne, 1962: 45. Robert Kenny, 'Tricks or treats? A case for Kulin knowing in Batman's treaty', *History Australia* 5(2), 2008: 38.1–38.14.
3 Dror Wahrman, 'The meaning of the nineteenth century: Reflections on James Belich's Replenishing the Earth', *Victorian Studies* 92, 2010: 91–99.

intensification and its peculiar position in the much broader history of how Britons imagined and treated Indigenous peoples. This collection ponders the strategies and practices developed by the colonisers to govern the Aboriginal people upon whose land this demographic flood unfolded. Indeed, historians have frequently asserted that the management and control of Aboriginal people in colonial Victoria was historically exceptional; the pace of settlement, the liberal temper of colonial politics and the regime of governance that emerged as a consequence all combined to make Victoria look distinctive. While it is widely acknowledged that Victoria was the first Australian colony to develop and legislate a system of 'Aboriginal Protection', what has been less well researched is how the dynamics of settler colonisation intersected with the peculiarities of the Victorian case to shape so-called 'protection' policy and its legacies.

Victoria: Exceptional or emblematic?

Even contemporary colonists noted the speed and scale of settler incursions into the south-eastern corner of the mainland in the years between 1840 and the 1860s with a mixture of pride, astonishment and trepidation.[4] As Geoffrey Blainey notes, 'in the space of half a century ... Melbourne [grew] from a patch of grass on the river-bank to a city larger than such ancient cities of Edinburgh and Lisbon'.[5] Moreover, this was no steady increase; initial settlement and then the mid-century gold rush produced distinct demographic bulges that each forced urgent consideration of settler obligations to Aboriginal people. Only 15 years after Batman's arrival, there were already a little over 75,000 settlers in the colony – most of which had arrived in the previous decade. By 1861, this would increase sevenfold to just under 540,000.[6] Indeed, the speed and scale of pastoral colonisation after 1835 and the density of settlement after the gold rush nearly overwhelmed Aboriginal Victorians.

Caught up in this revolution, Aboriginal communities across what became the colony of Victoria in 1851 substantially suffered as the lethal materialities of settler land-hunger were compounded and amplified by the explosive impact of the gold rush. The impacts of these demographic floods (both human and animal) were brutal. As one early Protector remarked in 1845, nowhere else

---

4 See, for example, William Westgarth, *The Colony of Victoria: Its history, commerce and gold mining*, John Ferres, Melbourne, 1864. David Goodman notes that the pace of this development prompted some very anxious responses from settlers about the possibility of social disorder and disruption, in some ways, the laments about the impact of colonisation on Indigenous peoples was caught up within these fears about the 'degrading' possibilities of colonial modernity. David Goodman, *Gold Seeking: Victoria and California in the 1850s*, Allen & Unwin, St Leonards, NSW, 1994.
5 Geoffrey Blainey, *A History of Victoria*, Cambridge University Press, Melbourne, 2006: 71.
6 JC Caldwell, 'Chapter 2: Population', *Australians: Historical Statistics*, Fairfax, Syme & Weldon Associates, Broadway, 1987: 23, 2.

in the empire did 'there exist a people so helplessly situated, so degraded, so neglected, so oppressed'.[7] Even before 1835, Aboriginal people in Victoria had been affected by European presence; many had been ravaged by disease. Smallpox epidemics in the 1790s and 1820s reduced a population that probably numbered at least 60,000 and contained at least 40 distinct language groups to somewhere between 10 and 15,000 in 1835. Further depopulation was 'massive and rapid' during those first 15 years through a combination of violence and disease; by 1850, only around 1,900 Aboriginal people were recorded as having survived.[8]

Crucially, however, the settlement of Port Phillip unfolded in the same decades as humanitarian concerns about Indigenous peoples reached their peak across the British world, largely propelled by a metropolitan evangelical paternalism that asked serious questions about what Elizabeth Elbourne termed the 'sins of the settler'.[9] The patterns and practices of settler colonisation on the south-eastern mainland, even as they swiftly dispossessed Aboriginal people through violence, disease and depopulation, were always tempered by powerful discourses of evangelical protection. As Catherine Hall notes, the moral foundation of the British imperial mission in the 1830s was textured by powerful notions of responsibility and respectability that entailed an obligation to care for others; the moral epistemology of empire in these years unevenly hew together ideas about imperial expansion with a powerful obligation to care for the less fortunate. Indeed, in various moments and locations across the nineteenth century, the humane treatment of Indigenous peoples even became a signifier of colonial modernity rather than its critique.[10]

The consequences of this moral economy, though, were complex. In the settler empire, assertions of political independence and self-governance in the mid-nineteenth century were frequently articulated through a claim upon the kind of respectability Hall identifies; at the same time, though, settlers asserted their political autonomy as independent Britons in discursive contrast to the

---

7   James Dredge, *A plea on behalf of the aboriginal inhabitants of Victoria*, Geelong, 1856: 29–30. While it may well have appeared to observers like Dredge that the Kulin were oppressed, it is highly unlikely they saw themselves in that way. Certainly the later actions of head men, leaders and others suggests the Kulin always had a strong sense of their own autonomy and capacity. Indeed, it is worth remembering that the identification of the oppression and misery of Indigenous peoples was also a mechanism through which to assert British freedom and autonomy. It is little wonder that settlers were so fond of outraged statements about the oppressions of Aboriginal people in the 1840s, this was also the decade in which settlers were attempting to demonstrate their own capacity for freedom and self-rule. The 'discovery' of Aboriginal oppression could, in this way, demonstrate both humanitarian concern and discursively concretise settler autonomy.
8   A measured discussion of this can be found in Richard Broome, *Aboriginal Victorians: A History Since 1800*, Allen & Unwin, Sydney, 2005.
9   Elizabeth Elbourne, 'The sin of the settler: the 1835–36 Select Committee on Aborigines and debates over virtue and conquest in the early nineteenth-century British white settler empire', *Journal of Colonialism and Colonial History* 4(3), 2003.
10   Catherine Hall, *Civilising Subjects: Metropole and Colony in the English Imagination, 1830–1867*, Chicago University Press, Chicago, 2005: 27.

very peoples they claimed to protect and whose territory they expropriated. 'Aborigines' functioned as a powerful imaginative counterpoint for settlers to assert their status as freeborn Britons who deserved to be unshackled from the interventions of metropolitan authorities. Claiming settler self-rule became a mechanism by which Indigenous people were once again denied political and territorial sovereignty. Propelled by these local claims and their part of the wider contagion of geopolitical reconfiguration in the British world, within a generation of Batman's 'first' contact, local colonists had been granted administrative separation from New South Wales and a form of self-government that curtailed the influence of the Colonial Office on local affairs. Crucially, responsible self-government, in this case, entailed a responsibility for the governance of Indigenous peoples without the ongoing interference of London in ways that metropolitan evangelicals had worked very hard to avoid a decade before.

By 1868, settlers in Victoria had in some ways 'made good' on the promise of respectability and responsibility; the colony had developed and legislatively authorised a system of Aboriginal protection unparalleled across the settler empire. In sharp contrast to the predictions of humanitarians in Britain who feared that, unchecked by metropolitan sensibilities, colonists would descend into a state of unrepentant violence, settler autonomy in Victoria saw the development of a system of 'protection' that soon found legislative authorisation and later even provided the model for the governance of Aborigines across the Australian colonies and beyond. Indeed, settlers in Victoria – all too fond of declaring their historical exceptionalism – were soon holding up Victoria as an example of how to solve what they deemed the Aboriginal 'problem'; Victoria had become a laboratory of colonial governance.[11] The irony here was that the notion of 'Aboriginal protection' imaginatively expelled violence from the present and future political culture of the colony and, at the same time, instrumentalised the epistemological violence of settler dispossession in the everyday lives of Aborigines through a system of intimate regulation, control and repression.

In this volume then, the authors ask how a form of governance developed in Victoria after 1851 at the intersection of these local and global transformations. How, for example, did 'protection' take shape between seemingly metropolitan humanitarian concerns and local contestations and anxieties about settler respectability? In what ways did the wider economic texture of the settler revolution produce local political peculiarities? In what ways did local humanitarians negotiate between transforming imperial racial ideologies and local contests over land? Crucially, Aborigines in Victoria posed (and continue

---

11   Thomas McCombie, *Free Colonisation and Trade: Three Papers, Read before the Social Science Association*, Lowe, London, 1864.

to pose) an irresolvable problem for settler society because their mere existence was (and is) a reminder of the territorial thefts of colonisation.[12] How, then did this 'new' colonial society develop a practice of governance that both contained this central dilemma and circumvented its potential to undermine a claim on exclusive territorial sovereignty?

In part, the inspiration for this collection (and the symposium where it originated) was produced by an emerging critical mass of scholars who are working in the wake of the postcolonial turn on the history of settler colonialism in nineteenth-century Victoria. A group of scholars – shaped in part by their intellectual proximity to the interactions between the 'Melbourne School' of ethnographic history[13] and the postcolonial turn in historical writing – has begun to ponder how we might write histories of nineteenth-century Victoria that both take seriously the political and theoretical imperatives of postcolonial thought but also are attuned to the ways in which rich archival research sustains a sense of the historically idiosyncratic and provisional. It cannot be a coincidence that so much recent Australian work that takes the postcolonial turn seriously has emerged in and about Victoria. In part, the particular historical characteristics of settler colonialism in Victoria make it a rich space to consider how settlers developed specific forms of settler colonial governance; the intellectual history of Melbourne in the late twentieth century, however, must also be considered here. This collection, in some small way, functions as a testament to the important intellectual work that unfolded in Melbourne during the 1990s, when crucial postcolonial theorists like Dipesh Chakrabarty and Gayatri Spivak contributed to a robust reconsideration of colonialism and Australian scholars like Patrick Wolfe took up the challenge. The echoes of this moment, we hope, can be heard reverberating through the chapters that follow.

These echoes and legacies mean that the collection of essays differs from previous works in several key ways. The pioneering work of anthropologist Diane Barwick still provides the historiographic foundation upon which so many historians of Aboriginal Victoria build.[14] Perhaps her Canadian origins produced an outsider's orientation towards the stubborn silences and occlusions of a specific national

---

12   See Chris Healy, *Forgetting Aborigines*, University of New South Wales Press, Sydney, 2008.
13   On the development of the 'Melbourne Group', see Tom Griffiths, 'History and the creative imagination', *History Australia* 6(3), 2009: 74.1–74.16.
14   Diane Barwick, 'Economic absorption without assimilation? The case of some Melbourne part-Aboriginal families', *Oceania* 33(1), 1962: 18–23; 'Mapping the past: an atlas of Victorian clans 1835–1904', Aboriginal History 8, 1984: 100; and 'Aborigines of Victoria', in Ian Keen (ed.), *Being Black: Aboriginal Cultures in 'Settled' Australia*, Aboriginal Studies Press, Canberra, 1988: 27.

Diane Barwick's legacy should not be understated, her work has been foundational to Aboriginal studies scholars, and to Aboriginal people, especially in the state of Victoria. In many ways the work that this volume undertakes, and the larger project from which it emerges, engages with and extends the work of previous anthropologists via an historiographical framework. Just as anthropologists, Barwick in particular, were interested in understanding both Indigenous and settler frames of reference and their comprehension of

historiography; her work, and the field of Aboriginal history she helped to found, refused to ignore the experiences these racialised narratives obscured, and attempted to recast the conventions of historical research to acknowledge the needs of Indigenous peoples in the present. The work of Michael Christie, Bain Attwood and Richard Broome that emerged in her wake continued the important tradition of centralising Aboriginal experiences and stories into the accounts of colonial contact and dispossession.[15] While the authors in this collection extend and build on these important contributions, they also draw upon the resources of postcolonial theory to reconceptualise the colonial process itself. Where these authors were concerned with the retrieval of Aboriginal people's history and experiences (and for good reason), this collection refocuses the lens to carefully examine how settlers apprehended and attempted to control Aboriginal people.

Developments in postcolonial thinking clearly open out new ways to consider the connections between the governance of colonised peoples, the technologies and knowledges that enabled these practices, and the territorial imperatives of specific forms of colonial rule. However, the governance of Aboriginal people in colonial Victoria was always more complicated than the blunt manifestation of yet more European orientalism. As Robert Dixon writes, many of the scholars that take these insights seriously have become notorious for their 'high level of theoretical abstraction and generalisation, their abstruse psychoanalytic accounts of the formation of colonial subject and their correspondingly meagre historical evidence'.[16] The theoretical potency of these meta-categories of postcolonial thought needs to be balanced against carefully formulated historical accounts of colonialism's formations and instances.

Indeed, the authors in this collection are the beneficiaries of recent scholarship theorising the specific character and complexion of settler colonialism.[17] However, there is much work to be done to move beyond the discernment of cultural logics and grammars of colonialism and instead ponder how the particular territorial imperatives of settler colonialism were oriented by their historical manifestations. In a recent public forum, Tim Rowse expressed severe reservations about the reifying functionalism of settler colonial studies, noting

---

one another, so too do we aim to examine ways of thinking about the past as well as of the past (Russell and Boucher, *Victorian Ethnographers: Collecting and Contesting Racial Knowledge in the Settler Colonial Laboratory*, Australian Research Council Project DP110100076).
15   Michael Christie, *Aborigines in Colonial Victoria, 1835–1886*, Sydney University Press, Sydney, 1979; Richard Broome, *Aboriginal Victorians: A History Since 1800*, Allen & Unwin, Crows Nest, NSW, 2005; Bain Attwood, *The Making of the Aborigines*, Allen & Unwin, Sydney, 1989.
16   Robert Dixon, *Prosthetic Gods: Travel, Representation and Colonial Governance*, University of Queensland Press, St Lucia, 2001: 2.
17   Lorenzo Veracini, *Settler Colonialism: A Theoretical Overview*, Palgrave MacMillan, London, 2011, and also 'Introducing Settler Colonial Studies', *Settler Colonial Studies* 1(1), 2001: 2–3; Patrick Wolfe, 'Forum essay: land, labor, and difference: Elementary structures of race', *American Historical Review* 106(3), 2001: 866–905; Patrick Wolfe, 'Settler colonialism and the elimination of the native', *Journal of Genocide Research* 8(4), 2006: 387–409.

what he considers a disturbing trend of self-referentiality in this developing field.[18] Rowse's critique is not without foundation, the attempt to theorise settler colonialism has produced some abstracted historical engagements. At the same time, however, surely the answer to these queries is not dismissal, but rather a more thorough engagement with and interrogation of the past. For all the reifying possibilities that might be produced by heeding Wolfe's advice to consider settler colonialism a structure rather than a singular event, it also reminds us that the making of settler political and cultural worlds never resolved the contradictions of settler colonisation. It was in this constitutive unsettlement that a quite specific set of relations between metropolitan authorities, settler political claims, and Indigenous lives unfolded. The collection takes up the challenge to think about what Patrick Wolfe terms the 'structure' of settler colonialism whilst, at the same time, trying to realise its potential to theorise and historicise the constitutive and generative contradictions of settler colonialism rather than its relentless operation.[19]

In many ways, the chapters that follow might be considered examples of the kind of 'new colonial history' that Zoe Laidlaw has recently tentatively identified. For Laidlaw, 'this scholarship is concerned as much with the quotidian as the exceptional, and with individuals alongside policies and ideologies'. This work draws theoretical and methodological nourishment from the ways in which 'new imperial history' has encouraged historians to critically investigate the categories through which colonialism is manifested whilst, at the same time, carefully attending to the specific practices and actions of individuals within these world-making historical processes. For Laidlaw, this has productively recast our sense of the different classes of 'colonizers ... which can only improve future investigations of the relationships between colonizers and colonized'.[20] We hope that a closer engagement between the tradition of rich empirical work on Aboriginal history in colonial Victoria and the critical spaces that postcolonial thinking necessarily and productively wrenches open can contribute to the kind of critical historiographic deepening Laidlaw forsees. By considering the ways in which settler cultures and practices emerged at the intersection between increasing claims to autonomy from the metropole, empire-wide cultures of humanitarianism, and the blunt materialities of territorial expropriation with its attendant paradoxes and contradictions, perhaps both the exceptionalism and subsequent influence of the 'Victorian model' of governance can be explained.

---

18 Tim Rowse, 'Rethinking Indigenous Histories', Australian Historical Association Plenary Panel, 2013. http://www.abc.net.au/radionational/programs/bigideas/rethinking-indigenous-histories/4823432.
19 Patrick Wolfe, *Settler Colonialism and the Transformation of Anthropology: The Politics and Poetics of an Ethnographic Event*, Cassell, London, 1999: 3.
20 Zoe Laidlaw, 'Breaking Britannia's bounds? Law, settlers, and space in Britain's imperial historiography', *The Historical Journal* 55, 2012: 807–830.

Contact, crisis and transformation

Who, then, were the Kulin people that Batman and Fawkner 'discovered' in the area around Port Phillip Bay? The land south of the Murray River that became known as the Port Phillip Colony and then later Victoria was and remains the home to nearly 40 different language groups and clans, whose ancestors first began occupying the region over 40,000 years ago.[21] The Kulin were the groups that occupied south-central Victoria. They are made up of the Woiwurrung (Wurundjeri), Boonwurrung, Wathaurung, Taungurong and Dja Dja Wurrung with mutually intelligible languages that share up to 80 per cent of their terminology. It was the Kulin who would have the closest contact with Europeans in the years between 1835 and 1851, particularity through the agencies of the Port Phillip Protectorate that took shape in the mid-1840s.

Across what became the colony of Victoria, the picture was a little more diverse. These Aboriginal groups were comprised of various clans with their own belief systems, governance and cultural protocols. Each group was associated with their specific territory or country, and while boundaries were politically and culturally important, these were also porous and local protocols managed the movement of people across and between them. These patterns of identification and identity were a complex mosaic of cultural forms related and overlapping, yet also independent and coherent. Although economically similar (all were hunter-gatherers) these were diverse groups with their own linguistic and cultural specificities. The hubris of settler colonial knowledge meant than only much later in the nineteenth century did settlers realise the cultural and political diversity that the category 'Aborigine' had made invisible.

The south-east of Australia is one of the most fertile and resource-rich zones on the Australian continent. It is therefore likely that it was the most densely populated in the pre-contact period. The Kulin and their neighbours to the west lived in large semi-sedentary groups, adjusting their locations as seasonal foods were available. To the west we know, for example, that the Gunditjmara lived

---

21 Archaeologists estimate that south-eastern Australia has been occupied for at least 50,000 years. Aboriginal people often reject this and simply state that they have 'always been here'. For Victoria, the oldest occupation dates to between 30 and 32,000 years ago. Geoff Hewitt and Jim Allen, 'Site disturbance and archaeological integrity: The case of Bend Road, an open site in Melbourne spanning pre-Last Glacial Maximum Pleistocene to late Holocene periods', *Australian Archaeology* 70, 2010: 1–16. Similar dates were identified by Richards and others, with a possibility of occupation dating back to 40,000 years ago. Thomas Richards, Christina Pavlides, Keryn Walshe, Harry Webber and Rochelle Johnson, 'Box Gully: new evidence for Aboriginal occupation of Australia south of the Murray River prior to the last glacial maximum', *Archaeology in Oceania* 42, 2007: 1–11. However, the earliest conclusive dates for human activity in the south-east comes from just north of Victoria in the Willandra lakes region where researchers confidently assert at least 50,000 years. Kathryn E Fitzsimmons, Nicola Stern, Colin V Murray-Wallace, 'Depositional history and archaeology of the central Lake Mungo lunette, Willandra Lakes, southeast Australia', *Journal of Archaeological Science* 41, 2014: 349–364.

in villages and practised 'eel farming'.²² The Kulin and their neighbours had a complex social structure that most European observers failed to recognise. It is unsurprising that both the men that signed the 'treaty' and those that later agitated on behalf of, and spoke up for, 'their people' were all headmen or leaders, who among the Kulin nations were called *ngurungaeta*.

Although the establishment and settlement of Melbourne is often perceived as the first contact between the Kulin people and Europeans, it clearly was not. Very early contact with outsiders in the first decades of the nineteenth century had already ushered in a time of great transition and indeed crises for the Kulin nations. It is highly likely that from the last years of the eighteenth century the Kulin and other south-eastern coastal Aboriginal groups knew of Europeans via maritime visitors, particularly sealers and off-shore whalers. Cryptic clues can be found in early exploration charts. Matthew Flinders and George Bass surveyed the Australian coastline in 1798 in their boat the *Tom Thumb*. Bass annotated his chart with the term 'Sealers Cove' at Wilson's Promontory, indicating sealers were semi-permanent visitors to the region, harvesting the rich seal grounds of the south-eastern Australian coast. In a later voyage, Matthew Flinders noted in his journal for 1 May 1802 that he and two of his crew met with three unnamed Wathaurung balug men west of the stony outcrops known as the You Yangs. According to Flinders, these men were familiar with outsiders as three friendly companions approached his party 'without hesitation' and offered to trade their weapons for tobacco and European goods with a familiarity that suggests this type of engagement had already become routinised. Together with Flinders and his men they shared a meal. Flinders observed a bag of rice in one of their huts, which he took to be evidence of earlier trade with white travellers.²³ Later that year, French naval officer Nicholas Baudin, commander of the *Géographe* and *Naturaliste*, estimated that in excess of 200 sealers were working among the Bass Strait Islands and further north.²⁴

Knowledge about the presence of Europeans was unlikely to be limited to coastal communities. Traditional trade networks meandered from the Port Phillip region across the Murray River into New South Wales, westward into South Australia and beyond. Due to cultural and linguistic differences there appears to have

---

22 Harry Lourandos, 'Swamp managers of southwestern Victoria', in DJ Mulvaney and JP White (eds), *Australians to 1788*, Fairfax, Syme & Weldon, Sydney, 1987: 292–307; see also Harry Lourandos, *Continent of Hunter-Gatherers: New Perspectives in Australian Prehistory*, Cambridge University Press, Cambridge, 1997; Ian J McNiven and Damein Bell, 'Fishers and farmers: historicising the Gunditjmara freshwater fishery, western Victoria', *La Trobe Journal* 85, 2010: 83–105.
23 Matthew Flinders, *A Voyage to Terra Australis*, 2 vols, G and W Nicol, London, 1978 [1814]: 20. See also Lynette Russell, *Roving Mariners: Australian Aboriginal Whalers and Sealers in the Southern Oceans, 1790–1870*, SUNY, New York, 2012.
24 Nicholas Baudin, *The journal of post Captain Nicolas Baudin, Commander-in-Chief of the corvettes Géographe and Naturaliste, assigned by order of the government to a voyage of discovery* [trans. Christine Cornell], Libraries Board of South Australia, Adelaide, 1985 [1754–1803]. See also NJB Plomley, *The Baudin Expedition and the Tasmanian Aborigines*, 1802, Blubber Head Press, Hobart, 1983.

been less contact with the Kurnai people of the Gippsland region although there is still much work to be done about the experience of contact and dispossession amongst the Kurnai. To the north, as settlement was 'expanding', concomitant dispossession of Aboriginal land most likely created territorial pressure on the neighbouring groups to the south. Decades before the reverberations of Batman's encounter in Port Phillip travelled northward, echoes were already being felt south of the Murray from the penal colony in New South Wales and its increasingly large pastoral tentacles. The Kulin people would almost certainly have been aware of this via their traditional communications systems (and related trade routes). As Robert Kenny puts it, 'this was not the kind of news that would not travel', and indeed it did.[25]

In 1803, the Kulin witnessed the majesty of British colonisation first hand as a dismal attempt was made to settle at Sullivan's Bay near the modern township of Sorrento. The former Judge-Advocate of New South Wales, Colonel David Collins, landed from Van Diemen's Land with over 300 male convicts and free settlers, including 40 women, 38 children and a group of marine guards. The settlement was extremely short-lived, its failure assured by the lack of fresh water and timber, and the difficulties in planting and raising crops. Interactions with Kulin peoples were varied, and while the Wathaurung across on the Bellarine Peninsula were considered 'difficult', the relations with the Boonwurrung appear to have been mostly peaceful.

As others have implied, we need to consider the Kulin's response to newcomers in the mid-1830s in light of these earlier contacts. It is highly likely that the Kulin were well acquainted with Europeans and what they brought with them: goods, materials and the less appealing consequences of contact. The most destructive of the latter was, of course, what Judy Campbell describes as the 'invisible invader': disease, especially smallpox.[26] It is difficult to ascertain the precise demographic impact of this invisible threat, however, recent work suggests previous understandings have significantly underplayed both the Aboriginal population in the late eighteenth century and the subsequent impact of disease upon it.[27]

Even before the 1830s these groups were exposed to two smallpox epidemics that unfolded sometime around 1788–89 and 1829. The *ngurungaeta* and other leaders would have been desperately challenged as they witnessed high levels of unpredictable deaths. Early explorers and later observers noted that the first

---

25   Robert Kenny, 'Tricks or Treats': 38.7.
26   Judy Campbell, *Invisible Invaders: Smallpox and Other Diseases in Aboriginal Australia 1780–1880*, Melbourne University Press, Melbourne, 2002: 10, 39–50.
27   Len Smith, Janet McCalman, Ian Anderson, Sandra Smith, Joanne Evans, Gavan McCarthy, and Jane Beer, 'Fractional identities: the political arithmetic of Aboriginal Victorians', *Journal of Interdisciplinary History*, xxxviii(4), 2008: 533–551.

wave of the disease reduced the population by half. Pioneer-settler and astute observer Peter Beveridge noted how, in the 1840s, the legacies of that first late eighteenth-century epidemic could still be seen:

> All the very old aborigines in the colony show very distinct traces of small pox, and in speaking of the scourge which has so indelibly left the marks of its foul presence they say that it came with the waters, that is, it followed down the rivers in the early flood season (about July or August), laying its death clutch on every tribe in its progress until the whole country became perfectly decimated by the fell scourge.
>
> During the earlier stages of its ravages, the natives gave proper sepulchre to its victims. At last however, the death rate assumed such immense proportions, and the panic grew so great, that burying the bodies was no longer attempted, the survivors who were strong enough merely moved their camps daily, leaving the sick behind to die unattended, and the dead to fester in the sun, or as food for the wild dogs and carrion birds, which fattened to their hearts content thereon.[28]

Despite these crises, in those decades after 1835, Aboriginal people across south-eastern Australia mounted various attempts to resist the invaders. Ultimately, as Michael Christie notes, the settlers had to 'take the land by force' because resistance inevitably followed the expanding boundaries of the pastoral frontier.[29] As settlers took possession of much of Victoria, a pattern of sporadic violence and conflict unfolded in which Aboriginal people usually focused their resistance on livestock but suffered severe retributions at the hands of frustrated settlers as a consequence. By the mid-1840s, however, most of this violence was confined to the Western Districts and Gippsland.[30] Aboriginal people soon realised that survival would require a complete transformation of their everyday existence and this became even more apparent as the gold rushes unfolded. These were, as Broome drily suggests, 'wild-times' in which Aboriginal people struggled to find a sure footing.[31]

Less than two decades after Batman and his companions arrived in Melbourne the official Aboriginal population was recorded as fewer than 2,000.[32] It is difficult to comprehend the grief and exhaustion that must have reverberated through Aboriginal communities in these early decades; those who managed to survive had witnessed the death of the majority of their kin and needed to quickly develop ways to carve out an existence within a speedily transforming

---

28 Peter Beveridge, 'The Aborigines and Small Pox', *The Argus*, 27 January 1877: 5.
29 Michael Christie, *Aborigines in Colonial Victoria*: 59.
30 On these zones of violence on the Western Districts see Jan Critchett, *A 'Distant Field of Murder': Western District Frontiers, 1834–1848*, Melbourne University Press, Carlton, 1990.
31 Critchett, *A 'Distant Field of Murder'*: 84.
32 In 1853 1,907 Aboriginal people were recorded for the region. Smith et al., 'Fractional identities': 539.

settler colonial social, cultural and economic system. The subsequent arrival of hundreds of thousands of gold prospectors and vast numbers of pastoralists meant access to traditional hunting and gathering lands was quickly curtailed. Violence and disease continued to exact a high mortality and with relatively few births the Indigenous population dramatically declined. The scale of depopulation and the inevitable social and cultural crises it must have produced must be remembered when we consider the ways in which settlers could exert so much control over Aboriginal lives so soon after 'first settlement'.

However, a year after the arrival of Batman and Fawkner, a different kind of force began to make its impact felt upon Australian shores; the politically uneasy influence of humanitarians would be felt by settlers and Aborigines alike. The attempt to temper the violent edges of colonisation across the empire was given its most concrete expression in the House of Commons *Report from the Select Committee on Aborigines (British Settlements)*. The 1837 report, greeted with disdain and outrage by settlers in other colonies, made forceful arguments for the humanitarian management of the impact of British settlement because the 'wild times' of Port Phillip were a common story.

In part because formal settlement in Port Phillip unfolded at the same time as this apogee of humanitarian intervention across the empire, protectors were sent to the fledgling colony to act as some kind of buffer between the territorial hunger of settlers and the Indigenous population struggling to remake their worlds in such a short space of time. The Colonial Office appointed George Augustus Robinson to lead the Port Phillip Protectorate with four Assistant Protectors to act in the interests of Aboriginal people in colonial courts and assist Aboriginal communities in adjusting to colonial society.[33] Robinson and his fellow protectors hoped the distribution of rations would encourage them to settle in one place.[34] Thus also began the first attempts at ethnographic study as Robinson and the others began to consider the precise racial 'character' of their charges.[35] Their ethnographic interests and expertise, however, did not seem to arm them with the means to achieve their ambitions. Massively under-resourced and faced with declining budgets from 1843, by about 1846 it was clear the Protectorate was going to fail.

In the years after the decline of the Protectorate, missionaries began to make their impact felt in Victoria. Unity of Brethren missionaries from the Moravian Church (a Protestant denomination) arrived from Germany and established a

---

33   Although officially referred to as Assistant Protectors (of the Aborigines), William Thomas, Edward Parker, James Dredge and Charles Wightman Sievwright are often simply referred to as Protectors. These four were managed and supervised by the Chief Protector of the Aborigines George Augustus Robinson.
34   See Christie, *Aborigines in Colonial Victoria*: 106.
35   Close connection between ethnographic imagination and colonial governance would remain strong for the next six decades.

mission at Lake Boga in 1851. Local Anglicans followed suit with a mission at Yelta on the Murray in 1855. Both Lake Boga and Yelta were failures, but after returning to Germany, the Boga missionaries returned and began again with the Ebenezer mission in the Wimmera in 1859. That same year, the Victorian Legislative Council directed a select committee to inquire into the conditions of Aboriginal people; the report painted a damning picture of hardship and despair. The solution, its chair Thomas McCombie suggested, would be a system of reserves that formalised what was already developing through ad-hoc missionary intervention and the under-resourced legacies of the first efforts at 'protection'. The Victorian legislature agreed, providing the means for the instantiation of the Central Board for the Protection of Aborigines to both manage the Aboriginal population and begin the work of setting aside lands for reserves and missions. The Kulin had, in fact, engaged in a campaign for land with the remaining protector William Thomas since 1850 and met with various colonial administrators in the late 1850s and early 1860s, but the Board provided a crucial bureaucratic nexus through which surveyors could be engaged, missionaries found and gazettings produced.[36]

The 1860s thus witnessed the ravaged Aboriginal communities in Victoria becoming subject to ever more close management in a system of reserves and missions, this formalised the mechanisms of governance that would mediate the settler colonial encounter for the next century in Victoria. By 1863, the Board collected reports from seven different reserves and managed the distribution of rations at a further 23 depots across the colonies. Five of the missions were run by missionaries paid for by specific churches and the other two were government controlled. By the early 1860s, the survivors of the 'culture of terror' that Barry Morris suggests always accompanied frontier expansion became subject to a local practice of governance that had evolved at a meeting point between settler self-interest, ad-hoc colonial bureaucracy and missionary intervention.[37]

The Board thus formalised perhaps the most coherent framework for the governance of Aboriginal people in the Australian colonies; it also began to produce the kinds of archives of governance with which students of colonialism are so familiar. Aboriginal people were increasingly surveilled and monitored after 1860 and, by 1868, Victorian parliamentarians approved this system with legislation that was, according to some historians, 'simply another agent of dispossession'.[38] This system forcefully moved Aboriginal people onto the missions and reserves and, as a consequence, both further smoothed settler access to Indigenous space and took intimate control over Aboriginal lives. The legislation empowered the Board, and through it the missionaries and station

---

36 This point made by Richard Broome, *Aboriginal Victorians*: 186.
37 Barry Morris, 'Frontier colonialism as a culture of terror', *Journal of Australian Studies*, 1992: 72–87.
38 Smith et al., 'Fractional identities': 551.

managers, to regulate where Aboriginal people lived, their mode and location of employment, their contractual relationships with settlers and, in a haunting prediction of the horrors of the stolen generations, gave these 'protectors' the 'care [and] custody of [all] Aboriginal children' in Victoria. So too, the development of this framework for governance and its associated (but uneven) bureaucracy supported (if not produced) an endless ethnographic chatter about Aboriginal people in colonial public life. It is no coincidence that colonial Victoria became a hotbed of the kinds of ethnographic enquiry that Jane Lydon investigates; as colonial administrators struggled to figure out how to manage the Aboriginal problem, a variety of self-proclaimed ethnographic experts promised to provide answers in a language of race.[39]

Less than two decades later, and after a series of controversies over the management of the reserves in the 1880s, parliament passed legislation that only further (mis)managed the racial arithmetic of the colony. So-called 'half-castes' were expelled from the mission and reserve system in an attempt to weaken the rumblings of political protest in the reserves by once again rearranging Aboriginal communities. The *Aborigines Protection Act 1886* (Vic), the 'Half-Caste Act', moved a group of people previously characterised as Aboriginal into a borderline category that seemed to infer a future in which they could be absorbed in the white community. As Katherine Ellinghaus shows, this kind of thinking would have a tremendous impact on the lives of Aboriginal peoples; station managers and missionaries exerted increasing control over the marriages of Aboriginal people in ways that attempted to enact this racial disappearance.[40] The authors of the Act clearly imagined a colonial future without Aboriginal people, and empowered the Board to control Aboriginal lives in ways that would manufacture this settler fantasy.

From the 1860s, then, the governance of Aboriginal people on the mission and reserve system provided a new mechanism for the settler state to take possession of Aboriginal people as well as their territory. Missionaries and station managers had tremendous power and usually understood themselves to be engaged in a mission to transform their charges through a project of intimate reform. As Bain Attwood notes, these institutions were designed to remake Aboriginal people through careful management and control. As a consequence, the 'seeds of oppression came to lie within Aborigines as well as without; making the task of liberating themselves even more herculean'.[41] Life on the missions and reserves, however, was much more complicated than the legislative and bureaucratic framework upon which it rested. The politics of personality always remade

---

39   Jane Lydon, *Eye Contact: Photographing Indigenous Australians*, Duke University Press, Durham, 2005.
40   Katherine Ellinghaus, 'Regulating Koori marriages: the 1886 Victorian Aborigines Protection Act', *Journal of Australian Studies* 67, 2001: 22–29.
41   Bain Attwood, *Making of the Aborigines*, 31.

these projects of governance, and the specific religious inflections of particular missions reworked these regimes of progressive governance. As Peter Sherlock remarks, 'missionaries did not always act in the interests of the imperial power in whose colonies they laboured' and we are only just beginning to unpick how the histories of specific missions inflected the practices of colonial governance in this period.[42]

The mission and reserve system also nourished important possibilities of resistance amongst Aboriginal communities. Armed with increasing knowledge of the colonial system, Aboriginal people rebelled in a variety of ways, ranging from potent collective protests about the management of reserves to 'eloquent' individual campaigns to reconnect with family members who were separated by the vagaries of the reserve system.[43] Moreover, recent painstaking work by demographers and historians suggests that the reserve system also provided the best possibility of Aboriginal survival in this period. Whilst the Board only assumed control over about half the Aboriginal population in Victoria in 1868, the population on the reserves remained fairly steady. Most contemporary Aboriginal Victorians trace their heritage to this original group, suggesting that those living outside the reserve system found it very difficult to physically or culturally survive in a colonial system that made access to their traditional resources ever more difficult.[44]

The attempts to recast colonial governance by its subjects faced an uphill battle that was shaped by more than demography alone. Aboriginal lives in colonial Victoria were inevitably and consistently governed by an imperative over which they had little control – insatiable settler hunger for the land. Even as the system of protection smoothed settler access to territory (and also attempted to contain a morally troubling population), land-hungry settlers began to covet the reserves that offered such miniscule compensation to the dispossessed. As the 1886 Act legislatively reduced the number people defined as Aboriginal, it consequently reduced the population on the reserves, satisfying the land-hungry settlers who neighboured the apparently 'troublesome' Coranderrk Aboriginal Station and had been coveting this land for over a decade. The

---

42 Peter Sherlock, 'Missions, colonialism and the politics of agency', in *Evangelists of Empire? Missionaries in Colonial History*, Amanda Barry, Joanna Cruickshank, Andrew Brown-May and Patricia Grimshaw (eds), eScholarship Research Centre in collaboration with the Schools of Historical Studies, Melbourne, 2008: 14.
43 'Eloquent' from Joanna Cruickshank, '"A most lowering thing for a lady": aspiring to respectable whiteness on Ramahyuck Mission', in Jane Carey and Claire McLisky (eds) *Creating White Australia*, Sydney University Press, Sydney, 2008: 95.
44 Important work by Penelope Edmonds traces how hard colonial authorities worked to manage Aboriginal people in the streets of Melbourne, *Urbanizing Frontiers: Indigenous Peoples and settlers in 19th-century Pacific Rim Cities*, UBC Press, Vancouver, 2010. However, we should also be suspicious about assuming that Aboriginal people could not survive outside the reserve system – though it is highly likely that this strategy of survival may have come at the cost of continued recognition as Aboriginal by colonial authorities and that ties to existing communities may have been lost. See Richard Broome, 'Aboriginal workers on southeastern frontiers', *Australian Historical Studies* 26(103), 1994: 202–220.

Act was, in some ways, a bureaucratic manoeuvre that provided a powerful justification to reduce the Kulin's meagre territory even further. This moment of blunt administrative reconfiguration reminds us how, texturing this history of governance, the knowledge upon which it depended, the practices through which it was enacted, and even the personalities that attempted to resist and recast it, was a seemingly structural territorial imperative that was far less distinctive than this local history might make it seem. Indeed, the specific form of colonisation that was unfolding here and the mechanisms of governance that were shaped by it, has a much wider history. It is to these much broader historical forces – and the ways in which postcolonial thinking has helped us to theorise their operation – that we now turn.

Settler colonialism, race and the governance of colonised peoples

The question of territory and land, it should be clear, was a bluntly organising principle for the interactions between settlers and Indigenous peoples in Victoria. As Denoon noted many decades ago, this was an encounter in which Britons sought to expropriate the ground under Aborigines' feet rather than to transform the local population into a productive labour force or trade with their existing economies for imperial benefit. Indeed, settler cultures, as Lynette Russell has elsewhere argued, often constructed narratives and developed policies based on the notion that settlers were taking possession of unoccupied or virgin territories – how else could such wholesale occupations be justified?[45] As Fiona Bateman and Lionel Pilkington describe, the 'discourse of settler colonialism describes how, fortified by modernizing narratives and ideology, a population from the metropole moves to occupy a territory and fashion a new society in a space conceptualised as vacant and free'.[46] The settler practice of renaming Indigenous landscapes violently reveals the extent of these imperialist delusions of political and cultural vacancy.[47] So too, legal cultures emerged from the late eighteenth century that upheld the rights of settlers to take control over the land and convert it to alienable private property; as Julie Evans notes, this usually involved an usurpation, if not outright denial, of Indigenous sovereignty.[48] It is little wonder, then, that Wolfe's discernment

---

45   Lynette Russell, 'Introduction', in Lynette Russell (ed.), *Colonial Frontiers: Indigenous-European Encounters in Settler Societies*, Manchester University Press, Manchester, 2001: 1–10.
46   Fiona Bateman and Lionel Pilkington, 'Introduction', in Fiona Bateman and Lionel Pilkington (eds), *Studies in Settler Colonialism: Politics, Identity and Culture*, Palgrave Macmillan, London, 2011: 2.
47   On the ambivalence and complexity of place names see Samuel Furphy, 'Aboriginal house names and settler Australian identity', *Journal of Australian Studies* 72, 2002: 59–68.
48   See Julie Evans, 'The formation of privilege and exclusion in settler states: Land, law, political rights and Indigenous peoples in nineteenth-century Western Australia and Natal', in Marcia Langton (ed.), *Honour*

of a 'logic of elimination' at the heart of the settler enterprise has become a powerful organising trope amongst students of settler colonialism; territorial hunger had little space for Indigenous peoples, and, more disturbingly, their mere survival functioned as a form of resistance to the settler enterprise that required psychological, cultural and legal suppression.

Settler cultures, then, had to work hard to make colonialism look both coherent and legitimate – in fact, like anything other than brute force. The maintenance of these settler entitlements (and the denial of Indigenous sovereignties) inevitably involved what Scott Lauria Morgenson terms a series of intellectual 'ruses' to make them look coherent.[49] These ruses could take a variety of forms – the most obvious being the notion of the 'dying race' that so powerfully fantasised about the inevitable disappearance of the Aboriginal problem whilst also justifying specific practices of governance that would enact it.[50] Moreover, Indigenous peoples across the settler world could always function as a constant reminder of the great territorial theft at the heart of this project. Writing from a North American perspective, Philip Deloria and Renee Bergland thus argue that settler encroachments into Indigenous territories inevitably dramatised the possibility of their own illegitimacy.[51] The importance, then, of Indigenous peoples to the imaginative lives of settlers should be no surprise. They were both a signifier of territorial belonging and dangerously imperilled the possibility that settlers could inhabit this position of legitimacy. Not only were Indigenous peoples, a 'major problem to be solved' in settler cultural and political life, they also occupied a particularly volatile discursive and psychic position in the settler imaginary.[52]

Ideas about and the treatment of Indigenous peoples were inevitably shaped by these imperatives and contradictions. Because settlers came to stay, Indigenous peoples had to be incorporated within settler regimes of sovereignty; not least because any competing claim on political autonomy could be an unmanageable reminder of the illegitimacy of settler colonialism. In an Australian context,

---

among Nations: Treaties and Agreements with Indigenous People, Melbourne University Press, Carlton, 2004.
49   Scott Lauria Morgensen, *Spaces between Us: Queer Settler Colonialism and Indigenous Decolonization*, University of Minnesota Press, Minneapolis, 2011: 17.
50   Russell McGregor, *Imagined Destinies: Aboriginal Australians and the Doomed Race Theory*, Melbourne University Press, Melbourne, 1997.
51   Renee Bergland, *The National Uncanny: Indian Ghosts and American Subjects*, University Press of New England, Hanover, 2000; Philip Deloria, *Indians in Unexpected Places*, University Press of Kansas, Lawrence, 2006.
52   'Problem to be solved' from Bateman and Pilkington, 'Introduction': 12. On the Australian Broadcasting Commission's topical television program *Q&A*, 9 June 2014, Rosalie Kunoth-Monks, Aboriginal elder and former actor, eloquently demonstrated that for many settler Australians there remains a perception that Aboriginal people continue to be a problem (to be solved): 'I have a culture, I am a cultured person ... I am not something that fell out of the sky for the pleasure of somebody putting another culture into this cultured being.' Referring to the documentary work of John Pilger she noted, that there was: 'an ongoing denial of me ... Don't try and suppress me, and don't call me a problem, I am not the problem.'

the possibility that Indigenous peoples might not be incorporated within the colonial polity was dismissed in settler jurisprudence in the early nineteenth century.[53] On the other hand, this incorporation was usually tempered by legal exceptions. Indigenous peoples frequently found themselves restricted to specific territories, subject to specific laws, and denied the rights of their apparent fellow subjects. As Morgan Brigg suggests, Aboriginal people in Australia have long been 'designated and governed as an excluded-inclusion in [the settler] political community' because complete incorporation was both legally mandated and psychically impossible.[54] The political problem of the 'Aborigine' could only be completely resolved by their elimination. Whilst the 'logic of elimination' that Wolfe identifies was rarely enacted by frontier homicide alone, the legal and political restrictions that tempered such a violent expression of settlerism also generated creative mechanisms to 'demographically erode' a politically unsettling Indigenous constituency including:

> territorial removal and/or confinement, the imposition of regimes of private property ... discourses of miscegenation, Native citizenship, child abduction, total institutional surveillance ... intensive educational programmes, religious conversion and related assimilationist interventions.[55]

Moreover, as Evans, Grimshaw, Phillips and Swain reveal, the uneven distribution of political rights to Indigenous peoples in British settler polities in the nineteenth century always aided and upheld the economic and political imperatives of British settlement.[56] Racially specific exclusions to the rights of subjecthood, restrictions on enfranchisement, confinement to specific territories, uneven applications of legislation through practices of policing, and the application of racially oriented (but formally unspecified) vagrancy laws were all deployed to limit the rights and capacities of Indigenous peoples across the British settler world.[57] Ideas about race, unsurprisingly, became a crucial mechanism to justify these legal exceptions as 'race restore[d] the inequality that the extension of citizenship [or in the British case, subjecthood] had theoretically abolished'. The explosion of racialising discourses and practices that always accompanied settler colonialism were inevitable products of a regime desperately managing its own contradictions. These ideas, however, were produced through and by colonialism's operation rather than preceding

---

53   Lisa Ford, *Settler Sovereignty: Jurisdiction and Indigenous People in America and Australia, 1788–1836*, Harvard University Press, Harvard, 2010.
54   Morgan Brigg, 'Biopolitics meets terrapolitics: political ontologies and governance in settler-colonial Australia', *Australian Journal of Political Science* 42(3), 2007: 404.
55   Patrick Wolfe, 'Race and the trace of history', in Fiona Bateman and Lionel Pilkington (eds), *Studies in Settler Colonialism*, Palgrave Macmillan, London, 2011: 272.
56   Julie Evans et al., *Equal Subjects, Unequal Rights: Indigenous Peoples in British Settler Societies*, Manchester University Press, Manchester, 2003: 2.
57   See Edmonds, *Urbanizing Frontiers*.

it – race was and is, to return to Wolfe, 'colonialism speaking' (continuously, it should be noted).[58] Whilst postcolonial scholars have long noted the fabrication of racial categories as a mechanism of colonial rule, the specific imperatives of these colonialisms always oriented their meaning and vocabularies.[59]

Underlying structures, the cultural constitution of meaning, the actions of the colonial state, and the management of specific populations are the kinds of processes that find their analytic fulcrum in a theorisation of governance, a term with increasing visibility in colonial studies in recent decades. According to Julia Emberley, governance can be understood as the practices that 'manage, regulate and govern' colonised peoples in ways that secure the colonial political order.[60] There are, of course, glimmers of Michel Foucault in this turn. Whilst not all scholars of colonial governance would necessarily orient themselves in relation to a narrow Foucauldianism, the rise of 'governance' as an analytic frame has occurred alongside (and has been nurtured by) the rediscovery of Foucault's notion of governmentality in a variety of fields. Mitchell Dean argues that by the mid-1990s, it seemed a term whose time had arrived because studies of governmentality ask:

> how we govern and how we are governed, and with the relation between the government of ourselves, the government of others, and the government of the state.[61]

In the classic Foucauldian turn, however, the very population to be governed is produced by these practices rather than simply being acted upon by them; acknowledging the ways in which the category 'Aboriginal Victorians' flattened (and flattens) out the complex practices of identification amongst and between the Kulin and their neighbours is a powerful reminder of the connections between knowledge, governance and the dispossessing imperatives of settler colonialism. Putting this another way, the possibility of regulating and managing Aboriginal people was produced by the constitution of a category to perceive them.[62] The ethnographic activity that flourished in the colonies was necessarily entangled within these procedures of governance. The relentless commissions of enquiry, reports and commissions upon which so many colonial historians now depend are thus not only evidence of the ways Aboriginal people were governed, but the part of the cultural work that made Aboriginal people governable subjects in the first place.

---

58 Patrick Wolfe, 'Race and the trace of history': 275.
59 Sherene Razack, 'When place becomes race', in Sherene Razack (ed.), *Race, Space and the Law*, Between the Lines, Toronto, 2002: 4.
60 Julia V Emberley, 'The Bourgeois family, Aboriginal women, and colonial governance in Canada: a study in feminist historical and cultural materialism', *Signs* 27(1), Autumn 2001: 61.
61 Mitchell Dean, *Governmentality: Power and Rule in Modern Society*, Sage, London, 1999: 3.
62 A similar point to that made by Bain Attwood in *The Making of the Aborigines*.

Importantly, the notion of governance implies that the state is not the only, or perhaps not even the most important, historical (f)actor at play in the management of colonial lives. As Sebastian Conrad and Marion Strange suggest, governance has evolved into a key concept in colonial studies because the term is

> used to refer to processes and structures of regulation and rule that ... are not exclusively based on hierarchically organized government action, but instead involve ... modes of action by private, semiprivate, and public actors.[63]

Unlike Foucault's notion of governmentality – or at least in the ways it has been used in political science – investigating colonial governance (as distinct from the colonial state and its always imperfect machinery) has opened out the possibility of considering the ways in which colonised peoples were variously 'managed' in accordance with the imperatives of colonial rule in a variety of ways and how a broader cultural mentality granted these variegated actions a contemporaneous consonance.

This is particularly relevant in colonial contexts like Victoria in the nineteenth century; the machinery of the state was often playing 'catch up' to try and contain the development of settlement, and the mechanisms of governance were always limited by the willingness of the settler polity to fund them. The readiness of missionaries to perform the work of colonial governance, then, found ample support with the colonial political elite; so too, the governance of Aboriginal people in colonial Victoria outside the mission system relied on a network of Aboriginal Protectors who sometimes performed these duties alongside a variety of other colonial offices.

The settlers shaping the governance of Aboriginal people, then, were not faceless examples of a disciplined and disinterested colonial bureaucracy (which is so often inferred by studies of colonial governance that take their cues from Foucault), they were interested individuals who brought personal and institutional agendas into an imperfectly defined and sometimes contradictory political field. Indeed, they were closely and intimately entangled with Aboriginal people. These were the 'tense and tender ties', to take Ann Laura Stoler's phrase, that were both the sites through which the governance of colonised peoples unfolded, and the sites of anxiety about their possible disruptions.[64]

---

[63] Sebastian Conrad and Marion Strange, 'Governance and colonial rule', in Thomas Risse (ed.), *Governance Without a State: Policies and Politics in Areas of Limited Statehood*, Columbia University Press, New York, 2011: 41.

[64] Ann Laura Stoler, 'Tense and tender ties: The politics of comparison in North American history and (post)colonial studies', *Journal of American History* 88(3), 2001: 829–865.

Indeed, the notion of governance allows us to consider how shaky and imperfect the management of Indigenous populations could often be. As Andrew Sharp notes, studies of the transposition of British government to its colonies has often focused on an

> array of impersonal and abstract instruments – sovereignty, the rule of law, natural rights – not least because such instruments can have quite concrete effects in establishing the terms of intelligibility ... for the exercise of colonial rule.

But as Sharp argues, we also need to carefully consider the ways in which colonial governance relied on a much wider set of practices for its operation. The concerns and politics of individuals always shaped these histories. Nowhere is this more visible than in the ways specific religious cultures reoriented and sometimes completely reworked specific colonial imperatives.[65] Aboriginal people – whilst subject to British jurisdiction after 1836 – were caught within an 'increasingly complex field of social governance' that managed their lives according to a variety of political and social imperatives. Protection policies – and the colonial spaces they instantiated – produced zones of exception for the governance of Aboriginal peoples; Aboriginal people were simultaneously subject to legislative regimes that granted the colonial state additional 'powers' over their lives and devolved the enactment of this power to missionaries whose cultural connections to the colonial enterprise were ambivalent at best.[66]

Centralising the question of governance, and the ways in which its changing formations attempted to legitimate settler colonialism and, ironically, could never quite manage to resolve its contradictions, offers the chance to both more carefully historicise the 'structures' to which Denoon and Wolfe drew our attention and, perhaps, reconfigure how we might deploy them as both method and historical explanation. Indeed, in some ways the work in this collection suggests that it might be time to reconfigure how we understand and read the structure to which Denoon and Wolfe drew our attention so powerfully. Writing in the mid-1990s, Denoon reflected that neither 'marxist [n]or orthodox scholarship' seemed able to offer 'satisfying explanations' for the specific formations and relations of settler colonialism. Indeed, he even suggested that his own work had been a 'flawed response' to that challenge.[67] Denoon

---

65 Andrew Sharp, 'Samuel Marsden's civility: The transposition of Anglican civil authority to Australasia', in Shaunnagh Dorsett and Ian Hunter (eds), *Law and Politics in British Colonial Thought: Transpositions of Empire*, Palgrave Macmillan, London, 2010.
66 Mark Finnane, 'The limits of jurisdiction', in Shaunnagh Dorsett and Ian Hunter (eds), *Law and Politics in British Colonial Thought: Transpositions of Empire*, Palgrave Macmillan, London, 2010.
67 Donald Denoon, 'An accidental historian', *The Journal of Pacific Studies* 20, 1996: 209–212.

and Wolfe, even as their work might – in some readings – suggest a kind of structural determinism, still force historians to try and account for the ways in which settlerism produced specific ways of being and thinking.[68]

More recently, Lisa Ford has argued for a return to 'empiricism' as an attempt to 'deal more honestly' with the governance of Indigenous people. For Ford, we need to reject the notion 'that settler states were ever total institutions and that settler colonialism is a structure bent inexorably on dispossession, subordination, erasure or extinction'.[69] For Ford, then, the choice that historians face is between 'structures' and 'empirical' idiosyncrasies. What might happen, though, if we recognise that the terms under which Aboriginal people were rendered empirically visible were artefacts of the colonial encounter itself whilst, at the same time, we acknowledge these discursive fabrications could never quite manage to smooth out the contradictions that inhered within settler colonialism. The structures about which Ford and others now express reservations do not have to be read for the ways in which they did or did not 'achieve their "aims"'. Rather, we could acknowledge that the terms under which settler governance would be imagined, fabricated and instrumentalised were contradictory from the start, and, in these contradictions might have even been historically generative.

A new colonial history of Victoria

The contributors in this collection and the preceding symposium were asked to consider three key registers of governance. These were broadly described as 'Cultures of Knowledge and Ethnography'; 'Bureaucratic and Legislative Frameworks'; and, 'Governing the Everyday'.[70] Thinking about the relationships between and across these 'registers', we hoped, might throw open useful questions about the relationship between ideas and practice, metropole and colony, settler and Indigenous.

In the discussion that closed the symposium, the question of Indigenous agency unsurprisingly emerged as a key political and psychological knot. After all,

---

68   Wolfe's interventions, moreover, need to be read against and within the context of late twentieth-century Australian politics – these were powerful and influential interventions into an historiographic landscape that sought an easy integration of Aborigines into the Australian political settlement. Wolfe reminded scholars to pay attention to the terms under which such an incorporation was offered and the long history of the ways in which these discursive terms were constituted by settler colonialism rather than offering a chance to resolve it.
69   Lisa Ford, 'Locating indigenous self-determination in the margins of settler sovereignty: An introduction', in Lisa Ford and Tim Rowse (eds), *Between Indigenous and Settler Governance*, Routledge, Oxon, 2013: 1–11.
70   These foci emerged out of a larger project being undertaken by Russell and Boucher examining the development of anthropological thought within Victoria in the period 1835–1915. As this project developed, the intersection between understandings of race and the governance and control of Aboriginal people became a core concern.

if we are – in different ways – committed to a broadly postcolonial approach (politically and theoretically), surely the retrieval of Aboriginal voices from the nineteenth century is a crucial project; importantly, contributors in this collection display a keen awareness of the ways in which the 'categories' of nineteenth-century colonial governance referred to and became people, with lives and experiences that deserve recognition. Perhaps, though, there is a careful distinction to be drawn between the political credibility of our studies in the present and the historical arguments we make about the past. Aboriginal people in the nineteenth century were struggling to survive, let alone reconstitute the ideals and practices of governance that were reshaping their lives. 'Discovering' Aboriginal agency in the constitution of colonial governance across its variegated registers after 1851 could severely underplay the almost unbearable discursive and material weight Aboriginal people had to bear in the nineteenth century simply to exist; these historical subjects were withstanding enough without asking them to retrospectively sustain politically blaming stories of agency and resistance to smooth the consciences of academic historians. Our political commitments, perhaps, should shape the kinds of questions we ask rather than the answers we find. Considering the form and impact these answers have in the present might be a more productive use of our analytic energies. For this reason, this collection includes important discussions of the dilemmas and possibilities of re-presenting these histories in our settler colonial present. It would underplay the weight of these forces, though, to suggest that Aborigines in Victoria were the central agents in development of practices of governance that settlers developed to contain them.

While the volume is organised chronologically those three initial themes thread throughout the narrative. Contributors Rachel Standfield and Jane Lydon explore the cultures of knowledge. Standfield's chapter is concerned with the ethnographic observations of William Thomas, Protector and later Guardian of Aborigines from 1839 through to the 1860s. Focusing on Thomas's contribution to the classic Victorian ethnographic compendium *The Aborigines of Victoria*,[71] she convincingly traces knowledge networks and considers how anthropological knowledge served as a handmaiden to colonial governance. Jane Lydon via the work of the cosmopolitan intellectual Italian Enrico Giglioli considers the role that visualisation and photography in particular had on the discourses of authenticity and the development of the *Aborigines Protection Act 1886* (Vic).

Several chapters are concerned with legislation and bureaucracy and the emergence of new governance practices and how these were shaped by local and wider racial cultures. Leigh Boucher considers the role of humanitarianism in

---

71 Robert Brough Smyth, *The Aborigines of Victoria: with notes relating to the habits of the natives of other parts of Australia and Tasmania compiled from various sources for the Government of Victoria*, John Ferres, Government Printer, Melbourne, 1878.

the period between 1851 and 1869 to contextualise and historicise the *Aborigines Protection Act 1869* (Vic) as a moment that attempted to reconcile the seemingly contradictory inheritances of evangelical concern and liberal governance. By contrast, Samuel Furphy traces the complex relationships that were key to the functioning of the Board for the Protection of Aborigines in the period after the 1869 Act and up to the emergence of the second Act in 1886. As Furphy shows, there was an intimacy and expediency to the structure of the Board in which the personal remade the political.

Three chapters are concerned with governing the everyday. The first is Lynette Russell's chapter which examines the economic relationships that Kulin people had with European society, primarily in the early colonial period. Melbourne was, she argues, an econoscape that the Kulin manipulated and negotiated in ways that were often misunderstood by the settler colonialists. In the chapter by Claire McLisky (with Russell and Boucher) the management of mission life in the period between the two Acts is examined in detail. In contrast to previous studies, this chapter moves beyond single mission sites and attempts a comparative analysis. Rather than suggesting that the missions offered sanctuary and 'home', Aboriginal people were keenly aware that they had few rights with regard to residence and freedom of movement. The chapter by Patricia Grimshaw and Joanna Cruickshank return to a single mission site – Ramahyuck in Gippsland. Considering a later period, 1890–1910, these authors examine the role of gender, in particular the women missionaries, and how this affected authority and power as it played out in the late nineteenth century.

The final two chapters open up the discussion to consider the impact of the Victorian 'case'. Ann Curthoys and Jessie Mitchell consider the exceptionalism of Victoria's models of governance and compare it to other settler colonial locations. These authors argue that Victoria was indeed distinctive and the governance models were widely influential. In part the distinctiveness emerged as a consequence of the rapid demographic shifts mentioned above. This was married to the development of a deeply urbane and metropolitan culture of the mid-nineteenth century (facilitated by the enormous wealth of the gold rush). In the contribution by Jennifer Balint, Julie Evans, Nesam McMillan, Giordano Nanni and Melodie Reynolds-Diarra we move into the contemporary ramification of this kind of historical research. They discuss how the verbatim theatre production *Coranderrk: We Will Show the Country* and the project from which this emerged might be an exemplar of both Aboriginal community engagement and partnership research. This chapter perhaps most importantly demonstrates that these debates are not mere dry history but for contemporary Aboriginal communities these represent tangible links between the past and the present.

This volume of essays presents a complex picture of settler colonial governance in nineteenth-century Victoria; it might well be called an unsettled history as, despite the colonial fantasy of pacification, protection and settlement the picture that emerges here is filled with idiosyncrasies, contradictions and inconsistences. While the contributors innovatively theorise and historicise settler colonialism and the governance of Aboriginal people, they do so with careful consideration of previous work. Threaded throughout the collection the 'logic of elimination' jostles with the historical specificity of Victorian Aboriginal history, revealing a complex mosaic of historical phenomena that ripple far beyond the colonial boundaries of the Port Phillip district. Future work will, no doubt, extend this even further, however, we are confident that the papers that follow are timely interventions into a regional history that has broader implications for studies of settler colonialism.

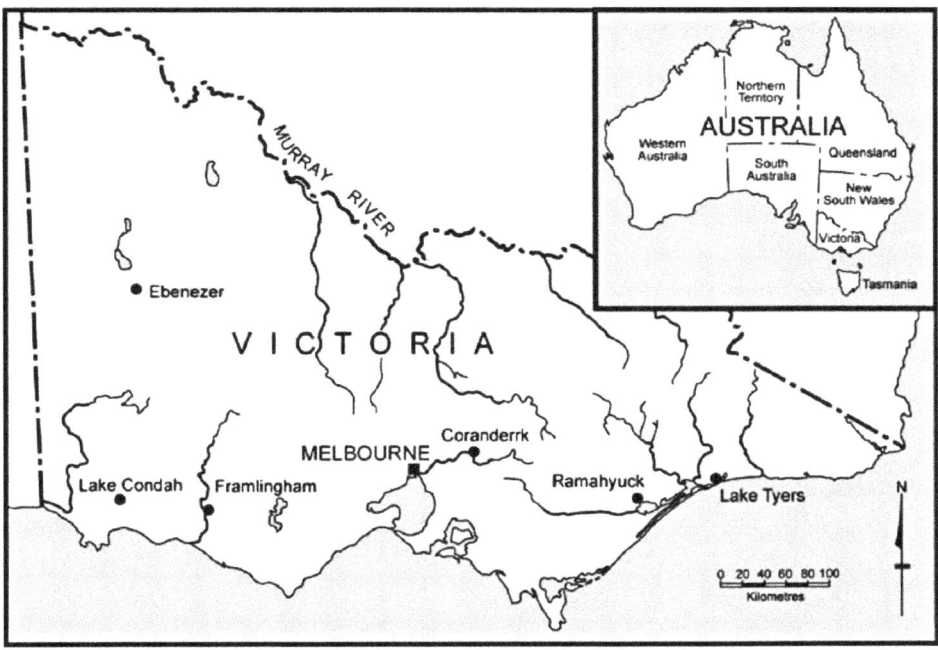

Kara Rasmanis' 'Aboriginal Missions and Reserves in Victoria', printed in Jane Lydon and Alan Burns, 'Memories of the past, visions of the future: Changing views of Ebenezer Mission, Victoria, Australia'.

Source: *International Journal of Historical Archaeology* 14, 2010: 39–55, reproduced with kind permission from Springer Science and Business Media.

1. 'Tickpen',[1] 'Boro Boro':[2] Aboriginal economic engagements in early Melbourne

Lynette Russell

European colonisation of south-eastern Australia brought Aboriginal people into contact with a vast array of new material culture items. These were often first introduced via 'gift giving' and exchange in an attempt to create and cement social alliances. Many Aboriginal people engaged in the new economy including the cash economy via trade and exchange, employment and what the Europeans described as begging. For the most part such engagements have not been systematically studied or analysed. In Melbourne, Kulin people used a form of economic action that Europeans perceived to be 'begging' as a means to engage with the settler economy from the very earliest days of contact. Although there were other mechanisms used by Aboriginal people to obtain funds and material culture, begging was highly visible and tended to elicit negative responses from the settlers. In this chapter, I explore Aboriginal economic engagement and what was described as begging. I argue that this was far from a mere opportunistic strategy for the acquisition of money, food and other goods, but was perceived by the Kulin as a viable, justifiable form of economic engagement – a kind of reciprocity for what they had lost. This was both economic entrepreneurialism and agency as the Kulin shifted their traditional econoscape to accommodate the new resources presented by European colonisation. In using the term econoscape I am drawing on the working of Arjun Appadurri, via the Australian analysis of Rae Norris.[3] An econoscape refers to the mode of production, its variability and capacity to change. It is overlain with cultural relevance and recognises that different cultural groups will perceive these differently. I use this term to describe the economic landscape of the Kulin. This framework allows an interrogation of three interwoven themes: begging and reciprocity; wages, employment and begging; and finally, the longevity of begging as a form of economic engagement.

---

1 *The Age*, 10 December 1883: 5.
2 'William Adeney diary sketch, Aborigines in Melbourne, 1843', William Adeney diary, State Library of Victoria (SLV), MS 8520: 306.
3 Rae Norris, 'The More Things Change: Continuity in Australian Indigenous Employment Disadvantage, 1788–1967', unpublished PhD thesis, Griffith University, 2006: 4; Rae Norris, *The More Things Change: The Origins and Impact of Australian Indigenous Economic Exclusion*, Post Pressed, Mt Gravatt, Queensland, 2010. See also Rae Norris, 'Australian Indigenous employment disadvantage: What, why and where to from here?', *Journal of Economic and Social Policy* 5(2), Article 2, 2001.

Images, paintings and etchings created by Europeans in the nineteenth century often featured Aboriginal people either begging or otherwise soliciting food, money and the benevolence of white settlers. Undoubtedly such images also depicted the supposed charity and generosity, as well as superiority, of the European settlers. Most of these are rural images highlighting the persistent historical (though erroneous) leitmotif that after the establishment of European cities Aboriginal people were confined to the edges and fringes of urban settlements. One particularly well-known and often exhibited image, painted in Adelaide by Alexander Schramm in 1850, is entitled *A Scene in South Australia*. Another, also in Adelaide, dated to 1857 was Charles Hill's tellingly entitled *The First Lesson*. In this image, a mother demonstrates to her children the importance of charity and kindness. These two paintings illustrate that pastoral care and Aboriginal welfare had always been a responsibility – as such they are both nostalgic and mythic. These images ostensibly created after the closure of the frontier can be seen to illustrate contact as benevolent and indeed charitable. In Victoria one of the most prolific nineteenth-century artists, ST Gill, produced several similar examples, in which Aboriginal people's wellbeing appears to be predicated on European largesse (Figures 1, 2, 3). In each of Gill's images, seated Aboriginal people are depicted on the margins of settler's huts, visually occupying a liminal space between two worlds – the domestic-internal and wild-outside. They sit between the old and the new, in subservient poses I take to imply begging. Aboriginal people are shown as dependent, dispossessed and figuratively marginal, while their dislocation from traditional modes of economy sees them unable to supply themselves with food, perhaps seeking employment, assistance and benevolence.

On the Melbourne streets from the beginning of first settlement in 1835, Europeans disapprovingly observed and commented on Aboriginal people 'soliciting sixpences'. This did not end, as was intended, with establishment of reserves and missions in the 1860s.[4] Even decades later, in the 1880s, as members of the Board for the Protection of the Aborigines visited Coranderrk Aboriginal Station at Healesville they observed a remarkable continuity. According to a contemporary report in *The Age*:

> An ancient warrior [known as] … Pretty Boy … [whose] principle acquaintance with the English language seemed to consist of being able to say "Gib it tickpen", and until that coin was handed over the visitors knew no peace'.[5]

---

4 An article in *The Argus*, 13 September 1860, described Aboriginal people as 'soliciting sixpences from township to township'. Leigh Boucher and I used this phrase in our article, '"Soliciting sixpences from township to township": Moral dilemmas in mid-nineteenth-century Melbourne', *Postcolonial Studies* 15(2), 2012: 149–165.
5 *The Age*, 10 December 1883: 5.

Figure 1: *Hut door*, 185?, ST Gill.

Source: National Library of Australia, nla.pic-an2351777.

Figure 2: *Bushman's hut*, 1864, ST Gill.

Source: National Library of Australia, nla.pic-an7150080.

Figure 3: *Stockman's hut*, 1856, ST Gill.

Source: National Library of Australia, nla.pic-an7178362.

It would seem that 'begging', as the Europeans called it, was an effective strategy for securing what was wanted.

In Melbourne's early days, as the embryonic city developed, the lives of the Kulin people were irrevocably changed.[6] The rapid nature of this development meant that the impact on the Kulin was pronounced and dramatic.[7] Disease and violence devastated the population and the survivors (often thought of as 'remnants') became a source of anxiety and concern for the European émigrés.[8] As explored elsewhere in this book, in the late 1830s humanitarian concerns led to the establishment of the Aboriginal Protectorate system which, at least in theory if not practice, aimed to remove the Kulin from the streets of Melbourne and deliver them to locales where they might be Christianised, educated, controlled and governed. Yet into the mid-1850s and beyond, Aboriginal people remained an unwelcome and uncontrolled feature of urban street life. The first mission station along the Yarra River, near the present-day botanical gardens, was close enough for groups to readily enter the fledgling city.[9] Similarly, the nearby presence of communities of Aboriginal people around Port Phillip Bay meant they had easy access to the city and its public spaces. Melbourne's officials instituted numerous mechanisms to confine Aboriginal people and keep them out of the urban environs. As Penelope Edmonds has clearly demonstrated, even into the 1850s Aboriginal presence on Melbourne's streets remained a concern to the governing authorities.[10] A major part of that concern was the activity of begging.

---

6   The Kulin people is a confederation of five related Aboriginal communities. They are known as the Woiwurrung (now called the Wurundjeri), the Boonwurrung, Taungurong, Wathaurung and the Dja Dja Wurrung. They occupied the area known now as south-central Victoria and included the location of present-day Melbourne. Information from the Department of Planning and Community Affairs: Aboriginal Affairs. See also Lynette Russell and Ian J McNiven, 'The Wurundjeri of Melbourne and Port Phillip', in J Fitzpatrick (ed.), *Encyclopaedia of World's Endangered Indigenous People*, Greenwood, New York, 2001.

7   The speed of Melbourne's development and its metropolitan nature is well documented in Asa Briggs, Victorian Cities, Harmondsworth, Penguin, 1968: 280; Geoffrey Serle, *The Golden Age: A History of the Colony of Victoria 1851–1861*, Melbourne University Press, Melbourne, 1963: 382; Edmund Finn, *The Chronicles of Early Melbourne*, centennial edition, Vols 1–3, Heritage Publications, Melbourne, 1976 [1888]; Thomas McCombie, *A History of the Colony of Victoria*, Sands and Kenny, Melbourne, 1858: 1.

8   Thousands of years of isolation meant that the Kulin were highly susceptible to a range of European diseases including influenza, smallpox, tuberculosis and syphilis. Coupled with violence, this massively reduced the population. While many regard the destruction to have been as great as 80–90 per cent, some more conservative estimates still claim a reduction in the population of least 50 per cent in the first two decades. See Richard Broome, 'Victoria', in Ann McGrath (ed.), *Contested Ground: Australian Aborigines under the British Crown*, Allen & Unwin, St Leonards, 1995; and Lyndall Ryan, 'Settler massacres on the Port Phillip frontier, 1836–1851', *Journal of Australian Studies* 34(3), 2010: 257–273.

9   AGL Shaw, *Victoria Before Separation: A History of the Port Phillip District*, Miegunyah Press, Carlton South, 1996: 115–116.

10 Penelope Edmonds, *Urbanizing Frontiers: Indigenous People and Settlers in 19th-Century Pacific Rim Cities*, University of British Colombia Press, Vancouver, 2010: 88.

Begging and reciprocity

European settlers in Melbourne were troubled by daily encounters that involved what *The Argus* newspaper often termed 'begging', which as Richard Broome observes, was more likely seen by Aboriginal people as a kind of reciprocal exchange for their dispossession, relocation and the disruption of their traditional hunting and gathering practices.[11] Wesleyan missionary Reverend Joseph Orton, writing in the mid-1830s, described the clash of worlds and the catastrophic impact this had on the Aboriginal economy. According to his reckoning, those that stayed near to Europeans in the 'settled districts [had] become pilfering – starving – obtrusive mendicants'.[12] Chief Protector of Aborigines, George Augustus Robinson, reflected that if whites were now hunting kangaroos, which were food for the Kulin, why then would the Kulin not be entitled to 'hunt sheep'.[13] Rev. Orton's point concurs with Robinson's idea of reciprocity, as he observed, the Aboriginal people:

> are almost in a state of starvation and can only obtain food day by day, by begging or hunting. The latter mode is however almost abandoned on account of their game being driven away by the encroachments of settlers, and the roots on which they used to partially feed have been destroyed by sheep.[14]

Henry Reynolds has shown that although many Aboriginal groups met the encroaching pastoral advance violently, others used what might be described as covert forms of resistance.[15] These included subtle weapons such as ritual and magic and the 'granting' of sexual favours which incurred reciprocity and obligation. Many of these forms of engagement and resistance were in a sense invisible to the Europeans.[16] Not all early black–white interactions, however, can be regarded as domination and resistance.[17] From the beginning of settlement significant numbers of Aboriginal men and women deliberately engaged with the society of the white newcomers and entered into the colonial economy as

---

11 Richard Broome, *Aboriginal Victorians: A History Since 1800*, Allen & Unwin, Sydney, 2005.
12 Michael Cannon (ed.), *Historical Records of Victoria (HRV)*, Volume 2A, The Aborigines of Port Phillip 1835–1839, Victorian Government Printer, Melbourne, 1982: 116–123.
13 In Shaw, *Before Separation*: 139.
14 *HRV*, Vol 2A: 122.
15 Henry Reynolds, *The Other Side of the Frontier*, University of Queensland Press, Brisbane, 1981: 108–109.
16 Ian McNiven and I have previously explored the role of these unseen forms of resistance see 'Ritual response: rock art, sorcery and ceremony on the Australian colonial frontier', in M Wilson and B David (eds), *Constructed Landscapes; Rock-Art, Place and Identity*, University of Hawaii Press, Honolulu, 2002: 27–41.
17 In my book *Savage Imaginings* I explore the discourses of resistance/domination/acculturation/assimilation at length, in short my argument is that these can not be easily distinguished from each other. See *Savage Imaginings: Historical and Contemporary Representations of Australian Aboriginalities*, Australian Scholarly Publications, Kew, 2001.

'economic agents'.[18] The exemplary work of Penelope Edmonds documented Kulin clan members venturing into Melbourne to 'barter, buy munitions, exchange their labour, and sell goods such as skins and lyrebird feathers'.[19] While some of the early colonists directly engaged Aboriginal people, it was usually on casual labour contracts. I suggest that these new entanglements were how the Kulin transformed their traditional hunting and gathering activities and accommodated the influx of new resources and new pressures and created a new econoscape. Fred Cahir, concentrating on the mid-century goldfields has indicated that actions 'construed as begging' were part of a cultural tradition that enmeshed and obligated newcomers, settlers and other non-Indigenous people to engage with local traditional owners by sharing food, supplies, tobacco, and so on.[20]

Miner Walter Bridges perceptively described the new econoscape in 1855. On the Ballarat goldfields, Bridges recorded an exchange that offers a neat summing up of how Aboriginal people might have perceived the act of begging or soliciting. He wrote:

> My mother and wife and small boy that come out from England with us was standing at the tent one day all alone, no other tents near when they saw a mob of native Blacks and Lubrias [lubras] … So up they come yabbering good day Missie You my countary [country] woman now… Blacks said You gotum needle missie you gotum thread you Gotum tea you Gotum sugar you Gotum Bacca [tobacco]. So Mother had to say yes to get rid of them and had to give them all they asked for …[21]

Bridges' family had pitched their tent on Aboriginal land[22] and it is clear from this interaction that the clan saw this as meaning they had rights to the miner's possessions. By referring to Bridges' mother as 'country woman', the Aboriginal people were emphasising that they were now related to each other and as kin, they the traditional owners were entitled to be provided with supplies. This activity of soliciting supplies or begging is an extension of the earlier exchanges,

---

18 I cover the idea of Aboriginal people engaging in the new colonial economic system in my book *Roving Mariners: Aboriginal Whaler and Sealers, in the Southern Oceans 1790–1870*, SUNY Press, New York, 2012.
19 Edmonds, *Urbanizing Frontiers*: 125, 138. Edmonds also notes that a man known as 'Pigeon' knew what were acceptable wages and complained vociferously when he had not been paid.
20 Fred Cahir, *Black Gold: Aboriginal People on the Goldfields of Victoria, 1850–1870*, Aboriginal History Inc. and ANU E Press, Canberra, 2012: 16.
21 Cahir, Black Gold: 16. Cahir is more ambivalent about this event arguing that: 'It is difficult, however, to discern how much of this invoking of kinship ties … had as much to do with opportunism and how much with the cultural rituals of sharing one's goods'. This event is also quoted in Ian D Clark and David A Cahir, 'Aboriginal people, gold, and tourism: the benefits of inclusiveness for Goldfields tourism in regional Victoria', *Tourism, Culture & Communication* 4(3), 2003: 132.
22 According to Clark the Keyeet baluk, a sub-group of the Burrumbeet baluk, a Wathaurung-speaking clan lived at Mt Buninyong. See Ian D Clark, 'Another Side of Eureka – the Aboriginal presence on the Ballarat goldfields in 1854 – Were Aboriginal people involved in the Eureka rebellion?', University of Ballarat, School of Business, Working Paper 2005/07.

which included gift giving as a way to create alliances and indebtedness. Gift giving as a means to secure relationships and engagements with Aboriginal people was a characteristic of early Victorian contact relations. Indeed Batman's illegitimate treaty was based on the settlers' assumption that they were entering into gift giving in exchange for land.[23] Though as Bain Attwood observed, it is highly unlikely the Kulin thought this is what the gift exchange involved. The Kulin, like other central and western Victorian Aboriginal groups, practised the tanderrum ceremony which was a diplomatic ritual involving hospitality and gift exchange.[24] Rather than being naïve about the meaning of Batman's treaty, Diane Barwick suggested the clan heads believed they were conducting a tanderrum, allowing the Europeans non-permanent access and use of their lands.[25] Two years later, in March 1837 when Governor Bourke toured the Port Phillip colony he continued the tradition, distributing blankets and clothing and issued the gift of 'four brass plates as honorary distinctions for good conduct'.[26]

EM Curr recalled of Melbourne in 1839 that Aboriginal people were a feature of the street life. He wrote that:

> These once free-born lords of the soil seemed to make themselves useful under the new *régime* by chopping firewood, bringing brooms for barter, and occasional buckets of water from the Yarra; and might be seen a little before sundown retiring to their camps on the outskirts of the town, well supplied with bread and meat …[27]

According to Curr both the Kulin and the settlers benefited from this arrangement. For the Aboriginal people it facilitated access to certain European goods, while the settlers obtained useful objects and materials. Assistant Protector of the Aborigines William Thomas commented in September 1840 that Aboriginal people were securing all they needed in Melbourne, which made relocating

---

23 For a comprehensive history and analysis of this 'Treaty' see Bain Attwood (with Helen Doyle), *Possession: Batman's Treaty and the Matter of History*, Miegunyah Press, Melbourne, 2009. See also James Boyce, *1835: The Founding of Melbourne & the Conquest of Australia*, Black Inc, Melbourne, 2011; James Bonwick, *John Batman the Founder of Victoria*, Wren, Melbourne, 1868.
24 Ian Clark, *Sharing History: A Sense for All Australians of a Shared Ownership of Their History*, Key Issues, no. 4: Council of Aboriginal Reconciliation, Australian Government Publishing Service, Canberra, 1994.
25 Diane Barwick, 'Mapping the past: an atlas of the Victorian clans 1835–1904, Part 1', *Aboriginal History* 8(2), 1984: 122. See also Robert Kenny, 'Tricks or treats? A case for Kulin knowing in Batman's treaty', *History Australia* 5(2), 2008, Monash University Epress.
26 *Historical Records of Victoria*, Volume 1, The Beginnings of Permanent Government, Victorian Government Printer, Melbourne, 1982: 102, March 8th 1837.
27 EM Curr, *Recollections of Squatting Days in Victoria, then called Port Phillip District from 1841 to 1851*, George Robertson, Melbourne, 1883: 21. Penelope Edmonds, however, has shown that there were many instances where 'beggars' went empty handed, or worse were subjected to violence.

them to distant sites much more difficult. He wrote: 'The fact is that ... [they] are so bountifully supplied by Melbournians that they not only get lazy but dainty, no longer begging bullocks' heads, sheep heads etc'.[28]

In this period Thomas was attempting to move the Kulin people from the township to a station at Arthur's Seat on the Mornington Peninsula 75 kilometres from Melbourne. Begging or the acquisition of food and provisions was sufficiently attractive to many Kulin that being persuaded to move proved difficult for Thomas.

In contrast, arriving in 1840, William Westgarth did not see any reciprocal benefits for colonists or the Kulin:

> The natives still strolled into Melbourne at the time of my arrival, and for a couple of years or so after; but they were prohibited about the time of the institution of the corporation, as their non-conformity in attire – to speak in a decent way – their temptations from offers of drink by thoughtless colonists, and their inveterate begging, began soon to make them a public nuisance.[29]

Westgarth, who demonstrated an almost evangelical zeal for improving society, was part of the intellectual elite that was then forming in Melbourne. He was one of the proponents of the Melbourne Mechanics Institute and went on to found a Benevolent Society. His interest in Aboriginal culture spanned both ethnographic and humanitarian perspectives and led him to publish a sympathetic and concerned booklet, *Report on the Condition, Capabilities and Prospects of the Australian Aborigines*.[30] Part of Westgarth's concern for Aboriginal welfare stemmed from his observations of what he termed begging and vagrancy. As Edmonds notes, 'begging and public nuisance' were constant concerns for the Protectors and other officials.[31] Indeed, she cogently argues that this was a key element in the establishment of reserves on land some distance from Melbourne. Furthermore, violence was regularly meted out to many Aboriginal 'beggars', often condoned or at the very least ignored by the authorities.

---

28   Quoted in Marie Hansen Fels, *'I Succeeded Once': The Aboriginal Protectorate on the Mornington Peninsula, 1839–1840*, Aboriginal History Monograph 22, Canberra, ANU E Press, 2011: 112.
29   William Westgarth, *Personal Recollections of Early Melbourne and Victoria*, George Robertson & Co., Melbourne, 1888: 9.
30   William Westgarth, *Report on the Condition, Capabilities and Prospects of the Australian Aborigines*, William Clarke, Melbourne, 1846. Geoffrey Serle, 'Westgarth, William (1815–1889)', *Australian Dictionary of Biography*, National Centre of Biography, The Australian National University, http://adb.anu.edu.au/biography/westgarth-william-4830/text8057, accessed 3 January 2013.
31   Edmonds, *Urbanizing Frontiers*: 126–127.

William Adeney was a contemporary of Curr and Westgarth, who in 1842 had recently arrived from London, and intended to 'take up' land in Western Victoria. In his earliest days in Melbourne he made a diary entry of a scene he had witnessed:

> I was sitting writing a letter the other day and rose to peep through between the blind and window frame to see how the day looked out of doors when at the same moment a black horrible looking face suddenly came into very close proximity to mine but on the other side of the glass. It was that of an old native woman who activated by the same curiosity as my own no doubt wished to see through the same aperture what was inside. As it happened I was regularly startled and could not imagine for a moment what it was. The old woman was as much surprised as I was and after gazing with open mouth a few seconds said boro boro but what she wanted I could not understand … [they are often seen] accosting passers by with "give me black money" and various other similar expressions begging bread.[32]

The term 'boro boro' is fascinating as a form of begging. To borrow (from which I take it this word drawn) is generally used to refer to taking and using something that belongs to someone else. There is the implicit assumption that the borrowed item will be returned. Not wishing to extend the analogy too far, it is nonetheless possible that this is a continuation of the expectation of reciprocity.

Aboriginal people were clearly aware that the presence of Europeans and the development of the city of Melbourne had disadvantaged them; that their lives had been fundamentally changed. They had been dispossessed without payment. In 1858, when the Victorian Select Committee into the condition of Aboriginal people collected evidence and testimony, politician William Hull observed that Boonwurrung elder Derrimut was alive and 'lay about in St Kilda'. According to Hull, Derrimut had said 'give me shilling, Mr Hull'. Hull refused, offering instead to 'give [him] some bread'. Derrimut fatalistically responded that:

> 'Derrimut soon die,' and then he pointed with a plaintive manner [to the area surrounding them] … 'You see, My Hull, all this mine, all along here Derrimut's once; no matter now, me soon tumble down'.[33]

---

32 Edmonds, *Urbanizing Frontiers*: 46; also Adeney diary, the extensive diary entry includes with it a delicate pen and ink sketch of an Aboriginal man, woman and small dog. 'William Adeney diary sketch, Aborigines in Melbourne, 1843', SLV MS 8520: 296–307.
33 Quoted in Ian Clark's article, '"You have all this place, no good have children…" Derrimut: traitor, saviour or a man of his people?', *Journal of the Royal Australian Historical Society*, 91(2), December 2005: 107–132. Quote on p. 177.

Wages, employment and begging

In the first few decades of European settlement there were few options for paid employment, though some Aboriginal people found work in tanneries, as farm labourers and bullock drivers.[34] In 1836, George Langhorne on the first government mission school, in an attempt to encourage the Kulin to attend, gave out rations, food and blankets. He emphasised that should they choose to work a few extra hours they would receive extra rations. Langhorne was convinced that by bringing the Kulin into a European economic system they would learn to value labour as an exchange for goods and rations.[35] For the most part, attempts to impose economic engagement failed. However, in those instances where Aboriginal people themselves exerted autonomy and control (limited as it undoubtedly was) they were more likely to succeed. Curr, above, offered an example of Kulin agency and autonomy when he noted that cutting wood had become a means of obtaining resources for men while some Aboriginal women were employed as domestic servants. For the most part, what little employment was available tended to be seasonal and cyclical.[36]

The most significant shift came with the 1850s gold rush when Aboriginal people could be recruited for harvesting and other work as so many European men headed to central Victoria to make their fortunes. Outside of Melbourne on the actual goldfields Aboriginal people (in particular Dja Dja Wurrung clan members) found work as trackers and native police.[37] In his expansive analysis of black and white relations on the goldfields, Cahir records a range of ways that Aboriginal people made money.[38] Aside from wood and bark cutting they did domestic service, laundry, labouring, babysitting, as well as manufacturing and selling baskets, possum skin cloaks and producing Corroborees as staged fee-for-service events.[39] However, many Aboriginal people were still regarded as 'neglected and degraded', as a correspondent in the *Gold Diggers' Monthly Magazine* of 1853 observed. They were perceived as beggars and intemperate vagrants:

---

34 Alan Pope, 'Aboriginal adaptation to early colonial labour markets: The South Australian experience', Labour History 54, May 1988: 1–15. See also Broome, *Aboriginal Victorians*: 148–149; R Castle and J Hagan, 'Centuries of Aboriginal unemployment in NSW', *Modern Unionist* 8, June 1983: 19, 52. For an excellent discussion of the colonial representations of Indigenous people as 'naturally idle' see Syed Hussein Alatas, *The Myth of the Lazy Native*, F Cass, London, 1977: 9.
35 Edmonds, *Urbanizing Frontiers*: 88.
36 Broome, *Aboriginal Victorians*: 148–149.
37 Cahir, *Black Gold*: 47–56.
38 Cahir, *Black Gold*: 67–72.
39 Cahir, *Black Gold*: 81–83.

> [Whose] revelries and quarrels disturb the camp at night, and disease, misery, violence and even murder follow in the train. We [Europeans] were horrified at the sight of an expiring blackfellow – the victim of the preceding night's drunken fracas.[40]

Associating drunkenness and violence with begging is a common theme in these descriptions.

As Edmonds has noted, vagrancy laws were only applied to white people who attempted to live around or loiter near Aboriginal people. Vagrancy laws – not applied to Aboriginal people – in a sense confirm the fact that they could not be homeless *per se*, as they were *sui generis* 'at home' – living on **their** country. It was prohibited to sell Aboriginal people alcohol, which as Penelope Edmonds notes was at odds with their status as British subjects.[41] However, concerns over Aboriginal drunkenness led to the administration of 'peremptory punishments' for those Kulin 'who drank excessively and caused serious disturbance'.[42]

Rarely, Aboriginal people's work was both admired and even celebrated. In the 1840s a group of young Aboriginal men (infantilised at the time as the 'Black Boys') were responsible for the construction of an important bridge across the Merri Creek, near to the Merri Creek Aboriginal School and the Yarra Bend Asylum.[43] The Merri Creek Aboriginal School was one of the earliest institutions in Victoria dedicated to the education of the Kulin people. Begun in 1845, the school sought to Christianise and educate, as well as enable a sort of self-sufficiency from the produce gardens and stock. When Edward Peacock, founding schoolmaster of the Merri Creek Aboriginal School, left in 1848 he was replaced by Francis Edgar who had arrived from Hobart accompanied by his wife, daughter Lucy and mother-in-law. Lucy wrote a detailed memoir 15 years after the family left in 1851. Although her memories are of her childhood adventures and the domestic circumstances of the family, aspects of her narrative are very useful.

According to Lucy Edgar, until 1848, crossing the Merri Creek was achieved by negotiating some gum tree logs that had been wedged together to form a makeshift bridge. A precarious hand rail had been added but many people were anxious about crossing. This presented an opportunity for the Kulin youths

---

40 Cited in Clark and Cahir, 'Aboriginal people, gold, and tourism': 130.
41 Edmonds, *Urbanizing Frontiers*: 151.
42 William Lonsdale in 1836, *HRV*, Vol 2A: 201, cited in Edmonds, *Urbanizing Frontiers*: 151.
43 Today the site where the Merri Creek Aboriginal School sat, is dominated by the footings of the Eastern Freeway bridge, constructed in the 1970s. No remains have been located of the school (or the nearby Aboriginal Protectorate Station) and it is most likely that the freeway construction and the redirection of the Yarra River has destroyed all evidence.

based at the school. According to Lucy Edgar: 'Little Jemmy had earned a good deal [of money] carrying passengers backwards and forwards in our cart, when the creek was not too high'.[44]

Unfortunately, heavy summer rains in 1848 saw the log bridge washed away.[45] The schoolmaster decided that he would oversee the construction of a new, serviceable and long-lasting bridge. On seeing how proud Jemmy was at 'earning' money, Schoolmaster Edgar insisted that only the labour of the Merri Creek Aboriginal students would be used:

> [He] called them [the 'black boys'] together, explained the project, and offered them wages at the rate of fourpence per diem for their work at the bridge, provided there was no sulking, and no necessity for driving them to it … their labour was persevering, so earnest. They never were lazy when called to work at the bridge – never sulky, never grumbling. And it must be remembered that this was all extra work; there was the stock to attend to, the harvest to get in, the garden to keep in order, all the same; and it was only in the afternoons they could work out of doors, because of their morning lessons. It was on account of it being extra work that wages were given.[46]

Lucy Edgar describes the construction of the bridge and the great pride the Kulin men had in their achievement. When the bridge opened in November 1849 the Chief Protector of the Aborigines George Augustus Robinson and his daughters attended.[47] The five bridge builders who remained at the Merri Creek Aboriginal School received payment for their bridge and in an act I regarded as attenuated economic independence and agency, instituted a toll system for anyone crossing the bridge.

> The boys were accustomed, after the completion of the bridge to run out when they saw passengers about to cross it, and demand a toll. They were always alert to their dues; they did not ask any particular sum, but took whatever was offered, and they ran in to show their gains. 'Me got white money this time – him gentleman;' or 'Him only poor fellar – give me penny'. And everyone seemed willing to add his mite [sic] towards remunerating the boys, remarking [on] the excellence of the structure.[48]

---

44   Lucy A Edgar, *Among the Black Boys; Being The History of an Attempt At Civilising Some Young Aborigines of Australia*, Emily Faithful, London, 1865: 48–53.
45   Edgar, *Among the Black Boys*; see also Ian Clark and Toby Heydon, *A Bend in the Yarra: A History of the Merri Creek Protectorate Station and Merri Creek Aboriginal School 1841–1851*, Aboriginal Studies Press, Canberra, 2004: 71–72; see also Thomas, 30 November 1848, Public Record Office Victoria (PROV), VPRS 44/P, Unit 669.
46   Edgar, *Among the Black Boys*: 49.
47   George Augustus Robinson Journal, 5 June 1849.
48   Edgar, *Among the Black Boys*: 54.

The 'black boys' in constructing the Merri Creek bridge were not merely using the European streetscape as their econoscape. In this instance they were creating an opportunity to control the movements of the Europeans and in so doing secure for themselves extra resources. The actions of the 'black boys' standing on the bridge demanding money was not described as begging, on the contrary it appears that those crossing bridge and the Edgars themselves saw this as a fair exchange. That they accepted a sliding scale of payments depending on whether those crossing were 'poor fellars' or 'gentlemen' certainly suggests that the Kulin were astutely engaged in the socio-economics of the situation.

Late nineteenth-century begging

Although instances of Aboriginal people on the Melbourne streets are rare in the 1880s, I have located two examples, both of which relate to begging associated with the Melbourne International Exhibition. The Exhibition, for which the world famous Melbourne Exhibition Building was designed, was held from 1 October 1880 until 30 April 1881. Despite the fact that many Aboriginal people were by this time housed in the reserve system, and in particular at Coranderrk, Kulin people frequented the area – perhaps attracted by the large number of well-heeled visitors. A writer in *The Argus* noted:

> It must be confessed that if our visitors are to judge the Victorian aboriginal from such specimens as may happen to be visible in, or about, Melbourne during this Exhibition time, they may be confirmed in the conclusion that he is all they have been taught to believe him ... For civilisation has not agreed with him. Contact with the white man ... has made him too familiar with the white man's habits, his vices, and his diseases. As he stands clad in the white man's cast-off rags, gibbering out a request for white money, there is none of the nobility of the savage about him. He is only an unpicturesque vagrant ...[49]

The newspapers of the day do not suggest a significant rise in the incidence of begging as recorded in court and magistrate reports and it is likely that this was mostly treated outside of the court/legal system. It is clear, however, that there were Aboriginal people begging in Melbourne, connected to the Exhibition, as depicted in the overt visual image which appeared in a French journal in 1881 (Figure 4).

---

49   *The Argus*, 17 December 1880, Supplement: 55.

1. 'Tickpen', 'Boro Boro': Aboriginal economic engagements

Figure 4: *Journal des Voyages* (The Travel Newspaper), 1881.

Source: Author's personal copy.

The title page of *Journal des Voyages* (The Travel Newspaper) carried an image of a group of Aboriginal people dressed in what appear to be cast-off (ragged) clothes begging for money which is tossed to them by a well-dressed woman.[50] The article is entitled: 'Throughout Australia – Melbourne Exhibition – The country's beggars'. The accompanying text notes:

> Everything in this city of 430,000 souls, save for the width of the streets, reminds one of England, and the colony faithfully reproduces that

---

50   I am grateful to Lorraine David, French technical specialist for assistance with this translation.

metropolis with an incredible exactitude, in a land which was unknown two hundred years ago, and which remained in its natural state until thirty-five years ago.

But sometimes a group of 'aboriginals' serves to remind you that you are separated from London by 73 days at sea.

The men and women have skin darker than that of crocodiles, their hair is crinkly and filthy, their faces forlorn and brutish. Ragged trousers tattered and torn clothe their repulsive bodies; worn out boots dangle beneath their naked thighs and legs, their European rags originally multicoloured but now as brownish as the skin they hardly even cover; opera hats reduced to the state of an old withered apple or feathered 'hats' all given by an Irishwoman who blushed at their lack of clothing; a miserable jumble of rags over scrawny torsos the colour of dirty ebony black; these are the original owners of this continent, whom every day the Europeans push further away into the bush.

And to think of that famous treaty, signed in 1836 between the first settlers and the original inhabitants, by which the latter exchanged *'one thousand square leagues of the* colony of Victoria *for three sacks of glass beads, ten pounds of nails and five pounds of flour!'*

Australia – which one usually thinks of as so remote and primitive – today, has all the luxuries of Europe ...[51]

The French may well have had their own political reasons for depicting Aboriginal people as vagrants and rag-clothed beggars. As a critique of British colonialism, this French article offers a damning commentary. However, this critique should be tempered by the history of antagonism between France and Britain that occupied much of the nineteenth century.[52] The article did, nonetheless, praise the British colonial city Melbourne regarding it as 'elegant and expensively built' with 'nothing to envy of Paris'.[53] Intellectually, the city demonstrated its civility via its

> public library, more scientific than literary, established ten years ago only and holds already 41.000 volumes. It has costs 120.000 pounds sterling to the colony, and attracts a considerable number of readers.

---

51 Translation of *Journal des Voyages*, No. 205, June 1881, Cover illustration by SC Perrichon, article by F Demays. Original emphasis.
52 Chris Cook and John Stevenson (eds), *The Routledge Companion To European History Since 1763*, Routledge, New York, 2005.
53 *Journal des Voyages*, No. 205, June 1881.

1. 'Tickpen', 'Boro Boro': Aboriginal economic engagements

The presence of Aboriginal people begging in Melbourne towards the *fin de siècle* is at odds with previous analyses that have suggested by the later part of the nineteenth-century Aboriginal people were largely absent from the Melbourne streetscape. Their begging, probably opportunistically related to the Melbourne International Exhibition, I suggest, implies a well-thought-out strategy of economic engagement via soliciting for money. As with the 'Black Boy's Bridge', the Kulin had marked out on their econoscape the most advantageous locations for them to secure resources.

Discussion

The new econoscape of the Kulin also included the use or reuse of European clothing. While numerous nineteenth-century observers referred to Aboriginal people dressed in cast-off clothes or rags it is difficult to know precisely how they came to have these. It is possible that the ragged clothes were merely clothing they had been issued which had become tattered, equally likely these might have been secured via 'begging' or indeed scrounging through the Europeans' cast-offs. Newly arrived William Adeney in the 1840s remarked that he had

> [m]et two of the poor aborigines looking almost like the inhabitants of another world. The man was clothed in some dirty pieces of blanket hung about him.[54]

So taken with this was Adeney that uncharacteristically he made one of the very few sketches in his diary. The sight of Aboriginal people wearing discarded European clothing or clothing that had become tattered and rag-like was challenging to the settlers. They stood as an almost satiric announcement that theirs had been an unsuccessful assimilation. These scenes were in many ways a mimetic reminder that such mimicry could be challenging and indeed unsettling. Covered in what the Europeans might consider to be rags the Kulin as an imperfect copy or replica disrupted the notion of the city as a white space. One powerful example is depicted in ST Gill's image *Native Dignity* (Figure 5). Penelope Edmonds regards this image, first published in 1866, as 'revealing the deep anxieties about the boundaries of civility and whiteness'.[55] I would suggest that this image might even represent a mimetic moment where the apparently 'Europeanised' Kulin represent an even bigger threat than they did before.[56]

---

54   Adeney diary, SLV MS 8520: 305.
55   Edmonds, *Urbanizing Frontiers*: 167.
56   In *Savage Imaginings*, drawing on the work of Walter Benjamin, Homi K Bhabha and Michael Taussig, I consider the range of ways Aboriginal people consciously used mimesis and mimetic faculties to resist and engage with white society. See also Walter Benjamin, 'On the mimetic faculty', in *Reflections*, Schocken Books, New York, 1986; Homi K Bhabha, 'Of mimicry and man: The ambivalence of colonial discourse', October 28, Spring 1984: 125–133; and Michael Taussig, *Mimesis and Alterity*, Routledge, New York, 1993.

In this moment the victim of invasion and colonialism has 'metamorphosed' and in so doing threatens the existence of the settlers, which also permits the settler's relief from guilt. Perhaps these were ironic though, as Edmonds notes by this date Aboriginal people were virtually absent from the Melbourne streets and their threatening presence was largely in the settlers' imaginations. For the Kulin themselves it is difficult to ascertain how they felt about their clothing or indeed if they regarded them as 'rags' or an adequate replacement for their traditional labour-intensive possum skin cloaks.

Figure 5: *Native Dignity*, 186?, ST Gill.

Source: National Library Australia, nla.pic-an7021882.

While the mid-nineteenth century might have seen many Aboriginal people vacate Melbourne environs, this was not meek acquiescing to the European settlers' takeover of their land. The settlers knew only too well that some Aborigines had maintained their social structure on their own terms and where many usually imagined a ruined, helpless people the Kulin continued to exert their presence in the imagination of the settlers in a range of uncomfortable and confronting ways.

As the poet George Gordon McCrae wrote with powerful melancholy in the 1860s poem, *Balladeadro*:

the Australian blackfellow, as we see him in the streets of Melbourne, is not a poetic looking object …. his thoughts must be of the gloomiest kind [because] his birth-right has been seized by the stranger.[57]

Based both in Melbourne at Abbotsford and also having a property at Arthur's Seat on Boonwurrung land, McCrae and his family were familiar with Kulin people. As a member of Melbourne's burgeoning intelligentsia – his mother was Georgiana McCrae – he was a sensitive observer of Aboriginal people. As such his works are telling for what they indicate about the perceptions of the time. In 1866, *The Australian* published a poem written by TB Shortfellow, an obvious and playful *non de plume* with homage to Henry Wadsworth Longfellow, author of *The Song of Hiawatha*. 'Shortfellow' wrote the 'Reminiscences and Reflections of an Aboriginal Chieftain'. Like the couple depicted in Gill's *Native Dignity* the chieftain was once a noble warrior who had been reduced to a 'debased' and 'conquered' victim – a mockery of white values. The Chieftain dreamed of a place:

> Where, free from the vice and follies of white men, he might live happy,
> Where no plant-distilling liquors to abase him could be found.
> And he thought no pale-faced stranger had a right, by force or cunning,
> To drive them back to the Mallee, or the parched and desert plain,
> And that allow seducing poison as a recompense to offer,
> Which destroys what pride the conquered and degraded might retain.

This is the image of a liquor-soaked dispossessed beggar. The Chieftain finishes with the begging plea: 'Mine poor fellow no got bacca, and mine big one want 'im smoke!'.[58]

It was a relatively simple segue to see Aboriginal people dressed in European cast-off clothing and soliciting for money as a conquered people begging for survival. It is highly unlikely that the Kulin saw themselves this way. Indeed it is possible that replacing their possum skin cloaks with blankets or other European dress items was seen as a sensible strategy given the labour intensity of the cloak manufacture. Similarly, begging for a few hours each day might well have been seen as preferable, indeed much easier than walking long distances for hunting and gathering resources, thus transforming their econoscape as they saw fit.

---

57   *The Australasian*, Wednesday 13 March 1867: 3.
58   *Australian Journal*, 6 May 1866; John O'Leary, 'The ethnographic verse of mid-nineteenth century Australia', *Australian Literary Studies* 23(1), 2007: 3–17.

Conclusion

Accessing European goods, clothes and money was a strategic economic concern of the Kulin throughout the nineteenth century. The assistant protectors, missionaries and other 'humanitarians' often distributed clothes and rations as a matter of course. This was recognised in the Legislative Council's Select Committee into the condition of the Aborigines questionnaire, which asked as question 4:

> Has assistance in the form of clothing , food or medical attendance, been bestowed on the aborigines of your district by the Government? What means have they of living? Are there any aboriginal reserves near you, or places well fitted for being granted as such?

As a consequence of the Select Committee's report the distribution of food, blankets and clothing became centralised through the establishment of the Central Board Appointed to Watch over the Interests of the Aborigines. In many ways it could be regarded as also the consequence of the Kulin's successful strategy of engaging with the new economy via soliciting and begging.

It is clear that the establishment of Melbourne and the colonisation of the Port Phillip Colony (Victoria) had a devastating and long-lasting effect on the Aboriginal people. Governing the Kulin was an immediate and ongoing concern for the settlers. Despite the establishment of the Aboriginal Protectorate in the 1840s designed to remove them from the city, the Kulin continued to be visible on the Melbourne streets in the mid-1850s and, as this chapter has shown, beyond. According to Edmonds, Melbourne authorities required a range of mechanisms to control the presence of the Kulin.[59] However, these were constantly challenged and Aboriginal people continued to exert their admittedly reduced presence up into the 1880s. What the Europeans termed begging was one of the ways the Kulin engaged with the imposed economic system. Begging was an effective means for obtaining money and other commodities as its continuity over five decades demonstrates.[60]

---

59 Edmonds, *Urbanizing Frontiers*: 88.
60 Richard Broome, *Aboriginal Victorians: A History Since 1800*, Allen & Unwin, Sydney, 2005; see also Alick Jackomos and Derek Fowell (eds), *Living Aboriginal History of Victoria: Stories in the Oral Tradition*, Cambridge University Press, Cambridge, 1991.

2. 'Thus have been preserved numerous interesting facts that would otherwise have been lost': Colonisation, protection and William Thomas's contribution to *The Aborigines of Victoria*

Rachel Standfield

Robert Brough Smyth, Chairman of the Central Board for the Protection of Aborigines, published his *The Aborigines of Victoria: with notes relating to the habits of the Natives of other parts of Australia and Tasmania, compiled from various sources for the Government of Victoria* in 1878.[1] Smyth's work is an example of an early Australian anthropological text. It is a large work, over two volumes and 938 pages, and collected together information gathered from multiple observers of Aboriginal life and society in Victoria and further afield. Smyth, as a noted colonial scientist as well as chairman of the Protection Board, was well placed to collate the work, and contribute to the burgeoning interest in collecting Aboriginal artefacts and documenting aspects of Aboriginal culture. In 1861, the President of the Royal Society of Victoria 'called for urgent research into Aboriginal "dialects and traditions" as whole tribes "are, under some mysterious dispensation, rapidly disappearing"'.[2] While the publication took a very long time to come to fruition, when it was published it was disseminated publicly at the expense of the Victorian colonial government, who distributed it to libraries and mechanics institutes.[3]

As well as taking significant time, the text was also the product of a significant number of contributions by a number of European observers of Aboriginal culture, including John Green, William Ridley and AW Howitt. The first source mentioned in Smyth's preface was William Thomas, Protector of Aborigines in the Aboriginal Protectorate in Port Phillip from 1839, Guardian of Aborigines when the original Protectorate was abolished, and involved in the Central Board

---

1 Robert Brough Smyth, *The Aborigines of Victoria: with notes relating to the habits of the Natives of other parts of Australia and Tasmania compiled from various sources for the Government of Victoria*, Melbourne, Government Printer, 1878.
2 Richard Broome, *Aboriginal Victorians: A History Since 1800*, Allen & Unwin, Sydney, 2005: 100.
3 Broome, *Aboriginal Victorians*: 101.

for Protection of Aborigines during the 1860s, but with a role that was curtailed by ill health. Thomas died in 1867, well before the publication of Smyth's work, but Smyth described Thomas's contribution in the following terms:

> When I commenced to figure and describe the native weapons, I asked the late Mr William Thomas … to write down under separate heads all that was known to him respecting the Aborigines; and thus have been preserved numerous interesting facts that would otherwise have been lost.[4]

'Collated texts' of the last quarter of the nineteenth century, like Smyth's work, Roger Lawrence concludes, are of limited use for understanding the connection between Aboriginal people and their environment from an anthropological perspective, because of the speed with which the material was collected and selective decisions to include material considered interesting or useful.[5] These collated texts do, however, offer an opportunity to trace the ways that knowledge was developed, reworked and remade in response to changing colonial circumstances and different contexts of colonial governance. In this chapter, I consider the contribution made by Thomas to Smyth's text, analysing Thomas's material and a notebook of collated material and looking at the way they were used in Smyth's work.

Exploring Smyth's collated text from the perspective of a selection of contributed material allows a view to emerge of the shifting currents of European thought in relation to Aboriginal people and culture, particularly from the perspective of changing systems for the governance of Aboriginal communities in Victoria. Through this chapter, I examine the way that Thomas's observations, with their particular emphasis on his early years of work with the original Port Phillip Protectorate, are utilised in a text associated with the second period of protection in Victoria, but one that was also written within an anthropological discourse.

Having worked with Thomas's papers housed in the Mitchell Library, my interest is in following the way that his views of Aboriginal people and their culture were reworked in this anthropological work. This chapter explores the way that Thomas's material, both from his own observations and that collated by Thomas for Smyth, was used within the published work, considering the way that observations drawn from one period of 'protection' of Victorian Aboriginal communities were utilised in a document borne from another. Thomas's ethnographic observations, largely based on his experiences living

---

4   Smyth, *The Aborigines of Victoria*, Preface: v–vi.
5   Edward Curr, *The Australian Race: Its Origin, Languages, Customs, Place of Landing in Australia, and the Routes by Which It Spread Itself Over That Continent*, Government Printer, Melbourne, 1886–1887; Roger Lawrence, 'Habitat and economy: a historical perspective', in DJ Mulvaney and J Golson (eds), *Aboriginal Man and Environment in Australia*, Australian National University Press, Canberra, 1971: 252.

with Indigenous people in the late 1830s and 1840s, while working as Assistant Protector in the Port Phillip Protectorate, were reworked to fit the anthropological text published in the context of the *Aborigines Protection Act 1869* (Vic). This chapter traces shifts from humanitarian discourses of the early period of protection in Victoria, which had often been critical of colonisation, to an academic discourse which while using these earlier sources, effaced their colonial dimension, in the search for a 'pure' anthropological type. Smyth, while 'preserving' Protectorate material he feared would be lost, also excised and reworked material about Aboriginal people and their social arrangements and culture. Thomas's writing often captured Aboriginal agency and Aboriginal resistance, but Smyth stripped this material of almost all aspects of the particularities of Aboriginal experience and engagement in the processes which governed their lives. In this sense, the chapter argues that Smyth's work is simultaneously an academic text and one related to processes of colonial governance, combining representation of Indigenous peoples from an anthropological perspective with discussions of governance and colonial history suited to the context of colonial governance in which the text had been developed and into which it was published. As Gillian Cowlishaw describes, anthropology as a discipline reflects both a critique of inequality and a 'deep complicity' with colonial discourses and power relations. Cowlishaw argues that two factors mitigate against anthropology's moral program of encouraging respect for Aboriginal culture – a focus on 'traditional Aboriginal society' and the manner in which anthropological texts ignore, or support, 'aggressive assimilationism' by governments.[6] This connection was perhaps even more pronounced with Smyth's text, being compiled 'from government records' by a scholar with deep connection to Victorian governance of Aboriginal people.

Ann Laura Stoler builds a powerful argument that the colonial archive is not merely a site of knowledge collection but also one of knowledge production.[7] Stoler's work looks at archives as 'cross-sections of contested knowledge', encouraging scholars to pay close attention to 'what subjects are cross-referenced what parts are re-written, what quotations are cited' as they 'not only tell about how decisions are rendered, but how colonial histories are written and remade'.[8] The archive examined here is a small part of a collection of papers, and yet, in examining this part of the Robert Brough Smyth collection, it is possible to see the impact that Thomas's contributions can make in Smyth's text, the way that they are utilised and employed to create new knowledge about Aboriginal people, to serve new needs in intellectual communities as well as, I argue here, in terms of governance of Aboriginal people. Stoler's work

---

6 Gillian Cowlishaw, 'Studying Aborigines: changing canons in anthropology and history', *Journal of Australian Studies* 16(35), 1992: 20.
7 Ann Laura Stoler, 'Colonial archives and the arts of governance', *Archival Science* 2, 2002: 87–109.
8 Stoler, 'Colonial archives and the arts of governance': 87, 107.

focuses on commissions, collections of statistics, and classification of state secrets, but by analysing a small portion of the archive of material that helped to form Smyth's texts it is possible to trace similar practices of the remaking and reworking of colonial knowledge, knowledge that was derived from an earlier system of colonial governance and applied to an emerging academic discipline, by an author himself connected to governance of Indigenous peoples.

Nicholas B Dirks, in examining the construction of works of 'pre-British Indian history' during the colonial period of Indian history, traces the way that European collectors, compilers and authors of these works made use of earlier material collected in the encounter between agents of empire and native peoples. Dirks read history back in to discourses which deny history to and essentialise colonised peoples, by interrogating the processes whereby the 'pasts of the colonized … were erased as soon as conquest made possible the production of new forms of knowledge that endowed colonialism with natural legitimacy'.[9] Dirks looks further back than 'texts of high imperialism' to examine the 'competing histories' created 'before colonized histories were ensnared and silenced'.[10] He looks for

> the ambivalences and contests within early colonial historicities, imagined when colonial historiographies were still dependent upon native informants and colonial histories were still unsecured by the political triumphs that made possible the illusion of permanence … Erasures were written over histories that were being actively recovered and rewritten at the same time they were being transformed into histories of loss and subjection. Mythical discourses were constructed out of historical encounters.[11]

Dirks traces the impact of these encounters, and the relationship between the European observer and the 'native informant' on later texts, and it is my aim here to apply the same approach to Smyth's text through an examination of the influence of Thomas's writing on his work. For Thomas's position and the knowledge derived from it was heavily 'dependent' upon 'native informants'.[12] Thomas, spent much of his early career living amongst the Woiwurrung and Boonwurrung communities and engaging with other Kulin peoples as they visited Melbourne. These experiences provided the basis of the information he provided for *The Aborigines of Victoria* and he was thus clearly indebted to his relationships with Aboriginal people for the ethnographic information he could

---

9 Nicholas Dirks, 'Colonial histories and native informants: biography of an archive', in Carol Breckenridge and Peter van der Veer (eds), *Orientalism and the Postcolonial Predicament: Perspectives on South Asia*, University of Pennsylvania Press, Philadelphia, 1993: 280.
10 Dirks, 'Colonial histories and native informants': 280.
11 Dirks, 'Colonial histories and native informants': 280.
12 Dirks, 'Colonial histories and native informants': 280.

contribute. These relationships, and the debt he owed to them, will be explored further in this chapter through an examination of material Thomas provided to Smyth and work within his own archive of papers, which appears developed for publication.

The publication of Smyth's two volumes occurred within the context of the establishment of the reserve system in Victoria and the passing of the 1869 Act, the first such Act in the Australian colonies, and the model for other colonial legislation to come. As Leigh Boucher and Lynette Russell have shown, this context of colonial governance allowed men of standing in Victoria to rest in the knowledge that 'the legislation effectively disbursed the moral obligation of settlers', after a period through the 1850s and 1860s when the 'nascent intellectual elite returned again and again to the moral problems of colonial expropriation'.[13] The sense of development towards 'progressive' legislation aimed at protecting Victorian Aboriginal people was palpable in Smyth's text. In the introduction to the work Smyth applauded the work of government on behalf of Aboriginal people (which he himself had, of course, been a part of), with the government having 'done much to benefit them'. Smyth, after documenting the rapid depopulation of Aboriginal communities, turned quickly to recognise the exertions of a lineage of Europeans who had worked to 'ameliorate the condition of the native that survived the first contact with the vices and contamination of the whites'.[14] Not only Secretaries of State for the Colonies or members of the Parliament of Victoria were applauded, but also missionaries – 'able, earnest and thoughtful men' – and 'gentlemen in Victoria – clergymen' who had 'voluntarily sacrificed all hopes of preferment, and have devoted their lives to the task of ameliorating the condition of our native population'. The previous system of appointing Guardians during the 1850s had not had results 'such as to satisfy the colonists' and Smyth concluded that the condition of Aboriginal people had been 'deplorable'; he could turn, however, to the 1858 Victorian Select Committee on Aborigines, the establishment of the Board, and the 1869 Act to provide for Aboriginal 'protection and management' as examples of progressive colonial governance. The parliament had been 'liberal in its grants of money' with Smyth suggesting that £100,000 had been spent on the system implemented since the 1858 Select Committee.[15] Thus the move to a 'moral' and 'progressive' system of governance allowed the author to be freed from any guilt of the failure of previous systems of governing the Indigenous population, and lent the text a congratulatory tone.

---

13   Leigh Boucher and Lynette Russell, '"Soliciting sixpences from township to township": Moral dilemmas in mid-nineteenth-century Melbourne', *Postcolonial Studies* 15(2), 2012: 161, 150.
14   Smyth, *The Aborigines of Victoria*: xx.
15   Smyth, *The Aborigines of Victoria*: xx.

Boucher and Russell also demonstrate that this new context of colonial governance had two impacts on Aboriginal people in Victoria, by offering both respite to communities 'from the onslaught of land-hungry and often violent settlers', while simultaneously depriving Aboriginal people of their ability to move throughout the colony and leading to increasing levels of government interference into Aboriginal lives. In removing Aboriginal people from urban spaces to reserves, Aboriginal bodies and voices were no longer constant reminders of dispossession, largely finishing a project of removing Indigenous people from the Melbourne environment which had constituted a core part of William Thomas's role from as far back as 1840.[16] In Smyth's text, increasing levels of government control were portrayed as natural and inevitable. Smyth's introduction included a short summation of colonial history, and it is one in which, while acknowledging settler violence, suggests that conflict between communities after white settlement was the principal form of conflict.

Firstly, Smyth described Europeans as 'invaders', providing a clear sense of contest over land in his description, but this contest, he felt, had changed Aboriginal communities. As colonisers 'established' themselves, 'and the natives were driven first from one spot and then from another' to make way for cattle and sheep, Indigenous people were mixed together – 'compelled to mingle' – in a way that had not been known before colonisation. The consequences of this, Smyth considered, were dire for Indigenous people and their culture:

> The ancient land marks were obliterated, the ancient boundaries had ceased to have any meaning, and the people, confused and half-stupefied by the new and extraordinary character of the circumstances so suddenly forced upon them, almost forgot the duties their tribal laws imposed upon them when they were brought face to face with strange blacks.[17]

Smyth thus suggested that as Aboriginal communities lost access to land and were thrown into new connections with other Aboriginal communities they simultaneously lost knowledge of country, that country lost its significance to Aboriginal cultures, and the people were merely confused and bewildered. Indigenous people have lost all agency here, they, according to Smyth, ceased upon colonisation to act deliberately or to defend themselves or their country. They were 'unable', he wrote, 'to combine and offer determined resistance to the invaders' but instead became 'the more savage and cruel', and this 'compelled' settlers to make reprisals.[18]

---

16   Boucher and Russell, 'Soliciting sixpences from township to township': 162; Broome, *Aboriginal Victorians*: 120.
17   Smyth, *The Aborigines of Victoria*: xviii–xix.
18   Smyth, *The Aborigines of Victoria*: xix.

Moreover, the actions of 'the rifle and the pistol' were less dangerous to Aboriginal people than disease and 'vice', such that it was the 'kindness of the civilised immigrant that swept off the native population', through the introduction of alcohol and 'attentions' to Aboriginal women.[19] Disease and the relationship between Aboriginal people and the colonial medical establishment became important to the text, alongside a strong theme of 'superstition'. Such emphases accord to the conclusions of Patrick Brantlinger, who stresses the centrality of accounts of disease and superstition within dying race discourses (which neccesarily downplayed the role of violence or European agency in the decline of Indigenous populations).[20] This is a point I shall return to in more detail later in this chapter.

While Smyth concluded that these European responses were 'not much to the credit of Europeans', he consigned them to 'the olden time'.[21] Thomas's material, being largely based on his experiences in the first period of Protection in what was then the Port Phillip District of the Colony of New South Wales, belonged to this earlier period. In Smyth's text, Thomas's observations represented a 'traditional' and 'authentic' Aboriginal culture on the cusp of the degradation caused by European contact and the loss of culture. Thomas appears to have provided a significant amount of material to Smyth.[22] Some letters in the Thomas papers are addressed to Smyth particularly and other material in his papers, included directly after the letters to Smyth, appear to have been annotated by Thomas and sent on. As well as contributing work from his own papers, Thomas gathered information. A notebook of this collected material is included within Smyth's papers in the State Library of Victoria. Running to 129 pages, it collates information gathered from different earlier sources, including material from Thomas Mitchell's exploration journals, published material on Aboriginal life from Victorian newspapers, and undated material from the Port Phillip Protectorate that has since been identified as the work of Assistant Protector James Dredge.[23] This, Fels suggests, is Thomas 'doing anthropology'.[24]

If we consider the presentation of Thomas's ethnographic information in Smyth's text, by taking as an example the depiction of Aboriginal weaponry, however, we can see the way that the processes of collating, cataloguing and editing Thomas's contribution worked to strip Aboriginal cultural information from this anthropological text. Smyth was particularly interested in weaponry,

---

19   Smyth, *The Aborigines of Victoria*: xix.
20   Patrick Brantlinger, *Dark Vanishings: Discourse on the Extinction of Primitive Races, 1800–1930*, Cornell University Press, Ithaca and London, 2003.
21   Smyth, *The Aborigines of Victoria*: xix.
22   In the papers which survive from Thomas's long career, there is a significant amount of writing which he had provided to others, including material provided to La Trobe for use in a book.
23   Marie Hansen Fels, 'The La Trobe library collection of the papers of Assistant Protector William Thomas', *The La Trobe Journal* 43, Autumn 1989: 14.
24   Fels, 'The La Trobe library collection of the papers of Assistant Protector William Thomas': 14.

and had initially gone to Thomas to ask for his input in his project to 'figure and describe the native weapons'. Subsequently, in providing information to Smyth, he focused on the importance of the use of weaponry and the role of conflict within Victorian Aboriginal culture; the particularly organised and ritualised nature of conflict, the presence of 'commanders' and the role of older men to manage conflict so that inter-clan relationships were generally restored without people coming to serious harm. He concluded of the resolution of conflict: 'There is an affecting feature after all. Combatants may be seen sucking each others wounds and spitting the blood from them.'[25] These insights were based on his observations of Kulin communities coming together for ritual conflict. He had initially tried to intervene to stop such conflict, and was physically removed and protected on one occasion by members of the communities he lived with, and had come to understand conflict as highly organised and with important cultural functions in ensuring the smooth running of clan relations.

The drawings of Aboriginal weaponry were reproduced in Smyth's text, with the features of the weapons being compared to descriptions by other European observers in other parts of the continent. In the process of including these images, beautifully presented though they were, the accompanying cultural information about the way that Aboriginal people used the weapons was removed from the images, some of it being woven into other parts of the text. The visual presentation of these allowed Smyth to explore the scientific and comparative aspects of Victorian Aboriginal weaponry, but strip out all sense of Aboriginal culture, reworking the information in another part of the text. As Lynette Russell describes, 'the failure to provide the necessary detail or text required to appreciate the object and its context – to hear its story – is a common omission in museum displays' and I would argue that the same is true in this text.[26] Within the development of the text, the cataloguing and classification of objects of material culture have taken on more importance than understanding their cultural context, their function in social life and community relationships, or indeed the context of encounter out of which European understanding of that significance was generated. Instead, selected information was paraphrased in the section entitled 'fights' within the chapter devoted to 'a native encampment, and the daily life of the natives'. Smyth included descriptions from William Buckley as well as Thomas, 'because there are probably not very many now living who have seen a well-contested fight, after the Aboriginal fashion, in this colony',[27] but not before he had drawn his own quite lurid picture of Aboriginal inter-clan conflict. He described Aboriginal conflict as 'not a brawl ... but generally a well-devised set-to between the fighting men of each side'

---

25   Thomas papers in the Mitchell Library, MS214, volumes 21 and 22, frame 136.
26   Lynette Russell, *Savage Imaginings: Historical and Contemporary Constructions of Australian Aboriginalities*, Australian Scholarly Publishing, Melbourne, 2001: 11.
27   Smyth, *The Aborigines of Victoria*: 157.

after which 'they come out ... most often scatheless', and yet the description itself is of disorder and savagery. Smyth focuses on 'the decorations of the warriors', naked except for paint and feathers, 'loud cries', 'shaking' of spears', 'rattling' of clubs, the 'violent motions of the warriors and their savage yells', combined with the 'yells and screams of the women and children' as 'wives rush in to protect their husbands and mothers cling to their sons to shelter and help them'. He suggests that such a scene would 'create alarm' for 'one new to the country'.[28] Thomas's discussion of wound care was used as evidence that no matter how much the scene might 'induce disgust and abhorrence, they are not altogether devoid of those elements which serve to elevate our species'.[29] Smyth's collating and categorisation of the information provided by Thomas, which Stoler might describe as 'information out of place' that 'underscores what categories matter', suggests that depicting material culture was of primary importance, with Smyth collecting objects of material culture to be catalogued, but excising the supporting context which explained Aboriginal life and could counter depictions of 'savagery'.[30]

While some information was 'out of place', other contextualising material was not used at all, but sifted through for the 'facts' of Aboriginal life. Assistant Protector Dredge's writing, included in Thomas's notebook amongst the Smyth papers, was clear about colonisation and the crisis it had engendered amongst the Aboriginal communities that he was sent to protect. Information in Dredge's papers did mirror that which Smyth eventually used, but, as the following example in relation to Aboriginal food resources might illustrate, the 'facts' were provided without reference to colonial intrusion into Aboriginal life. Dredge described 'Murnong', a staple Aboriginal food source, but quickly turned to a description of how the loss of Murnong had been felt by Aboriginal communities:

> In the unlocated parts of the country and such other places as have not been visited by the flocks and herds of the settler these roots are obtained in great abundance but like the other natural supplies of the Aborigines they diminish and soon disappear when sheep and cattle are depastured. Nor are the Natives insensible of the cause of such diminution.[31]

---

28 Smyth, *The Aborigines of Victoria*: 156.
29 Smyth, *The Aborigines of Victoria*: 156.
30 Stoler, 'Colonial archives and the arts of governance': 107.
31 William Thomas, undated notebook within the Robert Brough Smyth papers, State Library of Victoria (SLV) MS 8781, Box 1176/6: 97.

Dredge included a quote from an Aboriginal person in Melbourne that registered Aboriginal protest at the loss of food resources, which he translated thus 'no Murnong, no yam at Port Phillip, too much by one white man Bullock and sheep, all gone Murnong &c'.[32]

Smyth's treatment of this information was to excise all discussion of colonial process and Aboriginal perspectives on the loss of their resources. The same descriptions of Murnong are employed, the role of women and children in gathering the resource and the seasons in which it was gathered, and descriptions of the likeness to Europeans vegetables come from Dredge's material:

> *Murr-nong or Mirr-n'yong*, a kind of yam (*Microseris Forsteri*), was usually very plentiful and easily found in the spring and early summer, and was dug out of the earth by the women and children. It may be seen growing on the banks of the Moonee Ponds, near Melbourne. The root is small, in taste rather sweet, not unpleasant, and perhaps more like a radish that a potato. This plant grows throughout the greater part of extra-tropical Australia – and in Tasmania and New Zealand.[33]

All information about Aboriginal food gathering during colonial contact was removed, along with any sense of Aboriginal protest at the loss of the resource, replaced instead by scientific information about the diversity and extent of plant growth, not only in Victoria but in Tasmania and New Zealand.

Similarly, Dredge's papers included very important information about the way that Aboriginal communities recorded and communicated colonial experiences:

> They have a species of historical song which enumerates to a monotonous tune, the individual beating time by striking a couple of sticks together or beating with his hand upon his breast, the most material circumstances wished to be remembered. I have known a blackfellow lie on his back and sing to himself for an hour together, or till he had fallen asleep, about the coming of white fellow, the first appearance of the horse, bullock, wheelbarrow (cart), dog, sheep, flour &c &c and a great variety of other matters, indeed it is not unusual to hear them at their various fires when encamped for the night humming these things over till sleep overcomes them.[34]

---

32   William Thomas, undated notebook within the Robert Brough Smyth papers, SLV MS 8781, Box 1176/6: 97–98.
33   Smyth, *The Aborigines of Victoria*: 209, 'Food'.
34   William Thomas, undated notebook within the Robert Brough Smyth papers, SLV MS 8781, Box 1176/6: 105.

Descriptions such as these in the Protectorate material connect clearly to processes of colonisation. They show Aboriginal people remembering and reflecting on the momentous processes of change wrought by colonisation, and processes of oral histories within communities.

There was a natural place for this material in Smyth's text, in the chapter on 'encampment and daily life' which had a section describing a scene of an Aboriginal encampment at night:

> the old men and the old women devoted their evenings to conversation – and strange stories were told of phantoms and dim forms that had affrighted them in their journeys and when camping. The priests lost no opportunity of exercising and extending their influence, and many a night a camp was kept awake by the vagaries of some sorcerer. He would pretend to fly; he would pretend to bring wild blackfellows to the camp, he would make hideous noises and terrify the natives …[35]

And yet there was no description here of the remembrance of colonisation, of the committing to oral history the coming of white settlement. Instead, the focus of Smyth's text was on sorcery and superstition, rather than on Aboriginal people as active agents in colonial histories; it depicts Aboriginality as radically 'other' from the non-Indigenous community, rather than as people engaged in colonial situations remembered through distinct forms of historical remembrance.

Some of the most important observations on Aboriginal culture included in the Smyth text came directly from Thomas, particularly in connection to Aboriginal relationships to country, and descriptions of political leadership. Thomas's map of Aboriginal spatial arrangements was reproduced in the section on 'encampment and daily life'.[36] The map was based on Thomas's observations of the regular gatherings of the five nations of the Kulin alliance in Melbourne in the early years of the first Protectorate, while Smyth described how 800 people had gathered on the occasion when Thomas had produced his map.[37] While it was reproduced in the book in a simplistic manner, the value of this map, as Marie Fels describes is:

> This drawing is a representation on one plane of a birdseye view of an encampment when different tribes congregated together. Its huge significance lies in the fact that the map on the ground stands for or represents existing relationships of country, and, within relationships of country, social distance relative to family and powerful leaders.[38]

---

35 Smyth, *The Aborigines of Victoria*: 178–179.
36 Smyth, *The Aborigines of Victoria*: 124.
37 Smyth, *The Aborigines of Victoria*: 124.
38 Fels, 'The La Trobe library collection of the papers of Assistant Protector William Thomas': 13.

Thomas's map led Smyth to conclude that '[t]he Aborigines do not herd together promiscuously. There is order and method.'[39] Systems of Aboriginal leadership were also described in Smyth's text: 'the encampments of the natives, and indeed all their movements, are ordered by the old men.'[40] The theme of order in communities came through again, linked to Aboriginal leadership: 'They do not wander about aimlessly: there is order and method in what they do.'[41] Smyth linked this order to these depictions of spatial arrangements: 'when several tribes meet, the sites for the miams are selected in accordance with rules, the arrangement generally being such as to show exactly from what direction each tribe has come.'[42] This cultural information created a theme within Smyth's work that traditional Aboriginal communities had been organised, structured and contained, and he made use of the term nation to describe Aboriginal political organisation: 'Large tracts, with well marked natural boundaries, are peopled by "nations", each composed of many separate tribes, differing amongst themselves but little in speech, in laws, and in modes of warfare.'[43]

In fact, this is the material that proved to be the most controversial aspect, as Smyth, in his short discussion of Aboriginal politics, which noted consensus based decision-making and the role of clan heads in communities, went so far as to suggest that Aboriginal leadership could 'serve as a model to peoples claiming to be civilised but more inclined to vices than the Australians'.[44] What appears to be a quite simple statement was strongly contested within later Victorian anthropological writing. LR Hiatt describes how this was first disputed by Curr, who believed there was no Aboriginal government, only the fear of sorcery, and then subsequently defended by Howitt, who believed that while sorcery was important, government was also strong.[45] Diane Barwick describes how Curr's scathing criticism accused Smyth of being 'no bushman' and of not understanding Aboriginal people 'in their savage state', and yet, as she notes, these chapters 'came substantially' from information provided by Thomas, as a result of the years he had spent living amongst Woiwurrung and Boonwurrung communities.[46]

While Smyth's recognition of Aboriginal political systems was controversial, his arguments were not nearly so strongly stated as the depictions of Aboriginal political systems included in the records of the first Protectorate. One of Thomas's

---

39 Smyth, *The Aborigines of Victoria*: 124.
40 Smyth, *The Aborigines of Victoria*: xxx.
41 Smyth, *The Aborigines of Victoria*: xxx.
42 Smyth, *The Aborigines of Victoria*: xxx.
43 Smyth, *The Aborigines of Victoria*: xiii.
44 Smyth, *The Aborigines of Victoria*: 129.
45 LR Hiatt, *Arguments about Aborigines: Australia and the Evolution of Social Anthropology*, Cambridge University Press, Cambridge, New York and Melbourne, 1996: 87–88.
46 Quoted in Diane Barwick, *Rebellion at Coranderrk*, Laura E Barwick and Richard E Barwick (eds), Aboriginal History Inc., Canberra, 1998: 109.

pieces of earlier writing, which appears to have been written with an eye for publication, entitled 'my first journey with the blacks', clearly documents the extent he relied on the Woiwurrung clan head, and most senior Kulin leader, Billibellary, for his safety after his first attempts to move Aboriginal people out of Melbourne to establish a station at Arthur's Seat on the Mornington Peninsula.[47] In Dredge's writings in the notebook of collated material in Smyth's archive of papers, politics is even more clearly explained:

> It does not appear that there are any persons amongst them which have Kingly authority over the rest. Yet each sub division of a tribe has one or more leading man or men. And in all important matters which require the assemblage of the whole tribe these influential men debate upon Public Matters, and decisions are come to be mutual consent. This kind of debating usually occurs in the evening … and sometimes long and animated speeches are delivered.[48]

In Smyth's text, while Aboriginal political systems are outlined in a general sense, the vitally important role of Aboriginal leadership in mediating colonial relationships, and negotiating on behalf of communities, was not included. Both historical and contemporary leaders were barely mentioned, despite the continuation of Aboriginal political relations on reserves during the time when Smyth was Secretary of the Board, as described by Barwick: 'In the 1870s those Kulin assembled at Coranderrk were still influenced by ancient rules governing marriage, land ownership and political authority.'[49] The exception to including information about particular Aboriginal leaders was when Smyth was describing Aboriginal racial types; Billibellary, the most senior Kulin clan head at the time of first European settlement, was included in the text merely as a figure to illustrate that Aboriginal people also differentiated between racial groups. By contrast, Billibellary appears as a central figure in Thomas's narratives, as a leader on whom he relied for cultural information and for influence, as someone who had protected him physically on occasions.[50] Simon Wonga, Billibellary's son and successor, was described merely as 'the principal man of the Yarra tribe … Wonga has a mild disposition, and is always gentle and courteous. He is a good speaker, and has much influence with his people.' His photograph, as well as that of his wife, was included within a montage that was seen to exemplify an Aboriginal racial type. The names of other people living on reserves were included along with their height, weight and age to ascertain the characteristics

---

47 See Rachel Standfield, 'Protection, settler politics and indigenous politics in the work of William Thomas', *Journal of Colonialism and Colonial History* 13(1), Spring 2012.
48 William Thomas, undated notebook within the Robert Brough Smyth papers, SLV MS 8781, Box 1176/6: 106.
49 Barwick, *Rebellion at Coranderrk*: 12.
50 Standfield, 'Protection, settler politics and indigenous politics'.

of the Aboriginal racial type.[51] Information about Aboriginal leaders was included here as Smyth declared he was attempting to overcome the previous depiction of Aboriginal people in racial thought, having been

> harshly dealt with in nearly all the works that treat of ethnology. In many their faces are made to appear as like those of baboons as possible; and though it must be confessed that, as a rule, neither the men nor the women have pleasing countenances, they are as thoroughly human in their features and expression as the natives of Great Britain.[52]

Specific information about leadership was replaced with general points about racial characteristics, with Aboriginal leaders seen as exemplars of the characteristics and attitudes of Aboriginal society.

While politics, leadership and order in Aboriginal societies were themes in Smyth's text, they sat alongside another, that of 'superstition' and its supposedly central role in Aboriginal cultural life. Stressing the role of superstition in Aboriginal community life worked to undermine the idea of order within Aboriginal societies that Smyth's explanation of relationships to country, leadership and politics conveyed. No matter what admiration Smyth may have had for Aboriginal order, he could not admire Aboriginal life in general. In his introduction, Smyth described leadership and gathering by communities, but then goes on, 'there are endless sources of enjoyment when a large meeting takes place; but on the whole the life of a savage is one of trouble', said to be caused by hunger, the climate, sorcery and women.[53]

When Thomas had summed up Kulin leadership, he had done so in the following manner: 'Their government is patriarchal, the head of each family having control over his household … Each tribe has a chief who directs all its movements, and who, wherever he may be, knows well where all the members of the community are.' Thomas followed up this statement by identifying the other 'eminent men', including 'warriors, counsellors, doctors, dreamers who are also interpreters; charmers'.[54] As Hiatt shows, Smyth included a similar comment 'but embellished Thomas's formulation, and extended it to the whole of Victoria', suggesting that the 'principal man of the tribe' enacted the decisions of others:

> There are the doctors and sorcerers who under some circumstances have supreme power; there are the warriors who in time of trouble are absolute masters; there are the dreamers who direct and control movements of the tribe until the divinations are fulfilled or forgotten; there are the old

---

51 Smyth, *The Aborigines of Victoria*: 10, 9.
52 Smyth, *The Aborigines of Victoria*: 11.
53 Smyth, *The Aborigines of Victoria*: xxxi.
54 Quoted in Hiatt, *Arguments about Aborigines*: 126.

men – councillors – without whose advice even the warriors are slow to move; and finally there are the old women who noisily intimate their designs, and endeavour by clamour and threats to influence the leaders of the tribe.[55]

While Smyth, drawing on the observations of Thomas and Dredge, suggested that decision-making was consensus based, there was a subtle shift in wording here which places new emphasis on the role of doctors and sorcerers, as well as a focus on divination, and the suggestion that Aboriginal women were engaged in 'clamour and threats'. The original argument about order in politics and leadership is thus diluted into one of a chaotic society ruled by superstition.

Importantly, superstition supposedly undermined the Aboriginal community's ability to deal with disease, the cataloguing of which was an important aspect of Smyth's text, as was Aboriginal weakness in the face of disease and refusal to seek help from colonial doctors:

> It is undoubtedly true that the modes of treatment adopted by Europeans are not, as a rule, successful, if the black be at all under the influence of his own people ... Then the old superstitions are strong upon him ... He fears the white man, dreads his medicine, and shrinks from the outward applications which may, for aught he knows, be possessed of secret properties that will cause his destruction ... The European doctor indeed is always at a great disadvantage when dealing with the natives; and though medical men are in Victoria most zealous and painstaking at all the Aboriginal Stations, they are thwarted continually by the people for whose benefit they use their utmost skill.[56]

Patrick Brantlinger's work has documented this central role of superstition in dying race discourse, which allowed population decline in Indigenous communities to be explained away in ways that downplayed the effects of colonisation, allowing the idea of extinction of Indigenous peoples to become a 'massive and rarely questioned consensus'.[57] As Brantlinger argues, 'savage customs' including 'superstition' took precedence over violence and disease in many accounts of population decline, such that 'savagery, in short, was frequently treated as self-extinguishing'.[58] Smyth linked savagery to death by disease in a way that recognised the role of disease in population decline, but placed the blame back on Aboriginal people for its effects, and, at the same time, applauded the role of European doctors. Aboriginal belief in their own medical systems and wariness of European doctors, described in terms of the 'old

---

55   Hiatt, *Arguments about Aborigines*: 126.
56   Smyth, *The Aborigines of Victoria*: 259–260.
57   Brantlinger, *Dark Vanishings*: 1.
58   Brantlinger, *Dark Vanishings*: 2.

superstitions', led Smyth to depict Aboriginal people as a dying race, declaring that 'it is probable that the numbers will decrease, and that, as a race, they will ultimately be extinguished in Victoria'.[59] He did so even in direct contradiction to estimates from John Green he included in his text, and Board reports from 1869, which had concluded that 'the Board does not hesitate to declare that the oft-repeated statement that the race is rapidly disappearing is by no means in accordance with fact'.[60] So while Smyth was happy to contradict other accepted wisdom about Aboriginal people, he concurred with views that Aboriginal people would become extinct. He suggested this was because of Aboriginal loss of country and loss of liberty, but his lack of discussion of colonisation and his emphasis on superstition, meant that this seemed a mysterious force, rather than a clash between settlers and Indigenous peoples.

Robert Brough Smyth's text made heavy use of the work of William Thomas and other material from the Port Phillip Protectorate, the original attempt at 'protection' of Aboriginal people in Victoria during the late 1830s and 1840s. By interrogating just a small portion of the archive of ethnographic observation on which Smyth's two-volume work was based, it is possible to trace the way that this anthropological text sat within the context of colonial governance of Aboriginal people in Victoria, and trace the archive as a site of knowledge production rather than simply a repository of 'facts'. The relationships between ethnographic observation and Indigenous informants, which had been pronounced in the period of the first Protectorate, were removed in the context of developing a detached scholarly text. Smyth included material about Aboriginal cultural life derived from these early colonial relationships, but presented this as characteristic of a 'racial type'. In attempting to overcome negative perceptions of Aboriginal people, and counter racial prejudice, the text did explore issues of land and leadership, but did so in abstract terms. Smyth's text might have been based on descriptions of specific events and cultural characteristics, but in stripping them of detail rendered Aboriginal people ahistorical and timeless, their contemporary lives divorced from colonial history and dispossession. With the advent of a 'moral' policy of protection legislation to 'ameliorate' the conditions of Aboriginal life, the 'frontier period' of just a generation before was rendered as the 'olden times'. In Smyth's text, Aboriginal people required protection and government amelioration, not from the direct forces of white settlement, but from their own weakness and superstition, and ultimately despite the efforts of colonial governments, doctors and protectors, Smyth envisaged extinction for Aboriginal Victorians.

---

59   Smyth, *The Aborigines of Victoria*: 45.
60   Smyth, *The Aborigines of Victoria*: 44.

3. The 1869 *Aborigines Protection Act*: Vernacular ethnography and the governance of Aboriginal subjects

Leigh Boucher

In 1864, Theo Sumner, Vice-President of the Victorian Central Board for the Protection of Aborigines (CBPA) noted with some frustration that members of the Board worked 'under severe disadvantages at present [and] many of their schemes are thwarted'.[1] According to his annual report, the instantiation of the Board at the request of the Governor after an 1858 Select Committee represented a chance to 'attend to the wants of the blacks' who were clearly struggling for survival in the wake of the violent transformations of settler colonial dispossession and its continuing effects.[2] However, Sumner argued the CBPA occupied an untenably ambiguous position within the legislative and institutional frameworks of colonial governance. This was not simply an appeal for more financial support; the CBPA's projects of protection, Sumner argued, were 'thwarted and some have been abandoned solely for the want of power to give effect to them'. The CBPA asked for legislative authority to intervene into the lives of Aboriginal people, their relationships with the colonial state and their engagements with colonial employers. Sumner regretted that whilst 'a very short Bill would contain all that is necessary to enable them to extend their labours ... their urgent solicitations for some amendment of the laws affecting the blacks have not yet received attention'.[3] To be fair, endemic government instability in the 1860s in Victoria meant that many reforming projects struggled to negotiate the game of musical ministers that unfolded in colonial parliament. Finally, however, in 1869 the CBPA's desire for more power was fulfilled. As what would become the *Aborigines Protection Act 1869* (Vic) made smooth progress between the upper and lower houses of colonial parliament, legislators suggested this was 'the performance of a very tardy act of justice to a long neglected portion of the human family ... whose lands we have to a large extent usurped'. Sumner must have been pleased to finally hear parliamentarians acknowledge that the 'enlargement ... of the powers of the Board', would enable the CBPA and its

---

1   Many thanks to Jordy Silverstein and Kyle Harvey for research assistance on this article, to Kate Fullagar for her thoughtful comments, and to Lynette Russell for her ongoing conversations about the project from which it is drawn.

Fourth Report of the Central Board Appointed to Watch Over the Interests of the Aborigines in the Colony, John Ferres, Government Printer, Melbourne, 1864: 13 (henceforth, CBPA Annual Report).

2   First CBPA Annual Report (1861): 2.
3   Fourth CBPA Annual Report (1864): 13.

guardians to 'protect the members of this race' because previously 'they [had] not the power to protect the interests of the aborigines in such a way as to be of service to them'.[4]

The 1869 Act seems, in many ways, to represent the legislative embodiment of a 60-year-old humanitarian tradition long nourished by differing branches and styles of evangelical Protestantism. This tradition had criticised the impact of what James Belich terms the settler revolution in the British world almost as soon as it took shape in the 1780s.[5] Indeed, in its preface to a reprint of the 1837 Westminster inquiry into the treatment of 'native inhabitants ... of British Settlements', the Aborigines Protection Society in Britain called for 'immediate legislative interference'. They reminded the 'British public' that the committee had called for both 'protection' from settler violence and more fulsome support to ensure that Indigenous peoples could be led 'to the peaceful and voluntary reception of the Christian religion'.[6] The granting of self-government in the intervening years across the settler periphery, however, meant that after the 1850s any humanitarian legal intervention would have to come from colonial legislatures rather than Westminster.[7]

The successful campaign of the Victorian CBPA for a 'Protection Act' seemed to grant humanitarians and missionaries in colonial Victoria the kinds of authority and power that Michael Christie suggests their British forebears had so desperately wanted but had been unable to secure.[8] Ironically, the very settlers that humanitarians in Britain condemned produced the kind of legislative intervention they had sought. The echoes of humanitarian thought reverberated through the discursive landscape that surrounded the Act; an evangelical vocabulary that argued for 'protection and justice' for neglected members of the 'family of man' often framed public discussion. However, it was also one of the most far-reaching intrusions into the lives and liberties of Indigenous peoples yet seen in the nineteenth century. The Board would now be able to employ the mechanisms of the colonial state to control where Aboriginal adults lived, where their children went to school, what happened to any income they earned, and even the clothes they wore – simply by virtue of their legal status as an 'Aborigine'. Whilst evangelical claims for justice and compassion

---

4 Victorian Parliamentary Debates: Legislative Council and Legislative Assembly, Government Printer, Melbourne, 1869: 1726–1727, 1808 (henceforth, VPD).
5 James Belich, *Replenishing the Earth: The Settler Revolution and the Rise of the Anglo-world*, Oxford University Press, Oxford, 2009: 21–23.
6 Report of the Select Committee on Aboriginal Tribes (British Settlements): Reprinted, with comments by the 'Aborigines Protection Society', William Ball, London, 1837: 4, 7, 15.
7 Although this concern did have an impact on how colonial constitutions would be written and, indeed, the treatment of Indigenous peoples was a snag for campaigns for self-government in Western Australia. Ann Curthoys, 'Taking liberty: towards a new political historiography of settler self-government and political activism', in Kate Fullagar (ed.), *The Atlantic World in the Antipodes*, Cambridge Scholars Press, Cambridge, 2008: 237–255.
8 Michael Christie, *Aborigines in Colonial Victoria, 1835–1886*, Sydney University Press, Sydney, 1979: 177.

provided a powerful justification for this kind of intervention, they also granted the system of guardians, reserves and missions that had taken shape under the CBPA's gaze in the 1860s an exceptional form of legislative authority. As the Minister for Justice described to his fellow legislators, the Bill was 'intended to provide for the protection and management of the aboriginal natives of Victoria' and he predicted the legislation would enable 'the board to watch over the adult aboriginals throughout the colony' because the CBPA would now 'act *in loco parentis* to the aborigines'.[9]

In some ways, then, this piece of legislation exemplified the kind of racialising strategies that scholars like Ann Laura Stoler suggest buttressed colonial authority. This seems like a moment in which one of the 'powerful but false premises' of colonialism made its harder-edged logics more apparent; as Stoler argues, 'colonial control was predicated on constructing categories' that functioned to make racial difference seem 'self evident'.[10] In Victoria in 1869, Aboriginal people became governable subjects in a newly powerful assembly of legislation, bureaucracy, knowledge and practice. Perhaps, though, we need a more careful account of how this transformation occurred. Indeed, given the long history of ambivalent (if not hostile) engagements between colonial authorities and evangelical practices, how did the CPBA and then the Act suture together the long-standing discourse of evangelical protection with emerging ideas about the rights and entitlements of colonial subjecthood? As Andrew Porter notes, 'imperial control, colonial societies and the missionary movement intertwined in divergent and ambiguous ways' across the empire.[11] What kind of entanglement made such a powerful set of restrictions possible?

Historians, race and the 1869 Protection Act

Interestingly, of the two major pieces of legislation that took the 'Aborigine' as their direct object in colonial Victoria (the 1869 so-called 'Protection Act' and *Aborigines Protection Act 1886* (Vic) or 'Half-Caste Act'), the latter has secured far more attention from historians. Perhaps because the 1886 'Half-Caste Act' more clearly resonates with the dominant political concerns that have shaped both the field of Aboriginal History and the theorisations of settler colonialism that developed alongside it, the 'Half-Caste Act' has dominated the scholarship. The latter piece of legislation drew a distinction between 'full-bloods' and 'half-castes' in ways that now seem to presage the biological, social and cultural engineering whose legacies troubled the memory politics of late

---

9   VPD (1869): 1726.
10 Ann Laura Stoler, *Carnal Knowledge and Imperial Power: Race and the Intimate in Colonial Rule*, University of California Press, Berkeley, 2002: 43.
11 Andrew Porter, *Religion Versus Empire*, Manchester University Press, Manchester and New York, 2004: 40.

twentieth-century Australia. Moreover, if ever there was a piece of legislation that exemplified the 'logic of elimination' that Wolfe so carefully discerns at the heart of the settler colonial encounter, then the Act that bureaucratically expelled 'half-castes' from the meagre entitlements of state protection offered to 'Aborigines' seems paradigmatic.[12] So too, the temptation to read the 1869 Act only in relation to the 1886 Act is strong. For Henry Reynolds, these different strategies of management indicate a much wider instability in ideas about race in this period. In apparent contrast, Geoffrey Smithers and others collapse any distinction entirely and argue that both the 1869 and 1886 Acts were intended to 'facilitate the evolution of the half-caste Aborigines to white society'.[13] The lack of sustained anaylsis of the formation of the 1869 Act seems a little strange given the wider significance of this earlier legislation. As Katherine Ellinghaus notes, Victoria was the first Australian colony to 'legislate for a system of administration for Indigenous people living inside its borders', and others suggest the 1869 Act provided the model for protection legislation across the Australian colonies (and later, the states).[14] Perhaps, then, we should resist the temptation to read this legislation through or against the strategies of biological assimilation that were hinted at by the 1886 Act (regardless of whether this comparison reveals their origin or indicates that they were yet to be historically possible).

The scholars who do pay close attention to the 1869 Act have been much more concerned to trace its relationship to the development of the reserve system in the 1860s, or compare its stated ambitions to its material effects. Richard Broome and Michael Christie both argue that the Act exemplified the form of paternalistic management that had unfolded in the 1860s. Christie argues, for example, that the Act was 'framed by paternalistic, well meaning men, intent on protecting Aborigines physically and morally and yet it limited the rights and freedom of the Aborigines to such an extent that even the dignity of deciding their own fate seemed lost'.[15] Whereas Patricia Grimshaw's impressive body of work has regarded the significance of the Act in relation to the material effects it had on Indigenous lives across the late nineteenth century and the ways in which

---

12   Patrick Wolfe, 'Nation and MiscegeNation: discursive continuinty in the post-Mabo era', *Social Analysis* 36, 1994: 93–152. Indeed, according to historians like Michael Christie, the practices enabled by the 1886 Act were 'near-genocidal' in their focus on 'half-castes' being absorbed into the broader settler community. Christie, *Aborigines in Colonial Victoria*: 155.

13   So too Andrew Gunstone draws a contiguous line between the 1869, 1886 and then earlier twentieth-century Acts in administrative terms to discern a stubborn tradition of 'strong and discriminatory' practices from 1869 to 1957. Andrew Gunstone and S Heckenberg, *'The Government Owes a Lot of Money to Our People': A History of Indigenous Stolen Wages in Victoria*, Australian Scholarly Publishing, Melbourne, 2009: 17. Felicity Jensz similarly draws a contiguous line between the Acts to suggest that racialising dynamics simply became 'increasingly strident' in the intervening years. Felicity Jensz, *German Moravian Missionaries in the British Colony of Victoria, Australia, 1848–1908*, Brill, Leiden, 2010: 14.

14   Katherine Ellinghaus, 'Regulating Koori marriages: the 1886 Victorian "Aborigines Protection Act"', *Journal of Australian Studies* 67, 2001: 23.

15   Christie, *Aborigines in Colonial Victoria*: 177.

Aborigines carved out spaces within this draconian regime.¹⁶ With a similar focus upon the material effects of the Act, Attwood traces how it formed but one element in the repertoire of management that constrained life in the reserve system.¹⁷ In different, but related, ways, Marguerita Stephens argues that closer attention to the 'material ... and practical dispossession' of Indigenous Victorians reveals a substantial gap between the seemingly humanitarian character of the legislation and the blunt ideas about racial difference that structured everyday life in the colonies.¹⁸

What might happen, though, if we interrogate this piece of legislation and the discursive landscape that enabled its production not as a mechanism to reveal the gap between formation and material effect nor as a precursor to its 1886 revision? I would like to suggest that returning a sense of historical contingency to the 1869 Act, through a close analysis of shifts in thinking about 'protection' and the ethnographic 'character' of Aboriginal people, can more carefully explain how they became the objects and subjects of this form of settler colonial governance in the first place.¹⁹ As Catherine Hall argues, we need to remember that 'processes of differentiation ... were constantly in the making' rather than implying that colonised peoples were subjects acted upon by strategies of colonial rule.²⁰ This means, at the very least, carefully tracing how ideas and practices of differentiation mediated the tension that Indigenous peoples produced as equal (British) subjects with unequal rights.²¹ Indeed, this Act – and the decade-long campaign by the CBPA to produce it – might be understood as a moment in which Aboriginal subjects were constituted in relation to a transforming liberal state. Patrick Joyce suggests historians should consider how the 'rule of liberal freedom' was a technique through which specific entities (in this case people) became both comprehensible objects of government and, in doing so, rendered specific elements of their lives subject to rule and regulation.²² In the colonial context (a crucial site at which these liberal techniques and strategies were first expressed) an imagined boundary between settlers and colonised subjects

---

16 See, for example, Patricia Grimshaw, 'Rethinking approaches to women in missions: the case of colonial Australia', *History Australia* 8(3), 2011: 7–24.
17 Bain Attwood, *Making of the Aborigines*, Allen & Unwin, Sydney, 1989: 85. Indeed, for Attwood a key significance of the Act lay in the fact that missionaries often saw a resort to legislative authority as a threat to their religious legitimacy rather than its compliment.
18 Marguerita Stephens, 'White Without Soap: Philanthropy, Caste and Exclusion in Colonial Victoria' unpublished PhD thesis, University of Melbourne, 2010: 6.
19 Rather than considering the gap between the material governance of Aboriginal people and the legislation that fantasised about its smooth operation, or, regarding the legislation only in as much as it contained the seeds of practices and strategies that would take their full effects much later in the century, it is worthwhile remembering that this was the first piece of legislation that transformed Aboriginal people into distinct subjects of governance in the laboratories of settler colonial statehood.
20 Catherine Hall, 'Introduction', in *Cultures of Empire: Colonizers in Britain and the Empire in the Nineteenth and Twentieth Centuries: A Reader*, Manchester University Press, Manchester, 2000: 20.
21 This phrase is taken from the title of Julie Evans et al., *Equal Subjects, Unequal Rights: Indigenous Peoples in British Settler Colonies, 1830–1910*, Manchester University Press, Manchester, 2003.
22 Patrick Joyce, *The Rule of Freedom: Liberalism and the Modern City*, Verso, London, 2003: 2–7, 187.

provided a mechanism through which the repertoire of governable acts was both organised and differentiated. Moreover, the Act took shape in the wake of profound transformations in the relationship between the colonial state and its settler subjects – first in the devolution of self-government and then through the speedy achievement of manhood suffrage within these polities. These reformulations of colonial rule were, as Ann Curthoys and Jessie Mitchell have shown, profoundly and ambivalently racialised projects.[23]

In the chapter that follows, then, I draw together some of the competing ideas about practices of protection that took shape in the crucial years between the formation of the CBPA in 1860 (and the 1858 Victorian Select Committee that preceeded it) and the passing of the 1869 Protection Act. I ask how the endless political and bureaucratic murmurs about the management of the so-called Aboriginal problem legitimated a specific suite of techniques through which Aboriginal lives could be governed. Or, to put this another way, this chapter wonders how the 'Aborigine' became a governable subject of such coherence and specificity that the Act passed in 1869 without a single question raised about its exceptional powers. I do this by first tracing the emergence of 'protection' in colonial Victoria and the ways in which colonial administrators both adopted and adapted metropolitan humanitarian discourses. This adoption, I suggest, offered the solution to a series of uncertainties that took shape about the legal status of the 'Aborigine' in 1860s Victoria. This adoption and adaption, though, required some serious discursive work. Evangical ideas about protection were not simply implemented by the CBPA, they were recast in ways that offered the Board a unique way to imagine a settler colonial future that, for a brief moment, included Aboriginal people within it. In contrast to both the majority of evangelicals and settlers of a less humanitarian persuasion, in the years between 1860 and 1869 the Board suddenly argued that practices of protection might not only save the souls of Aboriginal people but secure their more earthly generational future. Returning a sense of contingency to those crucial years of debate and contestation can explain why this 1869 Act took shape in the ways that it did.

---

23   Ann Curthoys and Jessie Mitchell, 'The advent of self-government, 1840s–1890', in Alison Bashford and Stuart Macintyre (eds), *The Cambridge History of Australia*, Volume 1, Cambridge University Press, Melbourne, 2013.

The emergence of 'protection' in colonial Victoria

When the member of the Legislative Council Thomas McCombie called for a parliamentary investigation into the condition and treatment of Aboriginal people in 1858, he argued that there was 'scarcely a spot … where the weary aborigine could rest his weary feet [because] Victoria [was] now entirely occupied by a superior race'. Whilst few colonists could make a confident claim about the number of Aboriginal people who had managed to survive the onslaught of pastoral expansion in the 1840s and 1850s and the sudden explosion of unruly settlers during the gold rush, it was clear that Aboriginal communities had suffered severe depopulation because of that all-too-familiar settler colonial story of violence and disease. By the late 1850s, these decimated communities had been completely terrorised and traumatised by violence and death. Aboriginal communities in the 1850s, largely organised around kin relations, had lived through the death of at least half their family members in 20 years, and around 2,000 survivors were struggling to find a social and economic space in amongst a settler community that was indifferent at best and hostile at worst.[24] The practice of begging that Lynette Russell traces elsewhere in this collection was one example of how Aboriginal people were adjusting to this radically transformed environment.

In this context, McCombie spoke with force and conviction about the need to do 'something towards obtaining a measure of justice towards the aborigines' in colonial Victoria. Whilst he did 'not deny the right of the higher race to take possession of the land', he was convinced that the 'right' of the colonists also entailed an obligation to perform their 'duty to the original owners'.[25] McCombie's committee suggested that the colonial state should grant 'protection and assistance … to the aborigines of Victoria' through a series of land grants for missionary activity, a regular apportionment of state funds for their basic 'needs and wants' and a central administrative board to oversee their 'amelioration'.[26] In late May, six men with 'interest and knowledge' in the Aboriginal problem were appointed to oversee the 'protection' of this 'unfortunate race'.[27]

The idea that Indigenous peoples needed protection from the onslaught of settler expansion was hardly new to discussions about imperial policy. Nourished by the humanitarian turn of the early nineteenth century, evangelicals in Britain had long argued for less destructive forms of settler colonisation. So too, by

---

24   I owe a significant debt to Tracey Banivanua Mar for helping me to humanise these 'numbers' in this way.
25   *The Victorian Hansard Containing the Debates and Proceedings of the Legislative Council and Assembly of the Colony of Victoria: Volume 4*, W Fairfax, Melbourne, 1860: 110.
26   *The Argus*, 15 March 1860: 4.
27   *The Argus*, 13 May 1860: 6.

the mid-nineteenth century, claims to respectability by middle-class men were often justified by a demonstration of acute moral sensibility, this included the compassionate treatment of those in need of protection. As Catherine Hall notes, in British public life in the 1840s, 'to be a supporter of the weak and dependent – women, children, enslaved people and animals – constituted part of the independence of middle class masculinity'; it was no coincidence that McCombie was campaigning for colonial separation and self-government as he proposed a more sympathetic demeanour towards the Aboriginal population.[28] McCombie had mobilised precisely this kind of claim in his persistent assertions about the obligations of settlers since his arrival in the colonies in the mid-1840s. As he had written whilst editor of the *Port Phillip Gazette* in 1846, 'the community ... owe it as their solemn duty to do everything in their power to promote the welfare of the aborigines'.[29] In this sense, the history of protection was always constitutively entangled with ideas about collective legitimacy, the political order and practices of governance (both over an independent self and its dependent others).

The flowering of humanitarian sentiment in the decades before McCombie claimed political independence through assertions of moral responsibility was a crucial element of this transformation; like the anti-slavery campaign that recast British political life at the turn of the century, the project of offering 'protection' for native peoples amplified questions about the costs and responsibilities of historical progress both in the colonies and the metropole. For some historians, the 1837 Select Committee in London represented the high-water mark for this movement;[30] this committee and its recommendations sutured together a brief consensus at Westminster about the need to atone for the 'sins of the settlers' whilst also offering protection for the survivors of recent and future expansions.[31] Indeed, the impact of humanitarians on imperial policy in the 1830s – or at least, their impact on how it would be discussed in British public life – was enabled by the wider evangelical revival of the previous 30 years. Even by the 1820s, a broadly consensual form of British Protestantism had emerged that enabled missionaries to collectively craft a self-image in stark opposition to the violence of dispossession.[32]

---

28 Catherine Hall, *Civilising Subjects: Metropole and Colony in the English Imagination 1830–1867*, Chicago University Press, Chicago, 2002: 34.
29 *Port Phillip Gazette*, 11 May 1846, and 16 May 1846, np.
30 Alan Lester, 'Humanitarians and white settlers in the nineteenth century', in Norman Etherington (ed.), *Missions and Empire*, Oxford University Press, Oxford, 2005: 64.
31 Elizabeth Elbourne, 'The sin of the settler: the 1835–36 Select Committee on Aborigines and debates over virtue and conquest in the early nineteenth-century British white settler empire', *Journal of Colonialism and Colonial History* 4(3), 2003, online.
32 Hilary Carey, *God's Empire: Religion and Colonialism in the British World*, Cambridge University Press, Cambridge, 2013: 10; see also, Anna Johnson, *Missionary Writing and Empire, 1800–1860*, Cambridge University Press, Cambridge, 2003: 14.

The development of the Aboriginal Protectorate in Port Phillip flowed directly from these concerns and the committee in particular. In the year before his resignation from the stewardship of the Colonial Office, Glenelg – a figure already embroiled in contestation with settlers at the Cape over their treatment of Indigenous peoples – authorised the deployment of four 'protectors' to the new colony of Port Phillip. Having been first settled by entrepreneurial fiat a few years before, this accident of historical proximity meant that the Colonial Office was trying to manage the expansionist efforts of settlers in Port Phillip in the wake of the select committee. The 'protectorate' as Jessie Mitchell notes, was an early attempt to negotiate between the philanthropic efforts of missionaries and the ever-changing structures of colonial administration. Although this was always an ambivalent negotiation as missionaries usually contrasted their own form of religious interventions with the apparent moral paucity of colonial administrators.[33]

By the time the CBPA first convened in 1860, however, the earlier Protectorate was widely regarded as a complete failure (and frequently discussed in these terms in colonial public life).[34] In 1849, all but one of the Protectors had been dismissed (although figures like Edward Parker remained in the colony and attempted to forge ahead with humanitarian projects). Nonetheless, in the intervening years, missionary endeavours had begun to haltingly take root in the colony. Presbyterians formed missionary committees and Anglicans did the same, eventually producing enough support to sustain the employment of a missionary on land allocated by the colonial government at Mount Franklin. Moravian missionaries arrived in the early 1850s and stumblingly tried to encourage Aboriginal people onto their doomed Lake Boga mission. By the time the 1858 Select Committee made its recommendations, the ad-hoc system of government grants for missionary endeavour was beginning to take shape and the CBPA was designed to formalise, oversee and more carefully administer the disbursement of this obligation.

Ironically, then, even though historians like Lester suggest that the 1837 Select Committee seemed like the peak of humanitarian influence over colonial policy – and in the metropole it certainly was – in the newly self-governing Colony of Victoria in the late 1850s, the idea and practice of protection once again gathered steam. Over the 1860s, the CBPA would develop a network of guardians to oversee the distribution of clothing and rations across the colony, shape and support missionary practice (although this relationship was sometimes unclear), and secure a system of reserves within which, they thought, Aboriginal people

---

33 Johnson, *Missionary Writing and Empire, 1800–1860*: 33.
34 Although, as Jessie Mitchell notes, these claims about failure were as much about justifying certain practices of management in their own present rather than a reflection on the inadequacy of the Protectors. Jessie Mitchell, *In Good Faith? Governing Indigenous Australia Through God, Charity and Empire, 1825–1855*, Aboriginal History Inc. and ANU E Press, Canberra, 2011: 31.

could find respite from land-hungry settlers. By the end of the 1860s, the Board oversaw a network of six stations, including its own reserve modelled upon, but without the evangelical justification for, missions. However, questions about the relationship between Aboriginal subjects and the transforming colonial state constantly challenged the CBPA's activities in the 1860s. The Board was – in its original form – established as a mechanism to distribute near-evangelical care and compassion rather than necessarily 'govern' Aboriginal people. At the same time, however, the activities of the Board itself mobilised the strategies and techniques of governance that so many scholars have suggested were at the heart of an emerging liberal modernity in Britain and its colonies. The Board collected information about the health of Aboriginal people, monitored their presence and treatment in the judicial system and employed this knowledge in an attempt to control their behaviour. Whilst constantly hampered by their ambivalent position within the bureaucracy of the state, and their capacity to exert authority over their apparent charges, the Board did much more than simply distribute evangelical protection.

Protection as a strategy of governance

Recent work has begun to carefully consider the ways in which the progressive story of liberal modernity might be retold as a much more tenuous and inchoate process in which the relationship between the state and its subjects was constantly reconfigured and reassembled through boundary contests over the public and the private, the market and the family, and the individual and the collective. Rather than considering liberalism as a mechanism through which citizens could claim rights, we can, instead, ponder how liberalism functioned as a technique of government in which 'markets, civil society and everyday life' became sites at which the limits of state intervention would be negotiated.[35] The citizen of liberal modernity was only made possible through a shifting set of boundaries that established certain practices as private and others as subject to state intervention. Seen in this light, the history of the Board could be a story of how these boundaries were imagined through their suspension. In the 1860s, moreover, the colonial state was in the process of 'being put together', as probably the best known historian of the Australian state Alastair Davidson points out. Significantly, though, Davidson virtually ignores the history of the 1869 Protection Act, collapsing the 'failure' of the Port Phillip Protectorate into a story of systematic neglect over much of the second half of the nineteenth century, misdating the opening of Framlingham by 50 years and ignoring

---

35 James Gunn and Simon Vernon, 'Introduction', in James Gunn and Simon Vernon (eds), *The Peculiarities of Liberal Modernity in Britain*, University of California Press, Berkeley, 2011: 9.

the intersection between missionary practice and the CBPA completely.³⁶ If 'markets, civil society and everyday life' formed a crucial site at which the relationship between the state and its subjects would be imagined, then it is hardly a surprise that these three registers – and the place of Aboriginal people as subjects before the law – were central concerns for the Board in its first decade. Liberal governance is, moreover, not only a practice of managing the relationship between the state and its subjects; it is a technique through which subjects will manage their relations with each other. For the Board, the relation between settlers and Aboriginal people – and how they might be regulated – loomed large as their most pressing problem. Early in the decade the Board attempted to deploy various mechanisms of the state to manage the treatment of Aboriginal people in the colony, soon, however, it became apparent that attempting to moderate how settlers treated Aboriginal people specifically within the existing organisation of legal authority was almost impossible.

For example, the sale of 'intoxicating liquor' to Aboriginal people had been a concern of the CBPA since its first meeting and humanitarians in the colony had long suggested that the drunkenness was one of the more disturbing 'vices' that accompanied colonial expansion. Soon the Board would suggest the 'the necessity of taking strenuous measures to abate the sale of intoxicating liquors to the blacks'.³⁷ The sale of liquor to Aboriginal people was, in fact, already prohibited by the legislation the colony had inherited from New South Wales. This restriction had been instantiated to 'protect' settlers from the apparent violence of intoxicated Aboriginal people as much as 'protect' Aboriginal people from the 'vice' of drunkenness.³⁸ The Board in Victoria was not exempt from this kind of thinking, earlier suggesting that 'several murders have been committed by the blacks who have procured intoxicating liquors'.³⁹ In New South Wales, a shift away from the 'conception of Aborigines as enemy' meant this restriction would be removed in 1862. In Victoria at the same time, however, the Board engaged in a campaign to strengthen these restrictions – not to protect settlers but now to protect Aboriginal people.⁴⁰ From its earliest meetings, it sent letters around to police magistrates in the colony to remind them that the legislation inherited from New South Wales restricted the sale of alcohol to Aboriginal people to try and compel the enforcement of this restriction.⁴¹ The threat of financial punishment or the retraction of a licence to sell liquor was not, the CBPA argued, enough to compel publicans to halt these transactions. Settlers

---

36 Alistair Davidson, *The Invisible State: The Formation of the Australian State*, Cambridge University Press, Cambridge, 1991: 78.
37 First CBPA Annual Report (1861): 6.
38 Second CBPA Annual Report (1862): 6.
39 Third CBPA Annual Report (1864): 7.
40 Anna Doukakis, *The Aboriginal People, Parliament and Protection in New South Wales*, Federation Press, Sydney 2006: 6.
41 First CBPA Annual Report (1861): 8.

who sold 'spirits to the blacks should not be fined, but imprisoned', so grave was the offence.⁴² When the colonial parliament reformed its licensing laws in 1864, the Board worked hard to ensure that the restrictions inherited from (but since withdrawn within) New South Wales stayed in place in the Victorian 'Wine, Beer and Spirit Sale Statute'. Whilst the wish for imprisonment was unmet, they nonetheless achieved an increase of the penalty of sale to £10.

The Board attempted to shape economic relations between Aboriginal people and settlers in other ways as well. In matters of employment, the CBPA attempted to control how settlers would employ Aboriginal people and the conditions of contract under which that employment would unfold. Citing examples of settlers refusing to pay Aboriginal labourers and exploiting the Board's generosity in order to buck their responsibilities for sustenance, the Board noted that they had experienced 'difficulty in dealing with cases [where settlers] have taken Aborigines into employment [because] the responsibility resting on the settler and his duties towards his servant are, in some instance, unrecognised or misunderstood'.⁴³ In one case, the Board had tried to force a settler to 'give up' his servant – for reasons of apparent mistreatment – but floundered against their lack of authority.⁴⁴

Similar issues unfolded when settlers proposed to contract a successful team of Aboriginal cricketers to tour England in 1866. On the back of successful Aboriginal cricket teams in the Wimmera in the early 1860s, William Hayman and Tom Hamilton hatched a scheme to train the team locally and send them to England for a tour. The Board strongly objected, suggesting that these Aboriginal men were being exploited for settler gain and the efforts of the Board to civilise the population would be undone during such a prolonged absence. They were, however, unable to draw on any legislative power to prohibit the cricketers contracting to Hayman and Hamilton for the tour; in 1867 the Aboriginal team signed on the dotted line. Indeed, David Sampson's careful work reveals that settler signatories had contradictory understandings about the legal capacity of Aboriginal people to freely 'contract with' others; some considered them legally free subjects whereas others thought they were dependants and thus their capacity for legal consent was compromised.⁴⁵ The Board argued strongly that even if the latter was not the case legally, it certainly was in moral and civilisational terms. MacBain argued that if

---

42   Second CBPA Annual Report (1862): 10.
43   Fourth CBPA Annual Report (1864): 11.
44   Central Board for the Protection of Aborigines (CBPA), 'Minutes of meetings', March 1862, National Australian Archives (NAA), Series B314, Item 1.
45   David Samspon, '"The nature and effects thereof were by each of them understood": Aborigines, agency, law and power in the 1867 Gurnett contract', *Labour History* 74, 1998: 59.

the trip was undertaken for the purpose of improving the status and ameliorating the degraded state of those aborigines, and for raising them in the scale of the human family, then, indeed, I would gladly assist in carrying out an object so worthy and humane; but there is too much reason to fear that such desirable results will be altogether ignored in the proposed expedition.[46]

The Board discovered that attempting to force settlers to acknowledge this difference was impossible; legislative restriction was the only solution.[47] The 1869 Act, produced in the context of a debate between entrepreneurial settlers and the Board, granted it the right to 'prescribe the terms on which contracts for and on behalf of Aboriginals may be made with Europeans'.[48] The Board soon found that the notion of 'prescription' proved vague in judicial terms and the Act could not be applied retrospectively. Burnt by their experience with the cricket tour, the Board ensured that an 1871 legislative amendment meant that 'no contract with any Aboriginal for any service of employment for longer than three months shall have validity … unless such contract shall have been approved by the Board'.[49]

Similar ambiguities about the status of Aboriginal people as legal subjects had long unfolded in the practice of criminal law. As Lisa Ford discovered, questions about the jurisdiction of British law over Aboriginal people in the colonies seemed to have been resolved in a series of decisions about violence within Aboriginal communities in the 1830s.[50] However, as Mark Finnane notes, this did not resolve the questions about the legal status of Aboriginal people in the criminal system so much as establish they were subjects within it. Finnane's careful study of cases across the nineteenth century reveals that colonial jurisdictions frequently mobilised notions of custom, tradition, culture and race to specify and adjudicate criminal proceedings.[51] Whilst earlier governors in Victoria had suggested that making the Aboriginal population 'amenable as subjects to British law' would make them more 'civilised',[52] the Board argued strongly that the operation of criminal law needed to acknowledge the specificity of Aboriginal subjects as an ethnographic group.

---

46 *The Argus*, 14 October 1867: 6.
47 CBPA, 'Minutes of meetings', NAA, Series B314, April 1865.
48 *An Act to provide for the Protection and Management of the Aboriginal Natives of Victoria*, 11 November 1869, Victorian Parliament.
49 Sampson, 'The nature and effects': 64.
50 Lisa Ford, *Settler Sovereignty: Sovereignty: Jurisdiction and Indigenous People in America and Australia, 1788–1836*, Harvard University Press, Harvard, 2011: passim.
51 Mark Finnane, 'Settler justice and Aboriginal homicide in late colonial Australia', *Australian Historical Studies* 42(2), 2011: 244–259.
52 Quoted in Frances Thiele, 'Superintendent LaTrobe and the amenability of Aboriginal people to British law', *Provenance* 8, 2009: 3.

From 1860, the Board attempted to mediate between the colonial criminal system and Aboriginal people in Victoria. These subjects, the Board argued, represented an exception to the notion of equality before the law – nowhere was this more evident than in how sentences were handed down. From 1860 'criminal law as it effects the blacks was considered by the Board' and they soon argued that the judiciary needed to 'take steps' to 'mitigat[e] ... the severity of our laws, as they effect Aboriginal criminals'. Because of the

> character of the black ... the effect of close imprisonment on one of this people is to deprive him of all hope and gradually reduce him to a state of imbecility. Accustomed to freedom in its widest sense, the restraint of a gaol produced a lethargy which in cases of prolonged improvement results in death.[53]

The Board wrote letters to the Attorney-General to try and seek the reduction of specific sentences, mobilised its resources to try and produce more careful representation by counsel in criminal proceedings, and even sought pardons from the Governor in cases already heard.[54] From 1863, the annual reports began to tabulate the number of Aboriginal people currently incarcerated for criminal offences in the colonies, arguing 'that close imprisonment is not the kind of punishment to which an Aboriginal should be subjected'.[55] The great irony was, of course, that the Board was attempting to gain only a slightly different kind of disciplinary control over Aboriginal lives. Throughout the 1860s, though, the Board was constantly frustrated by the rigidity of the criminal justice system – just as it could not force settlers to adjust their engagements with Aboriginal people, so too, attempting to mediate between the judiciary and Aboriginal people was difficult. Even whilst they mobilised the powerful vocabularies of difference that were beginning to have substantive purchase in colonial life, they were constantly stymied by the difficulties of forcing a judicial system to acknowledge ethnographic difference with consistency. Unless Aboriginal subjects were recognised as having distinct legal status, they would be unable to govern them effectively.

Indeed, within six months of the Board's first meeting in 1860, its members had noted that their precise relationship (both to the colonial state and to Aboriginal people) was ambiguous at best. As soon as the Board was appointed, its secretary sought clarification about its position within an expanding colonial government and the 'Commissoner of Lands and Survey' had confirmed that 'the government would offer every facility to the Board to carry out its views'. The scope and limit of the Board's capacity to shape the purpose of its work,

---

53 First CBPA Annual Report (1861): 7.
54 CBPA, 'Minutes of meetings', NAA, Series B314, May 1861.
55 Second CBPA Annual Report (1862): 14.

organise the allocation of its resources and intervene into the lives of its charges was still unclear. In June, it was 'ultimately agreed' that the Board would 'stand adjourned … until the powers to be entrusted them should be clearly defined in a commission issued for that purpose, as to the control of officers and the disbursement of funds … which at present they cannot claim'.[56] The Board's place within the colonial bureaucracy was soon clarified, it would be 'subject to the political responsibility of the Department of Land and Survey' but would have the freedom to decide how its financial recourses should be distributed and the mechanisms by which this care and protection should be offered.[57] The question of how much control the Board would have over Aboriginal people was, however, left unanswered. Later that year, the Board had pleaded for legislative clarification about who would have 'custody of Aboriginal minors', suggesting that power might be granted to the governor, whose authority the Board could then mobilise to take control of Aboriginal children, but these negotiations stalled as their chairman Heales was soon entangled with the machinations of the rise and fall of government ministries and his brief episode as chief secretary.[58]

In 1862, the Board, in consultation with the Attorney-General, drafted a Bill to grant them more powers to control the movements and residence of Aboriginal people as well as custodianship of all Aboriginal children. In May, Brough Smyth reported on a meeting with the current minister of Justice 'who held out no hope of such a Bill being brought in this session'.[59] The Board took matters into its own hands, and submitted the Bill by deputation to the chief secretary in September of that year; it was continuously postponed due to the 'other pressing demands on the attention of the legislature'.[60] Heales attempted to form another select committee in the legislature in 1863 to provoke a discussion of the problem of governing Aboriginal people, but the attempt floundered after initial support in the Legislative Assembly, defeated by the apparent indifference of colonial legislators. Soon the Board registered their frustration in their annual report, noting in 1864 that 'their urgent solicitations for some amendment of the laws affecting the blacks have not yet received attention'.[61] Two years later their frustration was growing, and they noted that

> nearly three years have elapsed since they furnished the draft of a Bill; and they regret to say that the circumstances of the colony have

---

56   CBPA, 'Minutes of meetings', NAA, Series B314, June 1860.
57   CBPA, 'Minutes of meetings', NAA, Series B314, August 1860.
58   CBPA, 'Minutes of meetings', NAA, Series B314, September 1860.
59   CBPA, 'Minutes of meetings', NAA, Series B314, May 1862.
60   CBPA, 'Minutes of meetings', NAA, Series B314, November 1861, see also, September 1862.
61   Third CBPA Annual Report (1864): 4.

prevented your Excellency's advisors from taking those steps which are so urgently needed for the protection of the Aborigines ... under the present circumstances [the Board] can do little.[62]

Finally, in the next year, the Board would achieve the legislative authority it had so desperately sought. The Act passed in 1869 granted them control over where Aboriginal people lived, how their children were raised, how their employment with settlers would be managed and what happened to their earnings. The Board had effectively inserted itself between Aboriginal people and their relations with employers, their children and the state whilst, at the same time, claiming power to force them onto the system of reserves and missions. 'Protected by a just law,' the Board claimed, 'there is hope this people may yet be preserved.'[63]

Over the previous 10 years, the Board had developed a set of strategies that resonated with the key concerns of the emerging liberal state. Moreover, given the CBPA had 'scrambled' for authority in its early years and constantly complained about the ambiguous legal status of Aboriginal subjects, this was quite a transformation. Part of the explanation for this new-found legitimacy was, of course, the mobilisation of long-standing ideas about protection that were nourished by evangelical thought. Clearly, this legislatively empowered protection was, however, no straightforward adoption of evangelical practice. Crucially, some of the dominant elements of evangelical thought about Aboriginal people were recast and challenged by the Board in the mid-1860s – not least in a different imagining of the temporal future of Aboriginal people. Whilst the 1869 Act might be read as the combination of liberal strategies of rule and evangelical ideals of protection, their discursive entanglement only became possible after the CBPA recast some of the assumptions of their evangical allies.

Glimmers of an Aboriginal future

Questions about the future of Indigenous peoples had reverberated in discussions of the settler empire long before the instantiation of the Board in 1859. Settler colonialism was (and is) a project of (violent) historical transformation – it inevitably raised questions about the near and distant future of the peoples both propelling and struggling against its territorial imperatives. Whilst the hardening of racial categories as the century unfolded provided fertile, imaginative ground for the perception of Indigenous extinction (and thus a powerful vocabulary for settlers to enact it), earlier ideas about religiously ordained imperial progress and human difference could sustain similarly morbid predictions of the coming disappearance of native peoples across the settler empire. As Patrick Brantlinger

---

62   Fifth CBPA Annual Report (1866): 18.
63   Sixth CBPA Annual Report (1869): 8.

demonstrates, whilst the biological (and blood) based arithmetic of 'race' did not take shape until the later nineteenth century, what would become ideas about the 'doomed race' in the 1880s had their antecedents in earlier predictions about the demise of native peoples in the face of imperial expansion.[64]

Nontheless, there were important differences between these narratives of decline and disappearance. The later perception of the 'doomed race' was, as Henry Reynolds and Marilyn Lake note, deeply entangled with transnational ideas about the historical destiny of 'white man's countries' and the rigid categories of racial difference that underwrote them.[65] In the mid-nineteenth century, however, the ghosts of anti-slavery campaigns haunted British vocabularies of human difference and capacity; the various 'experts' who governed the empire were torn between assertions of human brotherhood and stubborn evocations of ethnographic difference. Importantly, though, Brantlinger points out that even evangelicals nourished by humanitarian turn in the 1830s were ambivalent about the possibilities of earthly Indigenous futures. Mid-nineteenth-century predictions of immanent disappearance – which were common to observers in both the periphery and the metropole – were powerfully shaped by a story of melancholic lament. Evangelical vocabularies provided powerful discursive mechanisms through which the colonising subject could both enact and lament the destruction of Indigenous peoples as both a loss and incorporation into the colonising self. To add even more complexity to this picture, the categories through which these mid-century discussions unfolded were sometimes understood as historically immutable and sometimes transitory – unstable ideas about the latter meant that even those who contested the notion of inevitable decline were uncertain about whether individual Aboriginal people could be 'civilised' or if the 'civilisation of the Aborigine' would unfold in generations to come.

As Lynette Russell suggests, moreover, narratives about the apparent 'demise' of Aboriginal Tasmanians reverberated through Victorian public life in the 1850s to provide yet more evidence for this kind of thinking.[66] The *Geelong Advertiser* declared in 1855 that the 'Aborigines of Tasmania [are] a race now nearly extinct … the inferior race has slowly but steadily yielded; and though long succoured and protected, there is now a mere handful of the aboriginal inhabitants left'.[67] So too, in a tidy disbursement of responsibility, the apparent failure of the Port Phillip Protectorate in the 1840s could be easily marshalled to suggest that settlers were powerless to effect any change. The Victorian 1858 Select Committee was

---

64 Patrick Bratlinger, *Dark Vanishings: Discourse on the Extinction of Primitive Races, 1800–1930*, Cornell University Press, New York, 2003: 17–44.
65 Marilyn Lake and Henry Reynolds, *Drawing the Global Colour Line: White Men's Countries and the International Challenge of Racial Equality*, Cambridge University Press, Cambridge, 2008: 137–165.
66 Lynette Russell, forthcoming.
67 *Geelong Advertiser*, 25 September 1855: 3.

keen to discover the cause of the 'great and almost unprecedented reduction in the number of the Aborigines' and McCombie's report suggested that, like other experiences of colonisation, the 'general occupation of the country by a white population ... the scarcity of game ... in some cases, cruelty and ill-treatment ... [and] the vices acquired by contact with a civilized race' had proved disastrous for Indigenous peoples in the colony.[68] It was a short step to remove any responsibility for this destruction from settlers themselves; they simply became signifiers of historical change rather than its agents.

Witnesses to the 1858 Select Committee were asked if 'they could be saved from ultimate extinction' and even humanitarians like William Thomas, who argued for a system of care and protection, suggested that 'extinction must be the sequel of this hapless race'.[69] Many other settlers, often whilst supporting the development of reserves, similarly predicted an eventual disappearance; landholding settlers and amateur ethnographers like William Beveridge suggested their 'final extinction' was inevitable. Frederick Godfrey similarly argued that because 'blacks were confirmed in, and by natural capacity adapted for, their wild roving life of freedom', they could not carve out an existence in the changed circumstances of colonisation. Godfrey worked hard to 'ameliorate' the conditions of Indigenous people around the Loddon district and was known as 'the Loddon blacks' best friend'. He nonetheless thought that even though many of the 'young could be reclaimed and civilized ... their final extinction seems the inevitable law of nature'.[70] Similarly pessimistic predictions were made in both parliament and the colonial press, soon, 'they would cease to exist, except in name' suggested *The Argus*, and any effort by the settlers to improve their condition was a moral and religious project in the present rather than an endeavour with an historicised future.[71] One settler gloomily predicted that 'attempts to reclaim the aborigines to the ranks of civilization' were doomed to fail.[72]

Even as these laments papered over a history of mistreatment and violence (or at least made this violence the exception rather than the logic of settler colonial rule), they did not necessarily justify indifference in their own present. Indeed, the notions of compassion and sympathy that often framed these predictions also worked as a mechanism to secure humanitarian intervention; evangelicals in the colony repeatedly imagined themselves in opposition to this apparent indifference suggesting that, instead, settlers owed a moral debt to the 'remaining

---

68 Report of the Select Committee of the Legislative Council on the Aborigines; together with the Proceedings of the Committee, Minutes of Evidence, and Appendices, Government Printer, Melbourne, 1859: v.
69 Report of the Select Committee of the Legislative Council on the Aborigines (1859): 27.
70 Report of the Select Committee of the Legislative Council on the Aborigines (1859): 21.
71 *The Argus*, 19 July 1861: 5.
72 *The Argus*, 7 September 1866: 7.

blacks'.[73] When McCombie tabled his report to the colonial parliament, he spoke powerfully about 'obtaining a measure of justice for the blacks' and ensuring their protection from the 'moral outrages [of] some colonists'.[74] So too, missionaries made potent claims that settlers owed Aborigines their 'protection'. As Anne O'Brien notes, humanitarians wove together ideas about justice and British rule to argue that colonists should deliver Aboriginal people a form of reparations for their dispossession.[75] When he opened a meeting of the Board of Australasian Missions, the Anglican Bishop of Sydney suggested that 'in the occupation of their soil we are partakers of their worldly things … natural and much more Christian equity points out [that] in justice they should be of our spiritual [concern]'.[76] Again and again, throughout the Australian colonies in the mid-nineteenth century, missionaries and humanitarians would argue for government support for missionary intervention; the revelation of the gospel and care for the physical 'wants' of Aboriginal people would represent a 'measure of justice' for dispossession.[77] As the chair of the Anglican 'Mission to the Aborigines' meeting noted in 1857, it was an 'act of pure justice that an effort should be made to convey to them the privileges of the Christian religion'.[78]

However, the actions of evangelicals were framed by a markedly different temporality than the (near and distant) earthly future that shaped the emerging institutions of colonial governance. As the chair of the 1860 meeting of the Church of England Mission to the Aborigines noted, 'God estimated the value of a single soul more highly than any more temporal matters'.[79] Spiritual reclamation was the crucial lens through which any material action unfolded. As the missionary Frederick Spieseke noted when he spoke to a capacity audience at the Melbourne Mechanics Institute regarding Moravian missionary efforts in Victoria, their endeavours were shaped not only by an attempt to ameliorate their 'fearful [material] state' but also to ensure their 'Christianization'. Moravian efforts were not only concerned with 'their bodies but [also] with their souls', which should be 'reclaimed' before their extinction. Indeed,

---

73   Report of the Select Committee of the Legislative Council on the Aborigines (1859): iii.
74   VPD (1859): 789.
75   Ann O'Brien, 'Humanitarianism and reparation in colonial Australia', *Journal of Colonialism and Colonial History* 12(2), 2011, http://dx.doi.org/10.1353/cch.2011.0016
76   *The Herald*, 2 November 1850: 2.
77   This phrase appears frequently, *The Perth Gazette* and *Independent Journal of Politics and News*, 14 November 1851: 4; *The Argus*, 27 October 1858: 4. What had taken shape as a claim for justice in the context of frontier killings had, in NSW, Vic and SA by the mid-century become a powerful mechanism to justify humanitarian intervention. Even the Catholic Bishop of Melbourne offered a scathing account of the culpability of settlers. The Bishop noted that it was 'a melancholy fact that the reason why the numbers of savage tribes had always diminished in every country in which civilized man had set his foot was in consequence of the wickedness of many of those people who professed and called themselves Christians. The mere fact of civilized men living in countries inhabited by savages was not the cause of the savages declining in numbers.' Receiving 'the gospel and manifesting the truth in their lives' could ensure their survival.
78   *The Argus*, 20 August 1857: 5.
79   *The Argus*, 20 January 1860: 5.

whilst the annual reports for the CBPA in the 1860s made careful calculations about mortality and living conditions, the Moravian missionaries in the 1850s calculated their success in spiritual terms; successful conversions functioned as the central economy of evangelicism.[80] So too, the Anglican missionary Thomas Goodwin encouraged his fellow Victorians with an account of the successful conversion he recently witnessed in South Australia. Whilst the 'blacks ... by many persons are deemed ... unsusceptible of religion', in South Australia he discovered 'a remnant, it is true, but yet a people ... worshipping Him whom their fathers knew not, but who, by His all-powerful grace, they have been brought to know and love'.[81] Moreover, like the long history of evangelical practice that preceded them, at the various public meetings held to secure support for missionary activity in the colony, stories of individual conversion provided crucial nourishment for the arduous project of mission work. Whilst the earthly treatment of Indigenous people in the present could be understood to exert a powerful claim on colonists, evangelical thought was not necessarily shaped by a concern to ensure the generational future of these communities.

Seen in these terms, it is no surprise that, unlike the broader public culture of the colonies, missionaries and their supporters did not adopt a uniform position about the earthly fate of Aboriginal people. Michael Christie argues that in the 1850s and 1860s, humanitarians adopted the twin projects of 'Civilization and Christianization' as the centerpiece of Aboriginal policy.[82] The entanglement of these ideas in the 1860s was not based, however, on an assumption that missionary intervention would produce Aboriginal futures. At the first meeting of the Anglican 'Mission to the Aborigines' in Victoria, the chair noted that 'in all probability, the opportunity of attending to [evangelical activity] will, with the natives themselves, be passed away for ever'. Even as he wanted to 'guard the Members of the Society against the idea that the mental standard of the Aborigines is so low that they are incapable of instruction', the Anglican Missionary Committee was far from certain this could produce a generational

---

80 See, for example, the discussion of Nathaniel Pepper's conversion: 'The object for which the Moravian mission was established, namely – the glory of God in the salvation of men,—has been attained in regard to at least this poor Native, and it is only due tribute of praise to God to acknowledge that every day's patient labour, every self-sacrifice of love, every dutiful act of every kind done for this Mission has been more than overpaid. God is greatly to be praised for the salvation of even one poor sinner, and each several victory over Satan and his hosts serves to inspire fresh zeal and love in the armies of the living God.' First Annual Report: Further Facts Relating to the Moravian Mission in Australia, Read in Connection with the Report of the Committee at the Annual Meeting of the Melbourne Association in Aid of the Moravian Mission to the Aborigines of Australia, Fergusson & Moore, Melbourne, 1862: 4.
81 *The Argus*, 23 January 1860: 5.
82 Michael Christie, *Aborgines in Colonial Victoria*.

future.⁸³ Four years later, the committee would suggest that 'the people are passing away – soon they will be all gone, and it is our duty to work while it is called to-day'.⁸⁴

The possibility of extinction could even add urgency to the missionary project. At a meeting of the Anglican Missionary Committee in Melbourne in 1855, the Archdeacon of Geelong assumed that the 'Aboriginal races [would] sink into non-existence before the appearance of civilization'. This did not, however, 'exonerate' the colonists from their duty. Indeed, inaction – even if it failed to ensure their survival – would make the entire colony 'virtually murderers'. The 'words of the gospel', for the Archdeacon, could 'reach [the Aborigine's] intellect and touch his heart' if only missionaries might learn the native language. At present 'the darkened minds of the aborigines were one of the strongholds of Satan, [and] God could with perfect ease overturn these strong holds, and influence their hearts to receive the Gospel'.⁸⁵ Conversion and reclamation, then, were the missionaries truest calling, in spite – or perhaps even because – of their imagined disappearance. As a fellow Anglican argued, 'the night cometh on so rapidly [for Aboriginal people] that the remaining hours of the day ought to be improved to the utmost'.⁸⁶

Missionaries and their supporters from other denominations were, however, less certain of this earthly demise. Even in the 1850s, Presbyterian leaders and the Moravian missionaries they supported argued that spiritual intervention could be the mechanism through which the 'decline' might be prevented. Perhaps because the theological history of both these denominations encouraged a more earthly orientation, or perhaps because ideas of progressive reform were deeply entangled with Presbyterian narratives of individual and collective improvement, the network that emerged between Moravian missionaries, their supporters and Presbyterian leaders sometimes suggested that the reforming projects of 'Christianization and Civilization' could 'save from extinction the races of fallen humanity'.⁸⁷ In Bendigo in 1865, the Presbyterian minister (and later vice president of Scotch College) Reverend Moir delivered a lecture on the 'customs and religious beliefs of the Aborigines of Victoria'. After the lecture, he engaged in a wide-ranging discussion of the missionary efforts in Victoria with the chair and local medical practitioner. Combining their spiritual and material expertise, Dr Boyd and Rev. Moir agreed that whilst the Aboriginal

---

83 First Annual Report of the Melbourne Church of England Mission to the Aborigines of Victoria, Mason and Firth, Melbourne, 1854: 4.
84 Fourth Annual Report of the Melbourne Church of England Mission to the Aborigines of Victoria, Mason and Firth, Melbourne, 1858: 10.
85 Second Annual Report of the Melbourne Church of England Mission to the Aborigines of Victoria, Mason and Firth, Melbourne, 1855: 9.
86 Fifth Annual Report of the Melbourne Church of England Mission to the Aborigines of Victoria, Mason & Firth, Melbourne, 1859: 7.
87 *The Argus*, 2 July 1851: 4.

population had decreased most rapidly 'from want of food, scant clothing and introduction of disease', missionary activity could 'teach them the civilization of the whites' so they might find a place in the colonial future.[88] Elsewhere, Presbyterians suggested that because their fellow churchman John Green acted as an 'evangelist among' Aboriginal people at Coranderrk, the 'civilization of Aborigines' could be possible when 'Christian habits (were) formed' (even though he was a secular appointment on the CBPA-run reserve).[89] By the late 1860s, Ramahyuck station in Gippsland, managed and supported by the 'Moravian Mission in connection with the Presbyterian Church of Victoria', was being discussed in similar terms. The *Illustrated Australian News* provided a sketch of the station and directed the reader to observe the schoolhouse and other buildings to suggest that spiritual 'salvation' could produce a generational future; 'the fences, gardens and other improvements [and] the general bearing of the natives in front to the place' suggested their 'fate' was not sealed.[90]

However, this Presbyterian and Moravian optimism was not widely shared. When the CBPA met for the first time in 1860, it faced a public culture in which predictions about the earthly future of Aboriginal people in Victoria was ambivalent at best and pessimistic at worst. Whilst some (but not all) evangelicals wove together the notion of 'Christianization and Civilization' to suggest that missionary action could save the spiritual and material futures of Aboriginal communities, most others found themselves in the intellectual company of wider public culture in colonial Victoria. A steady (or sometimes more sudden) generational decline was the only Aboriginal future they could imagine. In these terms, 'protection' implied moral and compassionate amelioration and a respite from settlers hungry for territory. In the first few years, the Board's practice largely reflected these ideas.

In those years, the CBPA's most pressing concern was to attend 'to the physical wants of the blacks'.[91] The instantiation of the Board, and the funds for rations and clothing that the parliament had offered for their task, could 'improve the welfare [of] the blacks generally' and 'preserve them from starvation'. Rather than the 'niggardly hand' the colonial state had previously proffered Aboriginal people, the Board suggested it would be an agent of 'warm sympathy' for these 'destitute' figures.[92] Moreover, given the political contention that surrounded the issue of state aid, it is little wonder the CBPA was keen to avoid anything that might resemble support for specific denominational missionary intervention. Requests for aid from the Moravians in addition to the standard allocations of rations and clothing for individual Aboriginal people were firmly rejected;

---

88 *Bendigo Advertiser*, 25 October 1865: 3.
89 *Australian News for Home Readers*, 25 October 1865: 11.
90 *Illustrated Australian News*, 1 January 1869: 5.
91 Sixth CBPA Annual Report (1869): vi.
92 First CBPA Annual Report (1861): 1, 6, 12.

funding the mission would be left to the missionaries and their network of denominationally specific supporters. The monthly meetings of the Board in the early 1860s were frequently dominated by the construction of careful distinctions between material support for Aboriginal people and financial support for missionary activity. Whilst the Board noted that 'every endeavour should be made to foster and encourage the self-denying efforts of the enlightened missionary', repeated requests for CBPA funds for the construction of mission buildings and the payment of missionaries provoked careful and lengthy discussions but were always rejected.[93] The CBPA was the mechanism through which the material obligations of the colonial state to Aboriginal people would be disbursed and missionaries could be the agents of this activity; whilst the members of the Board agreed that Christianisation was morally worthy, for the CBPA it was the mechanism through which a material obligation would be paid rather than its central object.

Adjusting the evangelical vocabulary

However, the Board faced an even bigger problem; for the state to manage the compassionate 'ameliorat[ion of] the conditions of the blacks', they needed to know where and how Aboriginal people were living. In the years after the Port Phillip Protectorate was disbanded, William Thomas – the lone guardian of Aborigines in the unruly context of gold-rush Victoria – had struggled to maintain an accurate picture of the number of Aboriginal people who were carving out a social and economic niche in the colony, let alone produce an empirically grounded account of their condition. Much like the 1858 Select Committee then, it is little wonder that the first years of the CBPA operated much like an audit. The committee's report had provided an estimate of the number of living Aboriginal people (and the 'conditions' in which they lived); but the Board was able to draw on its network of honorary guardians over a much longer period. In their first couple of months they issued

> a circular letter to the several honorary correspondents, wardens, police magistrates and respectable settlers throughout the Colony, asking information as to the numbers, condition and location of the Aborigines … This letter was published in the newspapers; it attained a wide circulation and the attention of all classes was directed to it … a mass of information was collected which has been of great utility to the Board.[94]

Soon, this information would be supported by regular inspections by the two employees of the Board, guardian William Thomas and secretary Brough Smyth.

---

93   CBPA, 'Minutes of meetings', NAA, Series B314, May 1864.
94   Second CBPA Annual Report (1862): 6.

Indeed, Brough Smyth's near-maniacal activities in the early 1860s crafted a geography of Aboriginal life through which the governance of Aboriginal people would unfold.

Whilst the early reports of the CBPA both recounted a litany of impoverishment and functioned as a sorry indictment of colonial indifference, soon, a sense of muted optimism shaped the discussion of the emerging system of reserves, missions and rations. Of course the condemnation of colonial treatment and the muted celebration of CBPA success must be read, at least in part, as a justification of expenditure. However, a firm rejection of inevitable extinction began to emerge. Soon after the replacement of Heales as chair, and drawing upon the geography of Aboriginal life crafted by Brough Smyth, the Board began to argue firmly against the notion of Indigenous disappearance. In his first report as President of the CBPA in 1865, James MacBain argued that 'there is hope this people may yet be preserved' not only from the 'harsher miseries' of colonial dispossession but disappearance altogether.[95] Drawing on accounts of the Board-managed station at Coranderrk in particular, the CBPA provided evidence of declining mortality rates. The blunt fact of Aboriginal survival functioned as a powerful disruption to the powerful narrative of extinction (which for the Board was a sign of their success rather than the agency of Aboriginal communities adapting to the harsh realities of colonial life). There was 'no reason to believe that there has been any great decrease in the numbers of Aborigines in the past few years [and] the Board does not hesitate to declare that the often repeated statement that the race is disappearing is by no means in accordance with fact'.[96]

Indeed, the Board mobilised this kind of thinking in spite of the evidence that many of its correspondents provided. Whilst evangelical zeal meant the missionaries could employ spiritual instruction as a signifier of success, local guardians who both distributed rations to those outside the reserve system and offered judgements about its success still tended to stubbornly mobilise notions of decline and disappearance. These correspondents, the Board noted, did not 'entertain any hope of their condition being greatly ameliorated'. These honorary gaurdians from the edges of the colony argued 'they still roam from place to place, frequent towns and goldfields where possible and remain sometimes for months out of the control of the Board'.[97] Few could imagine a colonial future in which Aboriginal people could carve out an existence in the colonies, and it was only through the actions of the Board that they could avoid complete destitution in the present. The Board received a litany of correspondence in which settlers still asserted 'they are rapidly disappearing',[98] they were about to

---

95   Fourth CBPA Annual Report (1864): 8.
96   Ninth CBPA Annual Report (1873): 4.
97   Second CBPA Annual Report (1862): 8.
98   First CBPA Annual Report (1861): 22.

'become extinct', and that no amount of 'moral and social' improvement could alter the fact that their 'indolence and carelessness' meant they were 'destined' for 'extinction'.[99] According to the narratives of Presbyterians like MacBain, however, the system of reserves and stations firmly demonstrated the folly of this kind of thinking. Holding up Coranderrk as the example of success, this 'prove[d] that the Aborigines living on these stations are not only civilized but equal to the performance of duties that civilization imposes'.[100]

The Board, then, had slowly adopted the strand of thinking that had shaped Presbyterian missionary support for the actions of Moravians in the 1850s. Material and spiritual action in the present might produce an earthly future. It cannot be a coincidence that after the death of Richard Heales, the Board was dominated by its agnostic secretary Brough Smyth, the Methodist Theo Sumner, the Presbyterian James MacBain, and was deeply indebted to the hard work of MacBain's friend and former employee the staunch Presbyterian John Mackenzie. (Mackenzie's own experiences of migration and hard work had elevated him from the life of a 'shephard' in Scotland to a landholder in Victoria; in some ways his own life resonated with the reforming project of the Board.) This was not, however, a straightforward mobilisation of the narratives of Christian reform and reclamation that characterised the 1850s network of Presbyterian support for evangelical action. There were subtle, but nonetheless important, shifts in ideas about the practices and actions that would underpin these humanitarian engagements. The different kinds of discursive work that the notion 'reclamation' would perform over the years between 1850 and 1870 exemplify these subtle but important differences in amplification.

Like so many other agents in the 'empire of religion' that Hilary Carey has so carefully traced, the missionary endeavour in colonial Victoria was determined to 'reclaim fallen' peoples – and, moreover, this practice granted empire moral legitimacy because it made imperialism the mechanism for evangelism.[101] As Porter argues, theological changes of the eighteenth century had recast Indigenous peoples as victims, not only of imperial violence and mistreatment, but also of their earthly location outside of God's empire. The promise of missionary work for Protestant faiths was 'that conversion of the world would usher in the millennium of peace, happiness and plenty, at the end of which Christ would return to earth'. The impacts of these theological transformations were, of course, socially and culturally uneven. However, they did encourage 'evangelism on the widest possible front' because it became possible to restore so-called savages to the grace of the gospel rather than assume their spiritual

---

99 Third CBPA Annual Report (1864): 8; see also CBPA, 'Minutes of meetings', NAA, Series B314, May 1861–62.
100 Ninth BPA Annual Report (1873): 3.
101 Carey, *God's Empire*: 23.

fate was sealed.¹⁰² The evangelical revival that followed, as Anna Johnson points out, was energised by a belief that everyday people (whether the poor in Britain or Indigenous peoples in the imperial periphery) had first 'fallen' from grace and thus could be 'restored'.¹⁰³ In evangelical terms, Aboriginal people in Victoria were thus understood as 'a degraded [people to be] brought to the knowledge of Christ'. They could, through missionary action, be 'reclaimed' to and by Christ.¹⁰⁴ As evangelicals sought support in the 1850s they recounted stories of missionary success from other colonies; a meeting of the board of the Anglican Mission in Victoria was encouraged by 'success … at Port Lincoln [which] proved there was no ground for the despair that some people indulged in as to the reclamation of the Aborigines'.¹⁰⁵

However, in the 1860s the notion of reclamation would be put to work to describe a process of a rather more secular character. A Victorian Presbyterian minister in 1864 argued that his fellow colonists could 'reclaim the aborigines from their primeval savagery' by teaching them the 'habits of civilisation'.¹⁰⁶ So too, *The Argus* suggested that to 'reclaim the aboriginal races from indolence' might be the only possible way to 'save them from extinction'.¹⁰⁷ A year later it noted that if Aboriginal people were allowed to 'grow up wild and no effort [was] made to reclaim them … [they would] fast die away', although humanitarian action was no guarantee of its success.¹⁰⁸ Even the most pessimistic accounts about Aboriginal futures adopted the narrative of reclamation – if only to suggest its impossibility. The *Ballarat Star* reported on 'their [slow] progress in civilisation' to argue that even 'the most favourable circumstances show no better results. [It is] futile to attempt to reclaim the mature savage'.¹⁰⁹ Settlers who took the Board's predictions of an Aboriginal future seriously suggested that actions of a 'very patient and zealous teacher might amend their condition and gradually indoctrinate their minds with rudimentary notions of industry and progress'; through this kind of activity they could be 'reclaimed and brought round to civilized habits'.¹¹⁰ For some settlers, whilst the system of reserves and compulsion the Board sought could be 'open to some objections [since] it interferes with the liberty of the subject – or rather *savage* … no such objection exists here'. In this mode of thought, the 'government … should lend itself to reclaim the natives'.¹¹¹

---

102 Andrew Porter, 'An overview, 1700–1914', in *Missions and Empire*, Norman Etherington (ed): 55.
103 Johnson, *Missionary Writing and Empire, 1800–1860*: 23.
104 Further Facts Relating to the Moravian Mission (1863): 2.
105 *Ballarat Star*, 4 July 1859: 3.
106 *Brisbane Courier*, 22 January 1864: 5.
107 *The Argus*, 12 December 1860: 5.
108 *The Argus*, 16 September 1861: 8.
109 *Ballarat Star*, 30 December 1862: 2.
110 *Sydney Morning Herald*, 7 June 1866: 2.
111 *Rodney Advertiser* (Heathcote), 25 September 1868: 4.

This was not simply paternalism, or the combination of 'Civilization and Christianization', but the adoption of an evangelical vocabulary to describe a social and possibly historical transformation. The Board, figures like Brough Smyth and James MacBain argued, could 'reclaim the black to civilisation', where that reclamation was carefully distinguished from the 'religious instruction of the natives'.[112] Nourished by the Presbyterian faith that reclamation could reverse the trajectory towards extinction, this kind of thinking easily reworked this notion of religious reclamation into a near ethnographic claim about reclamation to the 'habits of civilisation', if not shucked its spiritual consequences off altogether. Indeed, in 1869 the CBPA asserted that

> the most prosperous Aboriginal station in Victoria, or perhaps in Australia, has been exclusively managed by the Board and its officers with no extraneous [religious] assistance ... the complete revolution in the lives and habits ... have far exceeded the most sanguine expectations of the Board who have had the largest experience of the Aboriginal character.[113]

A vernacular ethnography

A crucial element of this shift in thinking (and the possibility of reclamation within it) was the development of a vernacular ethnography in both colonial public life in the 1850s and 1860s and the activities of the Board after its first meeting. Whilst missionaries had certainly pondered the spiritual and social 'character' of their charges and were often crucial translators of Aboriginal language and social practice, evangelical engagements with difference did not have nearly the same kind of discursive purchase (nor widespread intellectual activity) that an emerging network of amateur ethnographers and ethnologists would soon assume in the colony. Moreover, the production of these vernacular ethnographies was sustained by a steady murmur of interest in public life. Nourished by the intellectual activities of metropolitan institutions like the British Association for the Advacement of Science, the Social Science Association and the emerging (and constantly splitting) Ethnological and Anthropological societies in London, a network of colonial ethnographers began to seriously ponder the various ways in which they could understand the difference between Aboriginal people and the settlers who were responsible for their 'care and management'. In the 1850s the colony abounded with ethnographic lectures, displays of Aboriginal artefacts (and bodies), performances of Aboriginal ceremonies, and – perhaps most importantly – a steady population of middle-

---
112 Ninth BPA Annual Report (1873): 6.
113 Sixth CBPA Annual Report (1869): 34.

class men who claimed expertise.[114] Using their early experiences of the colony or their efforts to collect 'facts' about the remaining Aboriginal population, these men claimed status in colonial intellectual and scientific life. As others in this collection have noted, the work of William Thomas in the 1850s was a crucial example of this kind of enquiry. However, Thomas's work was nourished by the activities of a much wider network of amateur ethnographers (whose interests often moved between natural history, geology and other sciences of man and nature in the years when the divisions between these branches of knowledge and enquiry were ill-formed at best); these men were deeply engaged with the metropolitan debates about human difference and adapted and adopted these discursive frames to ponder the substance of racial difference. Victorian colonists, they often claimed, needed to investigate the character, temperament and capacity of Aboriginal people.

The parliamentary and bureaucratic practices that authored the governance of Aboriginal people in the late 1850s and 1860s were deeply entangled with this project of ethnographic investigation. McCombie's Select Committee in 1858 was as much directed by ethnographic enquiry as it was by humanitarian intervention. Making use of the extensive ethnographic questionnaire developed by the Aborigines Protection Society and the British Association for the Advacement of Science in Britain in the 1840s, the committee asked all its respondents and witnesses to provide information about the beliefs, language, social practices and bodies of Aboriginal people. McCombie had, in fact, published this survey in the *Port Phillip Gazette* in the late 1840s, but as chair of the select committee he could draw on parliamentary authority to produce the kind of information he sought. Over two thirds of the information collected by the select committee concerned ethnographically imagined character rather than the destructions of colonialism. (Moreover, like the inchoate development of anthropology unfolding at this time, there was little consonance in the differences these observers discovered.) The time had come, McCombie long asserted, to see if the 'Aborigine was fit for a political existence' and ethnographic enquiry would provide the answer.[115] Others agreed, noting that 'some singular ethnological facts may [produce] a better knowledge of our blacks [and] lead to their elevation in the social scale. If neither their morals nor their intellects can be improved, their physical condition may, at any rate, be ameliorated.'[116]

The connection between governance and ethnography did not, however, stop with McCombie. The Board itself became an avenue of ethnographic enquiry – whilst the Board acknowledged that their remit was limited to the 'amelioration of the blacks' they nonetheless supported the voracious ethnographic activities

---

114 *The Argus*, 3 January 1856: 5.
115 Report of the Select Committee of the Legislative Council on the Aborigines (1859): vii.
116 *The Argus*, 13 September 1860: 4.

of their secretary, Brough Smyth (in sharp contrast to their refusal of support for missionary endeavours). In the 1870s he would publish his work on the *Aborigines of Victoria*; in the 1860s he had used the Board and its network as a crucial mechanism to conduct his enquiries. Indeed, this work was originally commissioned by the Board in 1865 when the members acknowledged they could hardly expect to govern Aboriginal futures if they did not understand Aboriginal people. In his first report as president, MacBain acknowledged that 'though not properly within their functions' they could see the value of Brough Smyth's enquiries. MacBain wrote that 'the Board have encouraged the secretary in prosecuting this work, as the means of collecting information at their command'.[117] The Board, then, did not simply support this enquiry – it was also its agent. By 1866, its ethnographic collection was substantive enough to 'exhibit a very large assortment of native weapons, and also specimens of baskets, bags, nets, bonnets, pincushions, &c, the work of native hands'.[118] The network of honorary corrospondents, many of whom fancied themselves as ethnographic experts, had donated their own collections of 'weapons and utensils'.[119] As Samuel Furphy has noted, these objects became both a performance of difference and a demonstration of capacity, as goods destined for European consumption were displayed as evidence of the possibility of Aboriginal adaptation for a colonial future.[120]

Of course, there were important differences between the vocabularies through which evangelicals understood Aboriginal people and the project of ethnography. However, many of the practices they sustained were remarkably similar (the collection of language and social practices) and some colonists moved across and between these networks and the divergent vocabularies they produced.[121] The development of a vernacular ethnography allowed colonists to draw much stronger distinctions between Europeans and their colonised subjects than the universalising vocabularies of evangelical practice. Humanitarian compassion as it took shape in the early nineteenth century often employed notions of the 'family of man' and its 'brotherhood' to offer criticism of the treatment of both slaves and then Indigenous peoples. Missionaries and church leaders in Victoria in the 1850s agreed, Aboriginal people and colonists were part of 'one great family of mankind' the missionary Spieseke argued.[122] So too, the Bishop of Melbourne reminded the colonists that Aboriginal people were 'his fellow creatures, his fellow subjects, and his fellow inhabitants of the same land as

---

117   Fifth CBPA Annual Report (1866): 10.
118   *The Argus*, 25 October 1866: 5–7.
119   Second CBPA Annual Report (1862): 14.
120   See chapter 4 in this collection.
121   This should be no surprise, the men who spearheaded the British APS in the 1840s were the same figures who developed the BAAS survey in the same decade – these discursive distinctions emerged inchoately and untidily.
122   First CBPA Annual Report (1861): 22.

himself'.[123] They were all God's children and this familial connection produced obligations of care and protection. In contrast, these ethnographers produced a powerful language of difference that could legitimate distinct practices of governance (regardless of where they imaginatively located the source of this difference, or whether they thought it was intransigent, could be changed in individual Aboriginal people or transformed through generational change over time). The Aboriginal people who had been the object of evangelical compassion became, through this ethnographic vocabulary, a governable Aboriginal subject. Moreover, this negotiated another powerful contradiction of British settler colonialism, the distinction between the ostensibly undifferentiated rights of British subjecthood and the blunt inequalities of colonial rule.

Conclusion

What I have tried to suggest in this chapter, then, is that Aboriginal people became governable subjects in colonial Victoria through a set of subtle but important adjustments to extant evangelical vocabularies. The notion of 'protection', long understood to represent the compassionate amelioration of the destructions of settlers, was adopted and reworked by the Board into a strategy of liberal governance. In the context of a colonial state still assembling the mechanisms through which it would organise civil society, the market and private life (and the boundaries that would limit its intervention into those realms), the CBPA deployed a developing vernacular ethnography to justify arranging those limits and boundaries in quite different ways. This was, then, more than state support for missionary activity under the guise of Christianisation and Civilisation – the Board drew upon, reworked and sometimes contested evangelical ideas about human difference, reclamation and the dying race to legitimate a form of governance with almost unprecedented reach into Aboriginal lives. The ways in which the Board remained attached to narratives of individual reclamation – even when that process had been shucked of its spiritual dimensions – demonstrates the ways in which extant stories and practices could easily be reworked for more earthly consequence.

We need, I suspect, much more careful accounts of the ways in which denominational differences opened out different meanings of 'protection' and the ways in which these differences shaped how liberal governance would unfold. Evangelical practices and ideas clearly become a vehicle for working through liberal modernity in its settler colonial inflection. Elizabeth Elbourne suggests that around the middle of the nineteenth century, 'liberalism resolved the paradox of colonialism' by creating a grammar of racial difference through

---

123   *The Argus*, 17 January 1857: 4.

which certain subjects could have their rights suspended. For Elbourne, the universalising claims of humanitarianism could never quite 'fit' with the blunt territorial imperatives of settler colonialism.[124] That is certainly part of this picture, however, a rigid division between the political and the religious loses sight of the ways in which certain forms of religious belief and practice could become vehicles of liberal modernity. It cannot be a coincidence that these transformations unfolded as the Board came to be dominated by Presbyterians in the middle of the 1860s – indeed, the glimmers of many of these changes were beginning to emerge in Presbyterian thinking in Victoria in the 1850s. This, perhaps, should not be a surprise. The long history of free thought and dissent meant 'liberal impulses' could find an easy home within Presbyterian practice.[125] As one Victorian Presbyterian noted, a congregation characterised by 'freedom of thought and action' was an 'honour to the denomination'.[126] Presbyterian notions of individual reform as a spiritual work unfolding over a lifetime could be easily mapped onto projects of social reform and the improvement of others. Richard Sher's now all-too-familiar argument that moderate Presbyterians were key carriers of the Enlightenment project in Scotland would seem to have as yet unexplored colonial resonances. This might also explain why so many architects of the colonial state in Victoria were Scots radicals.[127]

These changes were not, however, simply the transformation of ideas. They had significant consequences for Aboriginal people. There is no question that this piece of legislation imagined and legitimated a regime of control and management that would continue the project of dispossession (by removing Aboriginal people from settler space). At the same time, this vernacular ethnography effectively short-circuited the languages of shared humanity that structured evangelical practice. Indeed, in the 1860s the CBPA materially reproduced its ideas about ethnographic specificity by ensuring as many Aboriginal people as possible were dressed in clothing with the 'same peculiar pattern'.[128] These were not people imagined to be individual liberal subjects.

---

124   Elbourne, 'The sin of the settler'.
125   AR Holmes, 'Covenanter politics: evangelicalism, political liberalism and Ulster Presbyterians, 1798–1914', *English Historical Review* 125(513), 2010: 340–369. Reformist and radical liberal thinking, much of which was united by a sense of historical progress, 'was underpinned to a large extent by Presbyterian ecclesiology … Many Scots Presbyterians expressed their dissatisfaction with an unreformed British government which failed to accord with Presbyterian principles. A desire to protect the independence of the Church of Scotland and an ideological objection to the position of bishops in the House of Lords – that is, the intermingling of the spiritual and temporal spheres – inspired reformist protests and democratic tendencies'. Valerie Wallace, 'Benthamite radicalism and its Scots Presbyterian contexts', *Utilitas* 24(01), 2012: 7.
126   A letter to the Mission Board on the United Presbyterian Church of Scotland … concerning the Geelong Congregation, Thomas Patterson, Geelong, 1858: 2.
127   Richard Sher, *The Enlightenment and the Book: Scottish Authors and Their Publishers in Eighteenth-Century Britain, Ireland, and America*, University of Chicago Press, Chicago and London, 2006.
128   *The Argus*, 25 June 1864: 8.

The question remains, however, whether the 1869 Protection Act energised a grammar of racial difference of a kind that that historians of race would comfortably identify 'qua' race. Historians of empire suggest that racial categories hardened somewhere around the mid century; this 'hardening' usually represents a loss of particular modes of relating to non-Europeans that, in turn, made violent repression more palatable.[129] This seems a strange narrative when the history of settler colonialism is considered – relationships between settlers and Indigenous peoples tended to become less rather than more violent as the century unfolded, closer rather than more distant. Clearly, however, mid-century understandings of human difference did not have the kind of biological instrumentalism ('hardness') that produced the possibility of 'breeding out the colour' half a century later. Perhaps for this reason, scholars often shy away from seeing race as an operative category in the 1869 Act.[130] However, just because the apparent differences between Aborigines and Europeans did not have the imagined immutability that we might recognise as 'race' does not mean that they were operatively insignificant. The explosion of what was termed either ethnological or anthropological inquiry in the 1850s and 1860s in Victoria suggests that grammars of difference were being elaborated that had some degree of purchase. Whilst colonists might have disagreed about the precise texture of these differences (and whether or not they would be historically stable) they nonetheless legitimated the possibility of different forms of rule.

The actions and practices of the subjects imagined by this form of governance were, however, unpredictable. The formalisation of the reserve system clearly offered communities moments of respite through which to adopt and adapt to their transformed worlds. So too, many Aboriginal people refused to mirror the Board's desires for a contained and disciplined population within that system. Even after the legislation, people moved on and off the reserve system and the Board struggled to enforce the kinds of limitations this legislation invoked. Moreover, soon Aboriginal people began to mobilise the notion of exceptional subjecthood in the 1870s to contest the actions and management of the BPA itself. The brief and fragile assemblage of ideas and practices that produced the 1869 Act began to transform almost as soon as the final vote was cast in colonial parliament.

---

129 See, for example, Catherine Hall, 'The economy of intellectual prestige: Thomas Carlyle, John Stuart Mill, and the case of Governor Eyre', *Cultural Critique* 12, 1989: 167–196.
130 See, for example, John McCorquodale, 'The legal classification of race in Australia', *Aboriginal History* 10(1), 1986: 7.

4. 'They formed a little family as it were': The Board for the Protection of Aborigines (1875–1883)

Samuel Furphy

In October 1876, James MacBain rose in Victoria's Legislative Assembly to explain why he had resigned from the Board for the Protection of Aborigines (BPA) after more than a decade's service, including several years chairing its meetings. After an absence overseas, he had returned to the board in January to discover a radically altered policy towards Aboriginal administration, making his membership untenable: 'During [my] absence in England,' he said, 'four new members of the board were appointed; they formed a little family as it were; and they appointed a gentleman as inspector ... for doing what [I do] not know'.[1] This essay will examine the 'little family' to which MacBain objected, and explore the internal politics of the Board for the Protection of Aborigines at a crucial time in its history. By characterising the board as a contested space, the essay will attempt to understand the political dynamics that shaped debate on Aboriginal policy, thus integrating Aboriginal history and political history in fruitful ways. At the centre of the analysis will be a trio of new board members appointed in July 1875: Frederick Race Godfrey, Edward M Curr and Albert Le Souëf. These former pastoralists almost immediately pursued the closure of the Coranderrk Aboriginal Reserve, near Healesville, sparking a sustained period of protest from Kulin people and their supporters in the settler community.

Many historians have identified the policy shift inaugurated by the new board appointments of 1875, and some have noted the similar political inclinations of the three men. Bain Attwood, for example, characterises them as 'English, politically conservative and closely associated with squatting interests'.[2] Diane Barwick, in her richly detailed and chronological account of the *Rebellion at Coranderrk*, hinted at deeper connections, but even she overlooked important sources that reveal a close friendship between the men.[3] A key strength of Barwick's account, however, is her attention to the complex motives and actions of the many individuals involved in the Coranderrk saga. She is able to trace the shifting alliances of Aboriginal policy debate, recognising the

---

1 Victorian Parliamentary Debates, Legislative Assembly, Session 1876, vol 25: 984.
2 Bain Attwood, *Rights for Aborigines*, Allen & Unwin, Sydney, 2003: 13.
3 Diane Barwick, *Rebellion at Coranderrk*, Laura E Barwick and Richard E Barwick (eds), Aboriginal History Inc., Canberra, 1998: 108–111. The key sources that Barwick did not cite include personal papers of both Edward M Curr and Albert Le Souëf, which are considered in more detail below.

significance of factors such as politics, religion, ethnological vanity and personal friendship. Building on Barwick's research, therefore, this essay will consider the backgrounds of the men who threw Aboriginal policy into a state of chaos, mapping the strong personal and professional links between them, describing the policy approach they championed, and exploring the ethnographic legacy left by two of them.

The politicisation of Aboriginal governance

The 1870s was a turbulent decade for Aboriginal administration in Victoria. After successive periods of neglect and then broad consensus in Aboriginal policy, the decade was characterised by sustained and sophisticated Indigenous activism, and disagreement within the settler community regarding the destiny of the Aboriginal population. The colony's first era of Aboriginal policy had ended in 1849 with the demise of the Port Phillip Protectorate. This scheme had been imposed upon colonists by the British Colonial Office, but faced considerable opposition from local settlers in a period when calls for self-government were strong.[4] Following its closure, Aboriginal governance became a marginal political issue, particularly after the discovery of gold demanded the attention of the settler population and sparked a period of exponential population growth. Only the Assistant Protector William Thomas was retained as a Guardian of Aborigines, and missionary activity was limited.

As Leigh Boucher outlines in this collection, however, the prevalence of liberal ideology in Victoria's post-gold-rush community sparked a reassessment of the plight and destiny of the colony's surviving Aboriginal people.[5] Soon after the achievement of responsible government in 1856, the new settler parliament conducted a Select Committee on Aborigines (1858–59), which investigated 'the present condition of the Aborigines of this colony, and the best means of alleviating their absolute wants'.[6] The inquiry was proposed and chaired by Thomas McCombie, a journalist, novelist, historian and member of Victoria's Legislative Council, who told his parliamentary colleagues that while the subject might now appear insignificant, 'in future times it would be deemed of far greater consequence'.[7] The committee concluded that 'great injustice has been perpetrated upon the Aborigines'; and although it did not question British

---

4   Jessie Mitchell, '"The galling yoke of slavery": race and separation in colonial Port Phillip', *Journal of Australian Studies* 33(2), 2009: 125–137, doi:10.1080/14443050902883355; Samuel Furphy, 'The trial of Warri: Aboriginal protection and settler self government in colonial Victoria', *Journal of Australian Colonial History* 15, 2013: 63–82.
5   See Leigh Boucher's chapter in this publication. See also David Goodman, *Gold Seeking: Victoria and California in the 1850s*, Allen & Unwin, St Leonards, NSW, 1994: 18–20.
6   *The Argus*, 13 October 1858: 5.
7   *The Argus*, 27 October 1858: 6.

sovereignty or the taking from Aboriginal people of 'their hunting grounds and their means of living', the report insisted that 'proper provision should have been made for them'.[8] The initial result of the committee's recommendations was a mission-style system of government-funded reserves, which was overseen by the prosaically named Central Board to Watch of Over the Interests of the Aborigines. The members of the new board were mostly urban philanthropic types, later described by Broome as 'radical and well-intentioned … if ignorant of Aboriginal people'.[9] The Scottish-born MacBain, a businessman and politician who had arrived in Melbourne during the gold rush, joined the board in 1864 and served as its president for the rest of that decade. With substantial pastoral interests, he was more moderate than many of his colleagues, but shared their progressive views on Aboriginal policy.[10]

The reserve system the Central Board pioneered was shaped in significant ways by the lobbying of Aboriginal people. In the wake of the Select Committee inquiry, the Woiwurrung clan head, Simon Wonga, assisted by an ageing William Thomas, pushed for the creation of reserves on land selected by Aboriginal people for that purpose. His efforts resulted in the creation of the short-lived Acheron reserve, in the territory of the Taungurong people, and subsequently, in 1863, the Coranderrk reserve, which was located in Woiwurrung territory near the newly surveyed town of Healesville.[11] While missionaries managed several of the reserves funded under the new scheme, the Central Board controlled Coranderrk directly. In 1861 it appointed John Green, a Presbyterian lay preacher, as general inspector of the reserves. He explained in 1863: 'My method of managing the blacks is to allow them to rule themselves as much as possible.'[12] A sympathetic overseer, Green played a particularly prominent role at Coranderrk and the Central Board praised his work there. Coranderrk's proximity to Melbourne resulted in it becoming a significant site for those wanting to experience Aboriginal culture, including tourists, photographers, and scientists.[13] Its location also enabled its leaders, including Wonga, and later William Barak, to visit politicians and government ministers in Melbourne and

---

8   Victorian Parliament, 'Report of the Select Committee of the Legislative Council on the Aborigines; together with the Proceedings of the Committee, Minutes of Evidence, and Appendices', John Ferres, Government Printer, Melbourne, 1859: iv.
9   Richard Broome, *Aboriginal Victorians: A History Since 1800*, Allen & Unwin, Crows Nest, NSW, 2005: 125.
10 J Ann Hone, 'MacBain, Sir James (1828–1892)', *Australian Dictionary of Biography*, The Australian National University, 1974, http://adb.anu.edu.au/biography/macbain-sir-james-4063.
11 Attwood, *Rights for Aborigines*: 7–10.
12 John Green to Central Board Appointed to Watch over the Interests of the Aborigines, 28 July 1863, quoted in Barwick, *Rebellion at Coranderrk*: 67.
13 See for example J Lydon, 'The experimental 1860s: Charles Walter's images of Coranderrk Aboriginal Station, Victoria', *Aboriginal History* 26, 2002: 78–130.

lobby for better conditions and greater autonomy on land they believed had been granted them in perpetuity. Coranderrk was to become a key source of debate in Aboriginal policy.

Despite the apparent success of the new system, a majority of Aboriginal people continued to live off the reserves. In 1869, however, the Parliament of Victoria passed its first *Aborigines Act*, based on a plan drawn up by the Central Board.[14] The Act granted the board extensive powers over Aboriginal people: to prescribe place of residence; to control employment contracts; to collect and disburse Aboriginal wages; and to assume guardianship of Aboriginal children. Reflecting this more aggressive paternalism, the Central Board was renamed the Board for the Protection of Aborigines. It did not immediately utilise its extensive new powers, but the proportion of Aboriginal people living on reserves increased from one third to one half by 1877.[15] Moreover, the legislation created a powerful framework for Aboriginal governance and brought it more overtly into the political sphere. The colony's Chief Secretary was the *ex officio* chairman of the new board; although he never attended meetings and left the elected vice-chairman to exercise effective control, the ministerial oversight provided the means for the politicisation of Aboriginal policy, and a focal point for Aboriginal protest. The scene was set for the controversies that followed over the next decade, which included a Royal Commission on Aborigines in 1877 and a parliamentary inquiry in 1881.

The Coranderrk Aboriginal Reserve was the focus of the vast majority of debate in Aboriginal policy during the 1870s and 1880s. Although John Green's management had been supported and praised by the Central Board in the 1860s, tensions began to develop in the 1870s when the economic potential of the Coranderrk land began to influence the decision-making of the reconstituted BPA. The board had resolved to make Coranderrk profitable by growing hops under the direction of agriculturalist Frederick Search, but in 1874 changes in legislation dictated that any profit from the farm at Coranderrk should be returned to the government's consolidated revenue. The underfunded BPA thus lost a financial incentive to persevere with Coranderrk. Meanwhile, Aboriginal residents protested against the hiring of European labour on the hops farm. John Green increasingly supported the Kulin and found himself at odds with Frederick Search. Consequently, the board dismissed Green in 1874, which in turn prompted the Coranderrk residents to submit a petition in protest. The vice chairman of the board, R Brough Smyth, was a key figure in the campaign against John Green. Other members of the board, who had known of Green's

---

14   *An Act to provide for the Protection and Management of the Aboriginal Natives of Victoria*, 11 November 1869.
15   Attwood, *Rights for Aborigines*: 12; Michael Christie, *Aborigines in Colonial Victoria 1835–86*, Sydney University Press, Sydney, 1979: 179.

work for more than a decade, were later concerned he had been mistreated. Smyth found support, however, from a trio of new members appointed in mid-1875.

The 'little family'

The three principal members of the 'little family' that so incensed MacBain were Frederick Race Godfrey, Edward M Curr and Albert Le Souëf.[16] The son of an army officer, Godfrey was born in India in 1828 and educated in England. Arriving in the Port Phillip District in 1847, he had a successful career as a pastoralist in the north of the district; he was a pioneer of irrigation and an early member of the Royal Agricultural Society of Victoria. After moving closer to Melbourne in 1863, he became a prominent lay Anglican.[17] In 1874 he was elected to the Legislative Assembly, but was embroiled in controversy when an opponent alleged that voters had been 'corruptly treated … to meat, drink and refreshments' by agents of Godfrey.[18] Exonerated by the Elections and Qualifications Committee, he took his seat in parliament, where he claimed to support measures not men, but was broadly aligned with moderate and conservative members. He was later a company director and president of the Melbourne Club.

Born in Hobart in 1820, Edward M Curr was the eldest son of English-Catholic parents. His father was agent of the Van Diemen's Land Company and later a prominent politician who campaigned for Victoria's separation from New South Wales. Curr was educated in England and France before establishing his father's pastoral empire in the Port Phillip District in the 1840s. He subsequently traded horses and cattle, and attempted to establish pastoral stations in New Zealand and New South Wales, before finding employment with the Victorian Government in 1862. He rose to the senior position of Chief Inspector of Stock, a handsomely paid position in a predominantly pastoral economy. Curr was an accomplished and published writer of non-fiction and, during the 1870s, developed an interest in Aboriginal languages and ethnology.[19]

Albert Le Souëf was a parliamentary official, having served as Usher of the Black Rod in the Legislative Council since 1863. Born in England less than a month

---

16 For an account of their appointment see Barwick, *Rebellion at Coranderrk*: 108–111.
17 Margaret Gravell, 'Godfrey, Frederic Race (1828–1910)', *Australian Dictionary of Biography*, The Australian National University, 1972, http://adb.anu.edu.au/biography/godfrey-frederic-race-3624/text5631.
18 'Elections and Qualifications Committee. Petition against Mr. F. R. Godfrey, M.L.A. for East Bourke', *The Argus*, 1 July 1874: 6.
19 Samuel Furphy, *Edward M. Curr and the Tide of History*, Aboriginal History Monograph 26, ANU E Press, Canberra 2013, http://press.anu.edu.au/?p=223251; see also Harley W Forster, 'Curr, Edward Micklethwaite (1820–1889)', *Australian Dictionary of Biography*, The Australian National University, 1969, http://adb.anu.edu.au/biography/curr-edward-micklethwaite-3301/text5025.

before Godfrey, he was educated at the Moravian Mission School in Neuwied, Germany, before joining his family in the Port Phillip District in 1841.[20] Le Souëf worked as a station overseer and profited from various pastoral and stock-trading ventures before taking up his parliamentary position.[21] In 1853 he had married a daughter of a prominent pastoralist and naturalist, John Cotton, and was also secretary of the Zoological and Acclimatisation Society.[22]

In referring to these men as a 'little family', MacBain might simply have meant that they formed a new faction on the board, which supplanted the influence of the urban philanthropists who had earlier dominated its affairs.[23] Certainly, their status as long-term colonists, who had arrived in Victoria long before the gold rush, set them apart from most other members. On closer inspection, however, it seems likely that MacBain was implying a strong personal connection between the three men, beginning with their common experience as pastoralists in northern Victoria in the 1840s. The eldest of the three, Edward M Curr, began squatting on the Goulburn and Murray rivers in 1841. Within a decade he and his family had acquired leases to 300 square miles of prime pastoral land.[24] His standard route to Melbourne passed by the Aboriginal Protectorate station on the Goulburn River, which was a convenient place to stop for the night or rest his horses.[25] The station was presided over by Assistant Protector William Le Souëf, who has been described as the 'failed protector'; he was dismissed in 1843 for, among other things, his harsh treatment of Aboriginal people.[26] His teenage son Albert lived at the station from 1841 to 1844, so Curr and Le Souëf must surely have met in this period. By 1847, Le Souëf was employed as an overseer on the Reedy Lake station, near Kerang.[27] In the same year, the recently arrived Godfrey took up nearby Boort station. Le Souëf and Godfrey were of a similar age and probably began their own close association in this period. It is likely that Godfrey and Le Souëf also fraternised with Curr, who later wrote that squatters from the region regularly met at Maiden's Punt (Moama) for fox hunts and other social gatherings.[28]

---

20   Allan McEvey, 'Le Souef, Albert Alexander Cochrane (1828–1902)', *Australian Dictionary of Biography*, The Australian National University, 1974, http://adb.anu.edu.au/biography/le-souef-albert-alexander-4013/text6361.
21   AAC Le Souëf, 'Personal Recollections of Early Victoria', Typescript, 1895, South Australian Museum.
22   D.H. Pike, 'Cotton, John (1802–1849)', *Australian Dictionary of Biography*, The Australian National University, 1966, http://adb.anu.edu.au/biography/cotton-john-1925.
23   Bain Attwood, *The Making of the Aborigines*, Allen & Unwin, Sydney, 1989: 87.
24   Furphy, *Edward M. Curr and the Tide of History*: 37–46.
25   Edward M Curr, *Recollections of Squatting in Victoria, Then Called the Port Phillip District (from 1841 to 1851)*, G Robertson, Melbourne, 1883: 66–67.
26   Christie, *Aborigines in Colonial Victoria 1835–86*, 96; Penelope Edmonds, 'The Le Souëf Box: reflections on imperial nostalgia, material culture and exhibitionary practice in colonial Victoria', *Australian Historical Studies* 37(127), 2006: 125, doi:10.1080/10314610608601207.
27   Le Souëf, 'Personal Recollections of Early Victoria': 18.
28   Curr, *Recollections of Squatting in Victoria*: 381–382.

The Le Souëf–Godfrey connection is easier to map. Between 1847 and 1863, Godfrey was in partnership with his brother Henry, who had earlier taken up the Gobur station on the Goulburn River. Gobur was in close proximity to the Seven Creeks station at Euroa, where Le Souëf was based for a time in the early 1850s. After selling Boort in 1863 and moving closer to Melbourne, Godfrey was a prominent member of the Acclimatisation Society of Victoria, to which Le Souëf was appointed secretary in 1870. Le Souëf was also appointed director of the fledgling Melbourne Zoological Gardens. An emphasis on acquiring exotic animals for public display resulted in a name change to the Zoological and Acclimatisation Society of Victoria in 1871, but Godfrey and Le Souëf continued to promote acclimatisation and created a farm for the purpose at Gembrook. Their interest in acclimatisation no doubt brought them into contact with Curr, who by then was the Chief Inspector of Stock, and had firm opinions against the importation of animals and livestock due to the threat of disease.[29] Nevertheless, at a conference of Stock Inspectors in 1886, when Curr advocated a blanket prohibition on the importation of exotic animals, he was careful to exempt the Zoological Gardens from his proposed regulations.[30]

Godfrey, Curr and Le Souëf were appointed to the Board for the Protection of Aborigines in 1875 during a period of conservative government under premier George Kerferd. MacBain later alleged that Godfrey had solicited membership for the three men.[31] Moreover, Barwick speculates that Smyth might have acted alone in authorising the appointments on behalf of the board. Whatever the circumstances of the new appointments, their effect was considerable, as Barwick explains: 'Three old pastoralists who knew nothing of Kulin history or social organisation – but prided themselves on their knowledge of "the blacks" – began to dictate Board policy.'[32] Godfrey soon replaced Smyth as vice-chairman and he and his friends voted together on most issues. It was a watershed moment for the board as Attwood has indicated: 'Control of its affairs was passing from its founding members, who were mostly liberal or radical in politics … to a small group of like-minded men'.[33]

The final member of MacBain's 'little family' was Sherbourne Sheppard, who joined the board in January 1876 as a replacement for George Syme, editor of the liberal *Leader* newspaper, who had ceased attending meetings in 1874 in protest against the dismissal of John Green. Godfrey nominated Sheppard in September 1875, but his appointment was not confirmed during the first brief premiership of the radical Graham Berry.[34] Sheppard was eventually appointed

---

29 Furphy, *Edward M. Curr and the Tide of History*: 106–108.
30 *The Argus*, 22 October 1886: 4.
31 Victorian Parliamentary Debates, Legislative Assembly, Session 1876, vol 25: 983–984.
32 Barwick, *Rebellion at Coranderrk*: 111.
33 Attwood, *Rights for Aborigines*: 13.
34 Barwick, *Rebellion at Coranderrk*: 122, ftn 47.

by Berry's successor, James McCulloch, a more cautious liberal who during his first premiership in the 1860s had rapidly promoted Edward Curr to the senior position of Chief Inspector of Sheep.[35] The town of Shepparton in northern Victoria is named after Sheppard, who in 1843 had purchased the Tallygaroopna pastoral run on the Goulburn River. Barwick describes him as an old friend of Curr's, which seems likely as both men occupied lands on the Goulburn River in Bangerang territory.[36] At the very least they were old acquaintances. There is no doubt, however, that Sheppard was a close friend of Le Souëf, who recorded the nature of their connection in his memoir. Around 1850, Le Souëf had helped Sheppard to reclaim Tallygaroopna by force, after it was illegally sold when Sheppard was overseas. By 1854, Le Souëf had joined Sheppard in partnership at Tallygaroopna.[37] In 1877, Le Souëf named his fourth son (who was later the founder of Sydney's Taronga Zoo) Albert Sherbourne Le Souëf.[38]

When complaining to parliament about the influence of the new board members, MacBain had noted 'they appointed a gentleman as inspector … for doing what [I do] not know.'[39] This man was Christian Ogilvie, a pastoral station manager with strong links to the new board members who appointed him. His closest association was with Albert Le Souëf. They had first met as young men in 1847 when they were both employees at Reedy Lake station; Ogilvie probably met Godfrey and possibly Curr in the same period. In 1852 Ogilvie and Le Souëf entered into a business partnership, borrowing money to buy cattle, which they sold on for a handsome profit during the gold rush. When Le Souëf married in 1853, Ogilvie was his best man.[40] Ogilvie also shared a close friendship with Edward Curr, who wrote to his son after Ogilvie's death: 'he was one of the few friends I had and I have regretted him much.'[41] Although Ogilvie had experienced pastoral success with Le Souëf, in the 1860s he lost all his money during a drought in the Gawler Ranges in South Australia.[42] Curr had experienced a similar failure on the Lachlan River a few years earlier, but had rebuilt his career as a stock inspector for the Victorian Government.[43] Ogilvie might have been in need of a job and his old friends delivered. He subsequently got a job as an inspector under Curr. For these various reasons, Barwick's suggestion that in appointing Ogilvie the board 'chose one of their own kind' is actually an understatement.[44]

---

35 Furphy, *Edward M. Curr and the Tide of History*: 99.
36 Barwick, *Rebellion at Coranderrk*: 122; Barwick does not cite evidence for the Curr/Sheppard friendship.
37 Le Souëf, 'Personal Recollections of Early Victoria': 30–32, 86.
38 A Dunbavin Butcher, 'Le Souef Brothers', *Australian Dictionary of Biography*, The Australian National University, 1986, http://adb.anu.edu.au/biography/le-souef-albert-sherbourne-7747/text12401.
39 Victorian Parliamentary Debates, Legislative Assembly, Session 1876, vol 25: 984.
40 Le Souëf, 'Personal Recollections of Early Victoria': 40–42, 74–75.
41 Edward M Curr to EMV Curr, 19 December 1883, privately held.
42 *South Australian Register*, 2 May 1898: 3; 19 May 1898: 7.
43 Furphy, *Edward M. Curr and the Tide of History*: 89–91.
44 Barwick, *Rebellion at Coranderrk*: 113.

The principal node in the close network of friends and associates that took control of Aboriginal policy appears to have been Albert Le Souëf, who also had significant connections with two subsequent board appointments, Friedrich Hagenauer and AMA Page. Le Souëf's Moravian education ensured a natural sympathy for the missionary Hagenauer, whose daughter Ellen later married Le Souëf's son Ernest.[45] Page, who replaced Ogilvie as general inspector and board secretary in 1877, was an elderly farm manager with whom Le Souëf had been partner in a farming property near Gembrook. Page subsequently appointed Le Souëf's son as his clerk, prompting suggestions of nepotism at the 1881 parliamentary inquiry.[46]

The Coranderrk controversy

At their first board meeting on 7 July 1875, Godfrey, Curr and Le Souëf encountered an unprecedented deputation of Kulin men, led by William Barak, who arrived to register their protests regarding the situation at Coranderrk. The Kulin were soon encouraged, however, to ignore the largely intransigent board, preferring to lobby parliamentarians, journalists and other sympathetic Victorians. Attendance at board meetings was poor in this period, partly due to the withdrawal of members concerned at the treatment of Green. This ensured Smyth and his three new colleagues were able to determine board policy. On 4 August 1875, Godfrey, Curr and Le Souëf formed a subcommittee to examine the future management of Coranderrk and visited it three days later. They immediately recommended that the station be closed and its residents moved elsewhere. Curr later recalled: 'We did this on the very first visit. We were all accustomed to blacks; we had no doubt about what we recommended. I knew nothing about the antecedents of the place or even the name of the manager.'[47] The new members cited health concerns, but it is clear that they were also concerned about the potential for political agitation, due to Coranderrk's proximity to Melbourne. Moreover, they believed that contact between the Indigenous residents and white sympathisers undermined discipline on the reserve.

The board's concern about interference with its management of Coranderrk was magnified by the sympathetic actions of Brother Johann Stähle, a Moravian missionary who had been appointed acting manager after John Green's suspension. On the very day Godfrey, Curr and Le Souëf visited Coranderrk,

---

45 Butcher, 'Le Souef Brothers'.
46 Barwick, *Rebellion at Coranderrk*: 154.
47 Coranderrk Inquiry (1881). 'Report of the Board appointed to enquire into, and report upon, the present condition and management of the Coranderrk Aboriginal Station, together with the minutes of evidence', in Parliament of Victoria, *Papers Presented to Parliament by Command*, Session 1882–3, Vol 3: 120.

Victoria's newly appointed premier and chief secretary, Graham Berry, received a letter from Stähle, who, on behalf of the Coranderrk residents, requested the dismissal of the hops farm master Robert Burgess. Stähle sent the letter by registered mail to the chief secretary because earlier complaints sent to Smyth had been ignored. Despite the fact that Berry was *ex officio* chairman of the BPA, the public servants Smyth and Curr were both furious that a subordinate officer had bypassed their authority, while Godfrey was embarrassed at having to provide an explanation to Berry, a political adversary.[48]

The BPA officially voted to abandon Coranderrk on 25 August 1875.[49] The new members hoped to convince the government that proceeds from the sale of the land would be more than adequate to meet the cost of setting up a new station. At the same meeting they resolved to employ Christian Ogilvie on a two-month contract to inspect all six Aboriginal stations in company with Curr. Three weeks later, the board dismissed Stähle and permanently appointed Ogilvie as 'General Inspector' of the Aboriginal stations.[50] Ogilvie was charged with implementing the vision of his friends on the protection board. He toured the Murray River region with Curr and recommended a new location for the Coranderrk reserve at Kulkyne, near Mildura.[51] Curr and Ogilvie thus became the key proponents in the campaign to close down Coranderrk, and their friends on the board supported them. In December, Curr successfully proposed that Ogilvie be promoted again to the position of General Superintendent of Victoria's six Aboriginal stations. Curr's motion, which was seconded by Le Souëf, gave considerable power to Ogilvie, even over those stations run by missionaries.[52]

The following month, James MacBain returned to the board and attempted unsuccessfully to limit Ogilvie's new powers and to reinstate John Green. He subsequently led a rearguard action by long-serving board members dismayed at the new policy direction. On 17 February, a compromise was reached and John Green was offered a role subordinate to Ogilvie, but he refused.[53] Meanwhile, the plans to close Coranderrk attracted protest from the Kulin people. In February 1876, for example, when the Kulin sent a delegation to Melbourne, the local member for Healesville, EH Cameron, was shocked to find Godfrey loudly berating them in the lobby of Parliament House, threatening to remove them from Coranderrk immediately if they dared to meet the chief secretary.[54]

---

48 Barwick, *Rebellion at Coranderrk*: 113.
49 BPA, 'Minutes of meetings', NAA, Series B314, 25 August 1875.
50 BPA, 'Minutes of meetings', NAA, Series B314, 14 September 1875.
51 BPA, 'Minutes of meetings', NAA, Series B314, 21 September 1875.
52 BPA, 'Minutes of meetings', NAA, Series B314, 14 December 1875.
53 BPA, 'Minutes of meetings', NAA, Series B314, 12 January 1876, 16–17 February 1876.
54 Cameron to Chief Secretary, 19 September 1876, quoted in Christie, *Aborigines in Colonial Victoria 1835–86*: 185; see also Barwick, *Rebellion at Coranderrk*: 128.

As opposition grew, the new board members lost a nominal supporter in Smyth, who resigned from all his public offices due to a controversy surrounding his management of the Mines Department.[55] Nevertheless, the dominant faction had consolidated its power through the appointment of Sherbourne Sheppard, whose vote was crucial in blocking an unconditional offer of re-employment to John Green, which was supported by longer-serving members at a meeting on 18 February.[56] Four days later, MacBain sent a letter of resignation to the chief secretary. When he explained his reasons for doing so to the parliament several months later, he noted Godfrey's vehement opposition to the reappointment of Green. In response, Godfrey implied that MacBain had resigned because there were no Presbyterians among the new appointments to the board. In a fiery debate, Graham Berry proclaimed from the opposition benches that the board should be abolished altogether.[57] By the end of the year, the government had announced a Royal Commission on Aborigines.

The resignation of MacBain, combined with the earlier withdrawal of George Syme and another long-serving member, John Mackenzie, ensured that the new faction on the board was able to determine board policy unhindered. Beyond the board, however, considerable opposition was mounting from the Coranderrk residents and their supporters in the parliament and in the settler community. In a tumultuous period for government in the Colony of Victoria, Coranderrk became one of many issues that defined the political landscape. A young protégé of Graham Berry, John Lamont Dow, took up the Coranderrk cause in the pages of *The Age*, while Coranderrk residents also received considerable support from the philanthropist Ann Bon. The BPA spread counter-propaganda through the more conservative *The Argus*, but even this newspaper was not uncritical of the board's management of Coranderrk.[58]

The Kulin people of Coranderrk played a shrewd political game, using petitions, letters and deputations to government ministers to win support for their cause. Younger men educated at protectorate and mission schools played a prominent role: both Robert Wandin and Thomas Dunolly were authorised to speak on behalf of their leader, William Barak, and exerted considerable influence through their command of written language. Their key role no doubt frustrated board officials, because a protectorate education was intended to further the assimilation of Aboriginal people, not empower them politically.[59] The board had previously carried out its duties with very little public scrutiny, but the

---

55   Michael Hoare, 'Smyth, Robert Brough (1830–1889)', *Australian Dictionary of Biography*, The Australian National University, 1976, http://adb.anu.edu.au/biography/smyth-robert-brough-4621.
56   Barwick, *Rebellion at Coranderrk*: 122.
57   Victorian Parliamentary Debates, Legislative Assembly, Session 1876, vol 25: 974–986.
58   Barwick, *Rebellion at Coranderrk*: 115, 178.
59   Michael Christie, 'Aboriginal literacy and power: an historical case study', *Australian Journal of Adult and Community Education* 30(2), 1990: 118.

politically mobilised Coranderrk residents ensured this would no longer be the case. The board's response to this challenge was notably stubborn: displaying both 'ignorance and a profound paternalism' the newer members dismissed the idea that the Kulin had adapted their traditional culture to accommodate 'a new kind of political expertise'.[60] The board was so convinced that the various letters and petitions were the result of outside interference that it twice hired detectives to analyse the handwriting on petitions from Coranderrk.[61] The detectives found that Thomas Dunolly had written the relevant documents, which represented the genuinely held views of the Aboriginal signatories.

The controversy peaked in April 1877 when the Royal Commission commenced its hearings. Appointed by the moderate McCulloch ministry, the commission did not seriously challenge the board's authority, although it must have been an unwelcome distraction. Broome has pointed out that Aboriginal voices were barely heard during the hearings, unlike the later parliamentary inquiry.[62] Moreover, Godfrey (a parliamentary ally of McCulloch) was appointed a commissioner and was the most regular in his attendance. The key spokesman for the board was Edward Curr, who was soon to replace Godfrey as vice-chairman. He was examined at length on 1 June and argued that removal of the Coranderrk residents was necessary for reasons of both health and discipline, as the climate was unsuitable and contact with outsiders was undesirable. Curr further argued that Coranderrk was not the traditional country of its residents and removal to the Murray River was thus perfectly justifiable. He had little sympathy for the views of William Barak, who had said in 1876: 'The Yarra ... is my father's country. There's no mountains for me on the Murray.'[63]

Although Curr's concern about the health of Coranderrk residents was genuine, he was clearly also motivated by a belief, shared by his colleagues, that 'outside interference' was undermining the discipline of a 'childlike' race. He told the commissioners:

> Members of the Board, casual visitors, cricketers, and Members of Parliament have probably little idea of how their visits interfere with

---

60 Barwick, *Rebellion at Coranderrk*: 114–115.
61 Penny van Toorn, 'Authors, scribes and owners: the sociology of nineteenth-century Aboriginal writing on Coranderrk and Lake Condah reserves', *Continuum: Journal of Media and Cultural Studies* 13(3), 1999: 335; see also Penny van Toorn, *Writing Never Arrives Naked: Early Aboriginal Cultures of Writing in Australia*, Aboriginal Studies Press, Canberra, 2006: 123–151.
62 Richard Broome, '"There were vegetables every year Mr Green was here": Right behaviour and the struggle for autonomy at Coranderrk Aboriginal Reserve', *History Australia* 3(2), 2006: 43.6.
63 *Leader*, 19 February 1876, quoted in Christie, 'Aboriginal literacy and power: an historical case study': 118.

discipline. The native is a child, and very little unsettles him and even makes him fractious, and probably the height of pleasure to him would be to get a Member of Parliament to listen to his grievances.[64]

In a final written submission, Curr committed himself to the closure of Coranderrk: 'With the proceeds of the sale of Coranderrk a fitting station might be set on foot, stocked, and possibly made self-supporting.'[65] When asked if Aborigines should be forced to relocate against their wishes, Curr responded: 'the black should, when necessary, be coerced just as we coerce children and lunatics who cannot take care of themselves. If they are not coerced, they cannot be preserved from extinction.'[66] Christian Ogilvie also gave evidence, and spoke freely as he had resigned shortly before the hearings to take up a pastoral opportunity in Gippsland. Unlike Curr, he was prepared to revise his earlier views, stating he now opposed abandonment due to the residents 'love of the place'. He did, however, state that 'parliamentary interference' had undermined the board and destroyed discipline at Coranderrk.[67]

The commissioners concluded that Coranderrk should not be closed, but the board's commitment to that course remained firm. Meanwhile, Graham Berry had formed government once more after winning the 1877 election. His protégé John Lamont Dow won a seat in the new parliament, and the following year he wrote a report for Berry on Coranderrk, in which he recommended John Green be reappointed and the BPA disbanded. Berry cautiously stayed his hand, but it was clear that the closure of Coranderrk was not on the new government's agenda.[68] A stalemate ensued, with the board still favouring abandonment, but Berry's sympathies lying with the Kulin. On 1 May 1878, for example, Berry received another delegation led by Barak, without inviting board members to be present.[69]

Meanwhile, cracks began to appear in the policy consensus promoted by the BPA's 'little family'. Curr's furious reaction to Berry's reception of Barak's delegation, and his intransigence on the Coranderrk issue more generally, began to concern his colleagues, who elected veteran member Henry Jennings to replace him as vice-chairman.[70] Godfrey resigned in March 1879 to travel overseas and Curr and Le Souëf began to disagree on significant issues, notably

---

64 Victoria, Royal Commission on the Aborigines (1877), 'Report of the Commissioners Appointed to Inquire into the Present Condition of the Aborigines of this Colony, and to Advise as to the Best Means of Caring for, and Dealing with Them, in the Future, Together with Minutes of Evidence', in Parliament of Victoria, *Papers Presented to Parliament by Command*, Session 1877–78, Vol 3: 77.
65 Royal Commission on the Aborigines (1877): 79.
66 Royal Commission on the Aborigines (1877): 78.
67 Barwick, *Rebellion at Coranderrk*: 153, 270; see also *Gippsland Times*, 28 May 1877: 3.
68 Barwick, *Rebellion at Coranderrk*: 162–163.
69 Barwick, *Rebellion at Coranderrk*: 161.
70 Barwick, *Rebellion at Coranderrk*: 161–162.

the treatment of 'half-castes' residing on the government reserves. The Royal Commission had not recommended sending 'half-castes' out to work, but Le Souëf proposed as much in December 1878. The liberal Dow had also advocated distinct treatment for 'half-castes' in his 1878 report to Berry. Curr was strongly opposed to such views and became isolated as assimilationist ideology took hold. He once again pushed for the abandonment of Coranderrk in May 1879 and was partially supported by Le Souëf, but the plan he had championed now seemed unlikely.[71]

The political situation became more volatile when Graham Berry narrowly lost the March 1880 election, returning to power a few months later at the head of a shaky coalition. There were ongoing protests from Coranderrk residents and in October the manager, Rev. Frederick Strickland, reported that 'not a man on the station' would do anything when ordered.[72] In March 1881 William Barak once again walked the 67 kilometres to Melbourne leading a deputation of 22 Coranderrk men. Their supporter Ann Bon joined the delegation, who was introduced to Berry by a young Alfred Deakin. The board, which had been warned by telegram of the deputation's mission, demanded representation at the meeting, so Le Souëf (now vice-chairman) and Page were both present. Barak requested the board be abolished and that his people be allowed to manage Coranderrk themselves under John Green's guidance. Le Souëf subsequently told his colleagues that Bon's role would convince Berry that the abandonment of Coranderrk was unavoidable because of 'continual interference'. In fact, Berry assured Barak that he would not be removed from Coranderrk and promised a parliamentary inquiry.[73]

In July, however, Berry resigned and was replaced by the radical liberal Bryan O'Loghlen. The BPA once again lobbied for the closure of Coranderrk, while Dow called for board reform through the pages of *The Age*.[74] The new government honoured Berry's promise of a parliamentary inquiry, to which it appointed the local member for Healesville, EH Cameron, as chairman. Despite attempts by the BPA to influence the membership of the inquiry, the new chief secretary, JM Grant, also adopted the recommendations Berry had received from Alfred Deakin, who had suggested the appointment of Ann Bon, among others.[75] Grant appointed two local landholders recommended by the BPA, but this did not satisfy board members, who protested against the Deakin-inspired appointments in September.[76] Grant added two further members to the inquiry

---

71 Barwick, *Rebellion at Coranderrk*: 167.
72 Barwick, *Rebellion at Coranderrk*: 174.
73 Barwick, *Rebellion at Coranderrk*: 178–179.
74 Barwick, *Rebellion at Coranderrk*: 183; see also *The Age*, 14 July 1881.
75 Barwick, *Rebellion at Coranderrk*: 183–184.
76 BPA, 'Minutes of meetings', NAA, Series B314, 7 September 1881.

after it began collecting evidence; one was a BPA recommendation but the other was John Lamont Dow, whose presence tipped the balance of opinion against the BPA.

Unlike the earlier Royal Commission, the Coranderrk inquiry provided ample opportunity for the people of Coranderrk to express their own views. It heard from 22 Aboriginal witnesses, including Barak, Wandin, Dunolly and four Aboriginal women.[77] Although Le Souëf was now vice-chairman, the board's spokesman was the confident and forthright Edward Curr, who again displayed his repressively paternalistic attitudes. When asked if he thought it desirable to relocate the Coranderrk residents against their will, he replied:

> Anyone who knows the blacks knows their will is nothing, that they might have a serious objection now which they would not remember three months afterwards. I would suggest that they should be moved for their own benefit ... If I saw my child playing on the brink of a well I should remove the child even if he cried. I should remove the blacks from Coranderrk whether they liked it or not. I do not believe they have any strong objection.[78]

Curr maintained his view that the problems at Coranderrk were due to outside interference and he singled out John Green: 'It has been the impression of the Board that Mr. Green has kept Coranderrk in a state of hot water for the last seven years.' He insisted that the key problem was discipline and boldly asserted: 'They are an easy people to manage. I managed four times as many as there are at Coranderrk when I was nineteen years old.'[79]

Reflecting the politicised nature of its appointment, the board of inquiry divided into two factions, but the report unanimously concluded that Coranderrk should not be closed and suggested the station was 'not so well managed as could be desired'.[80] A majority of five members (including Bon and Dow) signed an addendum, which included the following damning indictment of the board:

> The natives appear to have been chiefly stirred into a state of active discontent by the pertinacity of the Central Board in pressing upon successive Governments the gratuitous advice that the Blacks should be

---

77 Broome, 'There were vegetables every year Mr Green was here': 43.6. For a detailed history of the Coranderrk inquiry, and a verbatim theatre script based on its Minutes of Evidence, see Giordano Nanni and Andrea James, *Coranderrk: We Will Show the Country*. Aboriginal Studies Press, Canberra, 2013.
78 Coranderrk Inquiry (1881): 120. Curr gave evidence to the Inquiry on 8 December 1881.
79 Coranderrk Inquiry (1881).
80 Coranderrk Inquiry (1881): iii–iv.

removed from Coranderrk. The natives also bitterly complained of the removal of Mr. Green, who appears to have won their confidence and respect.[81]

The remaining four inquiry members, including the chairman, issued their own addendum, which argued that the problems at Coranderrk 'cannot be so easily laid to the charge of the Central Board'. They noted the board's apparently successful management of other reserves, and gave credence to the board's suggestion of outside interference by noting the access of Coranderrk residents to 'credulous sympathizers'.[82]

Although not a decisive victory for the people of Coranderrk, the inquiry decreased the likelihood of abandonment. The O'Loghlen Government did not formally respond to the report, but appointed four new members to the BPA in June 1882. One of these was Alfred Deakin, although he resigned soon afterwards in protest against the government's inadequate response.[83] These new appointments diluted the power of the 'little family' and increased the likelihood of policy reform, signalling a new era in Aboriginal governance. For Curr, the findings of the Coranderrk inquiry represented a major repudiation of the policies he had championed. He was firmly committed to a paternalistic policy of strict discipline and rejected the emerging assimilationist ideology of the period. He became increasingly isolated on the board, and unsurprisingly resigned in 1883. When Sheppard resigned the following year, Le Souëf was the sole remaining member of the 'little family'.[84] Nevertheless, he played a prominent role in negotiating the political compromise that resolved the tensions surrounding Coranderrk, although not in a way that benefited its Aboriginal residents.

The 1886 Act: from protection to assimilation

The protests of the Kulin people of Coranderrk corresponded with a period of significant change in Aboriginal policy, as earlier policies of containment on reserves gave way to a commitment to the gradual absorption of Aboriginal people into the white community. This shift culminated in the *Aborigines Protection Act 1886* (Vic), which drew an official distinction between 'full-bloods' and 'half-castes'. It was largely framed in response to the Coranderrk rebellion and it had the direct effect of undermining Indigenous protest, as

---

81 Coranderrk Inquiry (1881): vi.
82 Coranderrk Inquiry (1881): vii.
83 Barwick, *Rebellion at Coranderrk*: 248.
84 Godfrey re-joined the board in 1896. Le Souëf served until 1902, the year of his death, while Godfrey resigned in his eightieth year in 1907.

'half-caste' residents (many of them centrally involved in political activism) were denied further government support and forced to leave the reserve. Penny van Toorn, who has written extensively on the role of literacy in the Coranderrk rebellion, suggests that the 1886 Act separated the 'speaking generation from the writing generation, thus cutting a vital line of communication between Aboriginal communities and white government authorities'.[85]

Although members of the BPA's 'little family' were in furious agreement regarding the need for firm discipline of Aboriginal people, they diverged when it came to this emerging discourse of assimilation. Godfrey was an advocate of apprenticeship schemes and the hiring out of Aboriginal girls for domestic service, an approach that was considered by the 1877 Royal Commission.[86] Le Souëf supported Godfrey, but Curr did not, as his racialist views tended to preclude the possibility of assimilation. In fact, Curr was the only significant voice on the BPA to resist a distinction between 'full-blood' and 'half-caste'.[87] He remained committed to a strict segregationist policy, which assumed that Aboriginal decline was inevitable and that absorption, if possible at all, would be a long-term project. At the Royal Commission he had revealed the uncomfortable irony of his dual roles as Chief Inspector of Stock and protection board member when he observed: 'To begin, we should remember that as a mob of wild cattle cannot be tamed in a single generation, so we cannot at once civilize these people.'[88] For Curr, then, assimilation of the Aborigines would be a very gradual process, which would take many generations if it were to be achieved at all.

Patrick Wolfe has proposed three distinct phases in Aboriginal policy – confrontation, incarceration, and assimilation – all of which, he argues, are consistent with the 'logic of elimination' that characterises settler colonialism.[89] The 1886 Act was the culmination of a shift from the second to the third stage in colonial Victoria. Curr's resistance to such a shift reflected his view that assimilation could not be achieved simply by boarding out Aboriginal children or forcing adult 'half-castes' to leave the reserves. In 1877, he observed: 'This absorption to my mind is a mistake – there is no absorption in the case and I think never can be; substitute eradication for absorption, and I think you will be correct.'[90] Curr's conclusion was informed by a pessimistic assumption that Aboriginal people were less capable than white people, but also by a realistic

---

85 Van Toorn, 'Authors, scribes and owners': 341.
86 See, for example, Godfrey's questioning of Curr, Royal Commission on the Aborigines (1877): 77.
87 For a similar argument, see Marguerita Stephens, 'White Without Soap: Philanthropy, Caste and Exclusion in Colonial Victoria, 1835–1888. A Political Economy of Race', unpublished PhD thesis, University of Melbourne, 2003: 237, 243.
88 Royal Commission on the Aborigines (1877): 77.
89 Patrick Wolfe, *Settler Colonialism and the Transformation of Anthropology: The Politics and Poetics of an Ethnographic Event*, Cassell, London, 1999: 27–31.
90 Royal Commission on the Aborigines (1877): 77.

view that Aborigines would face discrimination and violence from white colonists: 'The Anglo-Saxon in Australia, as elsewhere, does not foster weakly races. He wants their lands. He is thinking of riches. He tramples them under feet without thinking what he does.'[91] Segregation on reserves was thus the only means of preserving Aboriginal people from extinction, in the interests of scientific inquiry if nothing else. It was not that Curr saw no difference between the categories of 'full-blood' and 'half-caste'; in his ethnological work, *The Australian Race,* he observed that the latter 'have more brains … and are more difficult to manage'.[92] Curr was unique, however, in that he did not believe such perceived differences should alter the board's segregationist policy.

Despite Curr's resistance, the new appointments to the BPA in 1882 facilitated a reconsideration of its policy and ultimately enabled the political compromise that ended the Coranderrk controversy. As the sole remaining member of the board's 'little family', Le Souëf was able to find common ground with liberals, such as Dow and Deakin, who advocated a distinction between 'full-blood' and 'half-caste', and the removal of the latter from Coranderrk. Significantly, James MacBain had earlier advocated sending 'half-caste' children away from Coranderrk, so Le Souëf's amenability to the idea represented a solution to the factionalism that had earlier dogged board proceedings.[93] For these reasons, Le Souëf played a key role in overseeing the policy shift that culminated in the 1886 Act. Moreover, he continued to exert influence through his close relationship with board employees Hagenauer and Page, who drafted recommendations in 1884 that all 'half-castes' under the age of 35 should be ordered to leave the government stations.[94] Both were to play a significant role implementing this policy under the 1886 Act.

The ethnographic legacy of Curr and Le Souëf

A necessary precondition to governing Aboriginal people is that Aboriginal people be defined. At a legislative level, definitions such as 'half-caste' and 'full-blood' became crucial; but, more broadly, the disciplines of ethnology and anthropology emerged as scholarly scaffolding for those who aimed to influence Aboriginal policy. The board members of the 1870s were no exception in this respect, with several combining their board careers with ethnographic pursuits. The most notable of these were Smyth and Curr, but Le Souëf also turned his hand briefly to the task of describing Aboriginal culture.

---

91   Royal Commission on the Aborigines (1877): 77.
92   Edward M Curr, *The Australian Race: Its Origin, Languages, Customs, Place of Landing in Australia, and the Routes by Which It Spread Itself Over That Continent*, John Ferres, Govt Printer, Melbourne, 1886: vol I: 42.
93   Victorian Parliamentary Debates, Legislative Assembly, Session 1876, vol 25: 984.
94   Barwick, *Rebellion at Coranderrk*: 238, 281–282.

Curr included an ethnographic chapter in his 1883 memoir, *Recollections of Squatting in Victoria*, and followed it in 1886 with a four-volume work, *The Australian Race*, for which he collected hundreds of Aboriginal vocabularies and proposed a theory of Aboriginal origins using the techniques of comparative philology.[95] The latter work was published by the Victorian government printer, but was controversial among rival scholars; pioneer anthropologist AW Howitt, who had served as a Royal Commissioner in 1877, attacked several of Curr's claims in scholarly journals.[96] Le Souëf's more modest contribution included an 11-page appendix to R Brough Smyth's *The Aborigines of Victoria* in 1878; he also wrote about Aboriginal people in a memoir he penned in about 1895.[97]

The alliance between Curr and Le Souëf in Aboriginal policy is complemented by their similar approaches to ethnography. Both men witnessed the early stages of European occupation in the Goulburn Valley and the devastating effect this had on Aboriginal livelihoods. Not surprisingly, therefore, each later displayed forms of what Rosaldo has called 'imperialist nostalgia'.[98] Penelope Edmonds has explored how nostalgia shaped the creation in the 1860s of the 'Le Souëf Box', which featured miniaturised Aboriginal weapons carved by Albert Le Souëf in a box decorated with idyllic pre-contact scenes drawn by his wife Caroline.[99] In his well-known memoir, *Recollections of Squatting in Victoria*, Curr also displayed nostalgia at the passing of his so-called 'sable companions' or 'sooty friends', whose jolly ways had entertained him in his youth.[100] Curr attributed the decline of Aboriginal people to the expansion of British 'civilisation', which he viewed as an inexorable process. Such forms of nostalgia routinely deflected personal responsibility for the decline of a colonised people.[101]

Despite their nostalgic admiration for pre-contact Aboriginal culture, both Le Souëf and Curr reveal a more general disdain for the Aboriginal way of life in their ethnographic writings. An obvious link is their characterisation of gender roles in Aboriginal society. Le Souëf describes Aboriginal women as 'unfortunate creatures [who] lead a wretched life of drudgery'. He recounts, for example, the story of an Aboriginal woman who was sent to the Goulburn River for water at night, noting that her husband was 'too lazy or frightened to go himself'.

---

95 Curr, *Recollections of Squatting in Victoria*; Curr, *The Australian Race*; for a detailed analysis of *The Australian Race*, see Furphy, *Edward M. Curr and the Tide of History*: 145–171.
96 AW Howitt, 'On the organisation of the Australian tribes', *Proceedings of the Royal Society of Victoria* 1, 1889; AW Howitt, 'The Dieri and other kindred tribes of central Australia', *The Journal of the Anthropological Institute of Great Britain and Ireland* 20 (January 1, 1891): 30–104, doi:10.2307/2842347.
97 AAC Le Souëf, 'Notes on the natives of Australia', in R Brough Smyth, *The Aborigines of Victoria: with notes relating to the habits of the natives of other parts of Australia and Tasmania compiled from various sources for the Government of Victoria*, John Ferres, Govt Printer, Melbourne, 1878: 289–299; Le Souëf, 'Personal Recollections of Early Victoria'.
98 Renato Rosaldo, 'Imperialist nostalgia', *Representations* 26, 1989: 107–122.
99 Edmonds, 'The Le Souëf Box': 117–139.
100 See, for example, Curr, *Recollections of Squatting in Victoria*: 435.
101 Furphy, *Edward M. Curr and the Tide of History*: 179–183.

The woman suffered a blow to the head during an ambush from an enemy tribe but Le Souëf ironically concluded that 'no doubt used to such treatment, she seemed to care little about it'.[102] Similarly, Curr observed that the Bangerang man was 'despotic in his own mia-mia' and was deliberately nonchalant in his description of violence between Aboriginal women: 'Their little disagreements were settled with their yam sticks, without much injury being done, their husbands interfering with their clubs if matters went too far.'[103] As Clare Land has recognised: 'Curr appears blind to Koori women's cultural and political power, consistently focussing on men's culture, work, skills and authority while denigrating those of women.'[104]

The links between Curr and Le Souëf's ethnographic writings are so extensive, that it is hard not to imagine them as two old friends, chatting about the quaint ways of 'the blacks'. They both, for example, noted the mutual avoidance of mother-in-law and son-in-law, Le Souëf proclaiming, 'I never could get at the meaning of this apparently absurd custom.'[105] Various other close similarities are apparent. Curr wrote, 'Religious worship the Bangerang had none', while Le Souëf observed, 'I never could discover anything among them approaching to religion.'[106] On linguistic origins, Le Souëf had suggested that all Aboriginal languages were probably of common origin, and Curr confirmed this view in his subsequent four-volume work.[107] Both men stressed the prevalence of infanticide.[108] Of particular relevance to their approach to Aboriginal policy was the view Curr and Le Souëf held about Aboriginal government. Le Souëf wrote: 'A good deal has been written and said about chieftainship, but nothing of the kind exists.'[109] Similarly, Curr recalled in his memoir that he did not observe 'anything resembling government' among the Bangerang, while in *The Australian Race* he mounted a spirited rebuttal of James Dawson's assertion that a form of Aboriginal government existed.[110] Such views informed, no doubt, the BPA's rejection of the chiefly authority of William Barak in the 1870s.

The theme of cultural disintegration is also strong in the writings of Curr and Le Souëf, leading to a nostalgic admiration for the traditional Aborigine and contempt for the survivors of the frontier times. Le Souëf observed that 'before they became so degenerated by contact with the whites, they were excellent huntsmen', while Curr, after describing a corroboree he witnessed in 1842,

---

102 Le Souëf, 'Notes on the natives of Australia': 290.
103 Curr, *Recollections of Squatting in Victoria*: 274.
104 Clare Land, 'Representations of gender in E. M. Curr's Recollections of Squatting in Victoria: implications for land justice through the native title process', *Indigenous Law Bulletin* 5(19), 2002: 7.
105 Le Souëf, 'Notes on the natives of Australia': 291; Curr, *The Australian Race*, vol I: 97.
106 Curr, *Recollections of Squatting in Victoria*: 274; Le Souëf, 'Notes on the natives of Australia': 295–296.
107 Le Souëf, 'Notes on the natives of Australia': 291; Curr, *The Australian Race*, vol I: 5.
108 Le Souëf, 'Notes on the natives of Australia': 290; Curr, *The Australian Race*, vol I: 76.
109 Le Souëf, 'Notes on the natives of Australia': 295.
110 Curr, Recollections of Squatting in Victoria: 244–245; Curr, *The Australian Race*, vol I: 56.

argued it was performed 'in a very different spirit from the tame exhibitions got up by our broken-spirited tribes during the last thirty years or more.'[111] Their nostalgic admiration for pre-contact Aboriginal people, and corresponding contempt for surviving Aboriginal culture, fits neatly with the notion of 'repressive authenticity' proposed by Patrick Wolfe.[112] In this formulation, the true Aborigine remains frozen in his 'savage state', leaving surviving Aborigines, and particularly 'half-castes', in a liminal state. The expression in policy of this ideology was the 1886 Act, and while Curr opposed separate treatment for 'half-castes', he certainly viewed them as distinct from 'full-blooded' Aboriginal people. Nevertheless, his resistance to assimilationist discourse is curious. A plausible explanation can, however, be found in his ethnological writings. Based on a linguistic analysis, Curr proposed that the Australian Aborigines were of Negro origin. In this matter he was swimming against the tide of scientific opinion, which generally held that Aborigines were of Caucasian origin.[113] The more prevalent theory of Caucasian origin encouraged Victorian policymakers to be optimistic about the possibility for biological assimilation.[114] By contrast, Curr insisted that assimilation, if possible at all, would take several generations.

Although Le Souëf's ethnographic writings were brief and had little impact, Curr's have had an enduring influence.[115] In 1975, AP Elkin described him as one of 10 founding fathers of Australian anthropology, although he implied Curr's key contribution was the wealth of material he compiled.[116] When one considers international impact, however, Curr pales in comparison to pioneers such as Howitt or Baldwin Spencer. Curr did not publish in international journals. Moreover, the journal of the Anthropological Institute in London did not review *The Australian Race*, despite the fact that the Victorian Government had earlier sent the manuscript to the institute's president, WH Flower, for critical comment prior to publication.[117] This lack of international recognition probably would not have concerned Curr, as he was generally suspicious of

---

111 Le Souëf, 'Notes on the natives of Australia': 297; Curr, *Recollections of Squatting in Victoria*: 140.
112 Patrick Wolfe, 'Nation and MiscegeNation: discursive continuity in the post-Mabo era', Social Analysis 36, 1994: 10; see also Wolfe, *Settler Colonialism*, Chapter 6.
113 Warwick Anderson, *The Cultivation of Whiteness: Science, Health and Racial Destiny in Australia*, Melbourne University Press, Carlton, Vic, 2002: 190; Russell McGregor, *Imagined Destinies: Aboriginal Australians and the Doomed Race Theory, 1880–1939*, Melbourne University Press, Carlton, Vic, 1997: 36; Furphy, *Edward M. Curr and the Tide of History*: 154.
114 Stephens, 'White Without Soap': 220–221.
115 The influence extends to a recent native title case; see Samuel Furphy, '"Our civilisation has rolled over thee": Edward M Curr and the Yorta Yorta Native Title case', *History Australia* 7(3), 2010: 54.1–54.16.
116 AP Elkin, 'RH Mathews: his contribution to Aboriginal studies: Part I: the founders of social Anthropology in Australia', *Oceania* 46(1), 1975: 12–15; AP Elkin, *The Australian Aborigines*, Angus & Robertson, Sydney, 1938: 389; see also RM Berndt and CH Berndt, *The World of the First Australians*, Ure Smith, Sydney, 1964: 537.
117 *The Argus*, 3 November 1884: 5; see also Furphy, *Edward M. Curr and the Tide of History*: 149.

anthropological theory and believed the integrity of his evidence and the validity of his arguments hinged on his personal experience of Aboriginal people.[118]

Curr stressed that his collaborators and correspondents were men with a similar background to his own, as he had sent his *pro forma* questionnaires about Aboriginal custom to 'stock-owners here and there'.[119] His text is littered with references to the ultimate authority of the bushman. When refuting certain claims by Howitt's collaborator Lorimer Fison, Curr exclaimed, 'I have never witnessed nor heard any bushman mention such a state of things'.[120] Similarly, of his erstwhile board colleague he wrote, 'Mr. Smyth as we know is no bushman and has no acquaintance with our Blacks in their savage state.'[121] The general tone of *The Australian Race* suggests that Curr was writing as much for an audience of fellow pastoralists as an audience of interested ethnologists. He assumed his readers would applaud his derision of ludicrous claims by 'new chums' such as Smyth, who had arrived during or after the gold rush and had pretentions to expertise about 'our blacks'. Yet because Curr wrote well, because he collected such a vast quantity of linguistic data, and because the Victorian Government published his work, his reputation in anthropology is not insubstantial. It is clear, however, that Curr's ethnological work is an extension of the coercive policies he pursued, with a little family of fellow pastoralists, while serving on the Board for the Protection of Aborigines in the 1870s.

---

118 Furphy, *Edward M. Curr and the Tide of History*: 157.
119 Curr, *The Australian Race*, vol I: xiv; one of Curr's trusted collaborated was Le Souëf; see vol I: 217–218; vol III: 523–524.
120 Curr, *The Australian Race*, vol I: 126.
121 Curr, *The Australian Race*, vol I: 238.

5. Managing mission life, 1869–1886

Claire McLisky (with Lynette Russell and Leigh Boucher)[1]

In settler colonies such as Victoria, missions and reserves were the sites where colonial legislation and missionary/humanitarian ambitions encountered Aboriginal people and their own goals, where theories about race, conversion and 'civilisation' were translated into everyday practice. Colonial power, in the words of David Scott, 'came to depend ... upon *the systematic redefinition and transformation of the terrain on which the life of the colonized was lived*',[2] and as the primary physical location in which these transformations were carried out, missions and reserves were laboratories both of Christian evangelical theories and of colonial rule. Granted astonishingly broad powers over Aboriginal people's lives, mission and reserve managers applied and tested a variety of approaches to achieve the related goals of Aboriginal pacification, protection, conversion and civilisation.[3] Their ability to do this was aided by the fact that missions and reserves were usually isolated from both rural settler populations and the metropolitan centres that often sought to dictate colonial and missionary policy. Yet despite this isolation, the flow of information and influence between 'centre' and 'periphery' was anything but unilateral; missions, reserves and Aboriginal people themselves fed 'knowledge' back into colonial, and metropolitan, understandings of race and 'Aboriginality', which in turn came to influence subsequent policy and legislation.

---

1   I would like to thank Alan Lester for his incisive comments on the review copy of this piece, and also the other, anonymous reviewer for his/her helpful feedback. In addition, Ben Silverstein and Felicity Jensz provided advice that helped to sharpen its argument. Most importantly, many thanks to my co-authors Leigh Boucher and Lynette Russell, whose input whilst I was on maternity leave made its publication possible.
2   David Scott, 'Colonial governmentality', *Social Text* 43, Autumn 1995: 205 (original emphasis).
3   During the period under consideration, missionary and official ideas about what the end point of Christian mission to Aboriginal people might mean were often contradictory. Discourses around 'smoothing the pillow of a dying race' through material assistance and deathbed conversions often co-existed with the ideal of creating a Christian Aboriginal population which, it was imagined, would eventually assimilate into settler society. With the advent of the *Aborigines Protection Act 1886* (Vic), however, a clear distinction was made between those who should be 'protected' (people of unmixed Aboriginal heritage), and those who should be immediately 'assimilated' (people of mixed Aboriginal heritage). The Act envisaged missions and reserves exclusively as places for the former 'category'. It should be noted, however, that not all missionaries and reserve managers agreed with this policy. John Bulmer, for example, was repeatedly cautioned by the Board for giving supplies to 'half-castes' (Clare Land, 'Law and the construction of 'race': critical race theory and the Aborigines Protection Act, 1886, Victoria, Australia', in Penelope Edmonds and Samuel Furphy (eds), *Rethinking Colonial Histories: New and Alternative Approaches*, RMIT Publishing, Melbourne, 2006: 155, ftn 107). Similarly, Daniel and Janet Matthews at Maloga Mission in New South Wales took in 'half-castes' who were no longer welcome at Victorian missions. See Claire McLisky, 'Settlers on a Mission: Faith, Power and Subjectivity in the Lives of Daniel and Janet Matthews', unpublished PhD thesis, University of Melbourne, 2009: 22.

This chapter focuses on one aspect of this dynamic – the ways in which missionaries and reserve managers interacted with colonial legislation in their attempts to redefine and transform Aboriginal lives on the six mission stations and government reserves in the Colony of Victoria during the period 1869–1886 (Ebenezer, Ramahyuck, Lake Condah, Lake Tyers, Coranderrk and Framlingham – see map in introduction). It considers the relationship between legislation, as imagined and set out by colonial policymakers, and the realities of everyday life on missions and reserves, paying particular attention to the ways in which the quotidian both reinforced and disrupted legislative goals. Missionary and reserve manager practice entailed the management not just of Indigenous time, space and resources, but also of emotions, behaviour and bodies – what Ann Stoler has called 'colonial habits of heart and mind'.[4] These intimate sites of governance and control were considered crucial to the larger goals of conversion to Christianity, 'civilisation' and assimilation, working hand-in-hand with the more structural methods of governance. They were also important loci of resistance and cultural transformation.

Victorian missionaries and reserve managers during this period served many different masters – their own faith and convictions, their Churches or, in the case of missionaries, missionary societies, and the Aboriginal people they built (or failed to build) relationships with. But they were all ultimately operating under the authority of the Board for the Protection of Aborigines (hereafter the BPA), a body with a specific colonial legislative mandate. Thus while missionaries and managers could challenge the methods and the outcomes of colonial legislation, they remained unable (and arguably unwilling) to disrupt its fundamental basis. This is particularly evident in the fact that even the most dissenting of the managers invoked colonial legislation when it suited them. In this sense, the many and variegated textures of mission life were not necessarily a case of the 'everyday' disrupting colonial culture and power so much as colonial culture and power operating on a different register, with different affects and effects. This chapter represents an attempt to survey the vast variety of individual approaches to mission management, placing them collectively in their common legislative context and asking what this overview can tell us about the *specific* nature of interactions between everyday and legislative technologies of governance in colonial Victoria during this period.

The first part of this chapter surveys the historiography on Victorian missions. While some authors have emphasised the structural nature of mission governance, others have argued for the importance of paternalism and interpersonal relationships, in explaining the ways in which missions were governed. Pointing to the limits of both these approaches, this section argues

---

4   Ann Laura Stoler, *Haunted by Empire: Geographies of Intimacy in North American History*, Duke University Press, Durham, 2006: 2.

for the need to consider both the affective dynamics of mission governance, and the legislative context which at once enabled, and troubled, them. The second section locates the missions and reserves in time and space, briefly elaborating the contexts for their foundations, and the circumstances under which they operated. Analysis then moves to the everyday ways in which missionaries and reserve managers attempted to 'manage' life on the missions, concentrating on four key areas: space and time; economic and spiritual life; sexuality, family and children; and disciplinary practices. Not all of these areas of 'everyday life' were directly addressed in the 1869 legislation under which the missions and reserves operated. However, the approaches of missionaries and reserve managers were all to some degree enabled and supported by this legislation, although the degree to which different managers relied upon the legislative framework, and the degree to which their subsequent chroniclers have emphasised this context, varied greatly from individual to individual.

Historiographical context

Because missionaries', colonial legislators' and Aboriginal peoples' understandings of the status and purpose of missions in Victoria often diverged sharply, the colonial archive of this period (which contains remnants, albeit unevenly distributed, of all parties' voices) can be read in a number of ways. Taking account of this complexity, recent scholars of single mission sites have tended to conclude that missions and reserves operated as both locales of incarceration and cultural loss, and as refuges and sites of cultural renewal for Aboriginal people. Yet a central problem for the historian of Victorian missions and reserves has been where to place the emphasis – on control and coercion, or negotiation and opportunity.

Another problem for those historians who have focused primarily on one mission or reserve is that they are inevitably influenced by the specificities and exceptionalities of 'their' mission's archives.[5] Archival traces are most obviously discernible in claims that a particular mission was 'the most successful', the 'most neglected',[6] the 'largest' or the 'most controversial',[7] or that certain

---

5 This is partly because much of this very important work has been undertaken as doctoral research, which lends itself to focused, localised studies. One exception to this is Felicity Jensz's *Influential Strangers: German Moravian Missionaries in the British Colony of Victoria, Australia, 1848–1901*, Brill, Leiden, 2010, which considers three Moravian missions – Lake Boga, Ebenezer and Ramahyuck. The first of these, Lake Boga, was closed before the period under consideration here.
6 Jan Critchett claims this of Framlingham in *Our Land Till We Die*, Deakin University Press, Warrnambool, 1992, and 'A History of Framlingham and Lake Condah Aboriginal Stations, 1860–1918', unpublished Masters thesis, University of Melbourne, 1980.
7 Diane Barwick claims this of Coranderrk in *Rebellion at Coranderrk*, Laura E Barwick and Richard E Barwick (eds), Aboriginal History Inc, Canberra, 1998.

missionaries or managers were the 'most authoritarian',[8] the 'most humane'[9] or the 'most influential'.[10] These traces are not surprising – mission and reserve archives were, after all, the product of a cast of eccentric, difficult and faith or ideologically motivated individuals competing for power, influence and affection. However, they do have implications for the ways in which the colonial context as a whole is understood, leading to the misapprehension that ostensibly idiosyncratic practices and encounters were shaped only by the personalities and intersubjective relations of the managers, missionaries and their Aboriginal subjects. By considering Victorian missions and stations individually rather than as a group, these authors lose the possibility of detecting and identifying the patterns of their common settler-colonial and legislative context.

These two problems are somewhat compounded by the fact that, while the number of single-mission studies (or single-mission society) continues to expand, only two comprehensive studies of Victorian missions and reserves have to date been published: Michael Christie's *Aborigines in Colonial Victoria* (1979) and Richard Broome's *Aboriginal Victorians* (2005). Both impressive works of scholarship in their own ways, these two volumes are also marked by the concerns of their time. Whereas Christie characterised Aboriginal reserves as 'total institutions' that governed all aspects of Aboriginal peoples' daily lives,[11] Broome emphasised the agency of Aboriginal people within these institutions, and found the fundamental basis for the Aboriginal-missionary dynamic in the concept of paternalism, which he defined as 'a subtle two-way form of power, that had governed relations between people in the British world for centuries'.[12] Within the paternalistic system, Broome argued, missionaries and reserve managers saw themselves in patriarchal relationships to 'childlike' Aboriginal people, while Aboriginal people in turn utilised the concepts of protection and paternalism to argue for their rights in what Broome called the 'patron-client relationship'.[13]

---

8   Critchett makes this claim for Stähle at Lake Condah in *Our Land Till We Die* and 'A History of Framlingham and Lake Condah'.
9   Diane Barwick makes this claim for John Green at Coranderrk in *Rebellion at Coranderrk*. See, for example, her claim that Green 'was the only one of a succession of managers who took charge of [Coranderrk] … who ever entrusted full responsibility for discipline to the residents' (pp. 67–69). Similarly, while Richard Broome does not overtly compare Green to other managers, his use of the adjectives 'benign', 'caring' and 'affable' positions Green as an exception in '"There were vegetables every year Mr Green was here": right behaviour and the struggle for autonomy at Coranderrk Aboriginal Reserve', *History Australia* 3(2), 2006: 43.1–43.16.
10 This claim has been made by several historians about Friedrich Hagenauer, who was undoubtedly one of the most important and influential missionaries of the era. See Felicity Jensz, 'Controlling marriages: Friedrich Hagenauer and the betrothal of Indigenous Western Australian women in colonial Victoria', *Aboriginal History* 34, 2010; Jensz, *Influential Strangers*; Bain Attwood, *The Making of the Aborigines*, Allen & Unwin, Sydney, 1989.
11 Michael Christie, *Aborigines in Colonial Victoria, 1835–1886*, Sydney University Press, Sydney, 1979.
12 Broome, *Aboriginal Victorians: A History Since 1800*, Allen & Unwin, Sydney, 2005: 128.
13 For another, more nuanced example of Broome's approach to this topic, see 'There were vegetables'. Broome has since shifted his notion of paternalism towards a more critical formulation. In a 2009 article on

In using paternalism as his central analytical framework, Broome, like the authors of many of the individual mission studies he drew upon, placed a strong emphasis on the importance of personal relationships, and the abilities of the individual missionaries and reserve managers to invoke either loyalty and cooperation, or mistrust and contempt in the Aboriginal people they were employed to 'manage'. He also highlighted Aboriginal agency within these relationships, an important corrective to Christie's focus on structural oppression. At times, however, Broome's emphasis on the 'personal' nature of mission life, and his efforts to distance his work from earlier scholars such as Christie, led him to some questionable conclusions, for instance his assertion that the Victorian Aboriginal reserves and missions

> were not 'concentration camps' as some have termed them, but places of refashioned community and identity: places that became 'home', complete with oppressions and opportunities like any home.[14]

In order to understand how Broome came to such a conclusion, we need to go back to David Roberts' 1979 work *Paternalism in Early Victorian England*, from which Broome's concept of paternalism was drawn. In this work, Roberts analysed the writings and practices of early nineteenth-century English paternalists who, he argued, believed that society should be at once 'organic, pluralistic, authoritarian and hierarchical'. Emphasising social duty and function, paternalists believed that each member of society had obligations to the whole, but could also expect to receive something in return.[15] In his work, Broome applied Roberts' findings to the colonial Australian context, arguing that the notion of paternalism could help to explain the often ambivalent relationships between Aboriginal and settler Australians. These relationships, he argued, were 'nuanced and complex and defy simple labels of oppression and exploitation, since both parties express some agency'.[16]

Drawing on Roberts' work allowed Broome to point out the continuities between nineteenth-century British domestic and colonial Australian paternalisms, and to draw important parallels between attitudes towards children and the poor in England and Aboriginal people in Australia. However, in applying Roberts' thesis (which was itself criticised for providing only a one-sided account of paternalism), Broome may well have over-emphasised the extent to which paternalism could operate in an organic, reciprocal manner in a settler colony like Victoria. In this context it is somewhat curious that Broome did not consult

---

Aboriginal freak show performers and their managers, he describes paternalism as 'an exploitative power relationship, even within the family on which it is modeled'. 'Not strictly business: freaks and the Australian showground world', *Australian Historical Studies* 40(3), 2009: 331.
14   Broome, *Aboriginal Victorians*: 128–129. It should be noted that it is the latter part of this point that I consider questionable.
15   David Roberts, *Paternalism in Early Victorian England*, Croom Helm, London, 1979.
16   Broome, 'Not strictly business': 331.

the body of work on paternalism in colonial settings, that is, discussions of the relationship between paternalism and violence in North American and South African plantation societies.[17] Perhaps the most significant work in this oeuvre is Eugene Genovese's 1974 work *Roll, Jordan, Roll*, which identified paternalism as central to planters' attempts to achieve 'total cultural hegemony' over their slaves.[18] Slavery in North America, Genovese argued, relied 'less on coercion than on paternalism – that is, on alternating acts of kindness and cruelty, on flattery and rebuke, on bribes and deprivations'.[19] Here, violence and paternalism were not separate or conflicting elements of planter behaviour, but rather two sides of the same coin. In this context, the slaves' only hope for resistance lay in responding to paternalism on their own terms, in turning their masters' need for gratitude and loyalty to their own ends. The ability of slaves to assert their own agency was not an integral virtue of the paternalistic system, but rather one possible response to it, something that had to be asserted and enacted again and again.

While the operation of paternalism in the Victorian mission context was unquestionably different from that of North American slave plantations, Genovese's findings regarding paternalism do open up some important lines of questioning, not least that of how different colonial contexts could put different pressures, and limits, on ideas and practices of paternalism. Unlike the domestic British paternalism of the late eighteenth and early nineteenth centuries, which relied on the idea of an affectively bonded and compassionate home, 'sharply differentiated from the public world of work, politics, production and capital',[20] paternalism in colonial contexts such as Victorian Aboriginal missions or North American slave plantations blurred boundaries between the private and the public, the personal and the commercial. It was also complicated by ideas about racial, cultural and religious difference, and the specific laws which embedded these ideas in the colonial legislature.

In the Victorian context after 1869, the system of reserves and missions was underwritten by legislation that bluntly organised power relations in ways that represented a significant expansion of paternal authority in this particular

---

17 See, for example, Eugene Genovese, *Roll Jordan Roll: The World the Slaves Made*, Pantheon Books, New York, 1972; R Ross, *Cape of Torments: Slavery and Resistance in South Africa*, Routledge and Kegan Paul, London, 1983; John Edwin Mason, 'Paternalism under siege: slavery in theory and practice during the era of reform c. 1825 through emancipation', in Nigel Worden and Clifton Crais (eds), *Breaking the Chains: Slavery and its Legacy in the Nineteenth-century Cape Colony*, Witwatersrand University Press, Johannesburg, 1995; Pamela Scully, *Liberating the Family: Gender and British Slave Emancipation in the Rural Western Cape, South Africa, 1823–1853*, Heinemann, Portsmouth, 1997. Whereas the first three authors consider the paternalism of slaveholders, Scully makes the important point that the emancipation of slavery was also conducted within the framework of paternalism. My thanks to Alan Lester for alerting me to these debates and sources.
18 Eugene Genovese, *Roll, Jordan, Roll*.
19 David Brion Davis, 'Slavery and the post-World War II historians', *Dædalus* 103(2), Spring 1974: 10.
20 Lester and Dussart, 'Masculinity, "race", and family in the colonies: protecting Aborigines in the early nineteenth century', *Gender, Place & Culture: A Journal of Feminist Geography*, 16(1), 2009: 64.

'domestic' space.²¹ Giving the governor power to regulate Aboriginal place of residence, employment, personal earnings, 'net produce', the expenditure of governmental grants and 'the care custody and education of children',²² the *Aborigines Protection Act 1869* (Vic) created a framework that enabled quite different practices of governance than those encapsulated in the reciprocal notion of paternalism proposed by Roberts and Broome.²³ Thus, despite becoming homes for the Aboriginal people who lived on them, mission stations and reserves were not envisaged, or managed 'like any home' by the missionaries and managers who controlled them; they were sites of heightened incarceration, surveillance and manipulation, which was only sometimes softened by the 'ameliorative' balm of familial affection.

This is not to say that legislation predetermined the conditions, or the outcomes, of life on Victorian missions and reserves, or the ways in which Aboriginal people viewed these sites.²⁴ Interpersonal connections, and the affective dynamics they both arose out of and created, were demonstrably important influences on the ways in which colonial legislation on the six missions and reserves played out. But given the unprecedented nature of the powers given to mission and reserve managers during this period, the specificities of the Victorian legislative context are important to keep in mind. It is with this awareness that we move to the next section, a brief consideration of the individual missions and reserves.

---

21 Lester and Dussart, 'Masculinity, "race", and family': 64.
22 The 1869 Act gave the Governor of Victoria the power to 'make regulations and orders':

'For prescribing the place where any aboriginal or any tribe of aborigines shall reside.

'For prescribing the terms on which contracts for and on behalf of aboriginals may be made with Europeans, and upon which certificates may be granted to aboriginals who may be able and willing to earn a living by their own exertions.

'For apportioning amongst aboriginals the earnings of aboriginals under any contract, or where aboriginals are located on a reserve, the net produce of the labor of such aboriginals.

'For the distribution and expenditure of moneys granted by Parliament for the benefit of aborigines.

'For the care custody and education of the children of aborigines.

'For prescribing the mode of transacting the business of and the duties generally of the board or any local committee hereinafter mentioned and of the officers appointed hereunder.'

An Act to provide for the Protection and Management of the Aboriginal Natives of Victoria, 11 November 1869, Victorian Parliament.

23 Roberts' book was in fact criticised in one review for the fact that it studied paternalism only 'through the paternalists themselves' (John Harrison, 'Paternalism in early Victorian England', *American Historical Review* 85(2), April 1980: 394–395). While this criticism does not apply to Broome's work, which gives considerable space to Aboriginal perspectives, his model of paternalism, based as it is on Roberts', would appear to be more weighted towards how the paternalists believed paternalism functioned than how it was experienced by its 'beneficiaries'.

24 Jane Lydon and Alan Burns, 'Memories of the past, visions of the future: changing views of Ebenezer Mission, Victoria, Australia', *International Journal of Historical Archaeology* 14, 2010: 39–55.

The reserve and mission system takes shape

Of the six Aboriginal stations operating in colonial Victoria between 1869 and 1886, three (Ebenezer, Ramahyuck and Lake Tyers) were Church-funded missions, and three (Coranderrk, Framlingham and Lake Condah) government-operated reserves.[25] While the mission stations were managed by missionaries whose wages were paid by the Churches or mission societies, government-appointed managers ran the reserves; the sole exception was Lake Condah which, as a partnership between the Board and the Anglican mission, operated under a mix of government and Church funding and control.[26] With two sources of income, the Church-run missions in Victoria have been represented as more stable and prosperous than the government stations, although contestations over the comparative efficiency and order of Church- and Board-run stations were often the subject of public debate. Indeed, contemporary accounts of stability and effectiveness were as much a claim on legitimacy as a reflection of actual conditions on the reserves, and accounts by those involved in these contestations need to be read accordingly. It is certainly true that the turnover of managers on Church-run missions was much less frequent, yet despite the apparent relative autonomy and job security of the missionaries, all mission and station managers ultimately came under the Board's control.

Population numbers on the missions and reserves waxed and waned over time, and as shown in Table 1, at different times almost all could have made the claim to have the 'largest' population of Aboriginal residents in the colony, though generally Coranderrk and Lake Tyers had the most residents. The population of Ebenezer was reasonably stable whereas Framlingham and Lake Tyers tended to show the most significant movement (indeed much of this movement may well have been between these two stations). It is important to note, however, that although the missions and reserves housed between 400 and 550 people, many other Aboriginal families were living away from these stations and, while probably under the gaze of colonial administrators, their daily lives were certainly less restricted.[27]

In 1869, at the time of the *Act for the Protection and Management of the Aborigines*, the Victorian missions and reserves were all established and receiving varying levels of government support. Development at Coranderrk was considered by the Board to be progressing well, with James MacBain, president of the BPA, calling it 'the most prosperous Aboriginal station in Victoria, or perhaps

---

25 Framlingham had begun as an Anglican mission, but had reverted to direct Board control in 1866.
26 Critchett, 'A history of Framlingham and Lake Condah': 81. Critchett says the managers at Lake Condah were employed by the Church of England, but van Toorn says Stähle's salary was paid by the BPA (p. 17), and Broome classifies Lake Condah as a government reserve and not a mission.
27 See Richard Broome, 'Aboriginal workers on south-eastern frontiers', *Australian Historical Studies* 26(103), October 1994: 202–220.

in Australia', and writing that its results had 'exceeded the most sanguine expectations of those amongst the members of the Board who have had the largest experience of the Aboriginal character'.[28] This glowing report contrasted notably with his assessments of the Moravian and Anglican missions at Ebenezer (Lake Hindmarsh), Ramahyuck (Lake Wellington), Lake Tyers and Lake Condah, where he observed deaths were rife and intoxication and the securing of liquor were a constant concern.[29]

Coranderrk was unique among the Aboriginal reserves and missions operating in Victoria between 1869 and 1886 in that no Church or mission society was involved in its foundation. The result of years of campaigning by Wurundjeri, Taungurong and Bunwarrung peoples and their white supporters, the station was finally established at the junction of Badger Creek and the Yarra River in March 1863, on traditional lands of the Wurundjeri. John Green, a long-time friend of local Aboriginal people, and exponent of their interests, was chosen by the residents as its manager.[30] Aboriginal people had clearly identified that emerging ideas about colonial governance could also provide them with space to make claims upon the colonial state as Aboriginal subjects. Green remained the manager at Coranderrk until 1874, when, after a falling out with Board Secretary Robert Brough Smyth, he gave an informal resignation.[31] He was succeeded by Heinrich Stähle, a Moravian missionary who had been sent to Ebenezer in 1872 but had left in 1874 after the death of his wife. Stähle is an important (if controversial) figure in the history of the Victorian missions, as he worked across several missions. First based at Ebenezer, then Coranderrk and later Lake Condah, Stähle had significant experience and influence. Throughout his time as manager of Coranderrk, Stähle supported the Kulin peoples' wishes to have Green reinstated. Partly because of this, he was in turn replaced in 1875 by Christian Ogilvie, a local settler chosen by the Board members who remained openly hostile to Green.[32]

Of the six missions and reserves under discussion in this chapter, Ebenezer Mission, located on Lake Hindmarsh in the Wimmera region, was the first to

---

28 *Sixth Report of the Central Board appointed to watch over the interests of the Aborigines in the Colony of Victoria*, John Ferres, Government Printer, Melbourne, 1869: 4 (henceforth, Sixth CBPA Anuual Report (1869)).
29 Sixth CBPA Anuual Report (1869): 6–8.
30 Jane Lydon, 'Charles Walter's images of Coranderrk', *Aboriginal History* 26, 2002: 79. Green had first come into contact with the local Aboriginal people in around 1860, when he would ride over from the goldfields, where he was a Presbyterian lay preacher, to hold services for the young Woiwurrung couples camped at Yering. In 1861, Green's wife Mary began a school for the Woiwurrung children at Yering, and in August of the same year Green was appointed temporarily as General Inspector for the newly formed Central Board Appointed to Watch Over the Interests of the Aborigines in the Colony of Victoria (the CBA). Heavily involved in the negotiations that finally led to land being gazetted for the reserve, Green was then appointed as Superintendent of Coranderrk at its foundation. Diane Barwick, *Rebellion at Coranderrk*: 55.
31 Barwick, *Rebellion at Coranderrk*: 102.
32 Barwick, *Rebellion at Coranderrk*: 113.

be founded. Established on the traditional lands of the Wotjobaluk in 1859 by two Moravian missionaries, Friedrich Wilhelm Spieseke and Friedrich August Hagenauer, the mission was intended, at least in part, to make up for the failure of the first Moravian mission in Victoria, which had been located at Lake Boga.[33] In the Moravian model, missions were 'ideally self-sufficient, hierarchically ordered communities of the converted, living lives of discipline and dedication, obedient to the missionary mentors and the rules and regulations they imposed', and Spieseke and Hagenauer attempted to run the mission along these lines.[34] However, the relationship between Hagenauer and Spieseke was strained,[35] and when in 1862 the Presbyterian Church joined forces with the Moravian Church to establish a new mission, Ramahyuck, in Gippsland, Hagenauer was chosen as its superintendent.[36]

Located on the Avon River at Lake Wellington outside Sale, Ramahyuck was built on the traditional lands of the Brayakuloong people of the Gunai Kurnai nation. At Ramahyuck, Hagenauer's ascent continued. The Moravians from the outset had an ambivalent relationship with the colonial state, however, they came to rely on it for support in their missionary endeavours. This tendency is epitomised in the person of Hagenauer, who throughout his colonial career built alliances not only across denominations, but also across the sacred-secular divide. By the 1870s, according to historian Felicity Jensz, Ramahyuck 'outshone Ebenezer as the role model for all other mission stations within the Colony of Victoria', with 'many converts and markers of European civilization'.[37] Having been given the 'full status of a minister' of the Presbyterian Church in 1869, Hagenauer was further honoured in 1871 by being made superintendent of Lake Tyers. Finally, in 1889 he completed his rise to the apex of colonial politics by being promoted to the position of acting secretary and general inspector of the Victorian BPA in 1889. These developments in Hagenauer's political career, combined with his continuing allegiance to the Moravian Church, had implications for the way Hagenauer ran Ramahyuck, and exerted his influence at Lake Tyers. However, Hagenauer was not alone amongst colonial missionaries in perceiving the necessity of cooperating with colonial authorities. All the missionaries discussed here relied at least to some extent on external regulations to enforce the legal code on Aboriginal peoples living on their missions.[38]

The fourth Aboriginal station in operation in colonial Victoria during this period was Lake Tyers. Founded by the Anglican Church in 1861, the mission

---

33 Felicity Jensz, *Influential Strangers*: 113.
34 Timothy Keegan (ed.), *Moravians in the Eastern Cape, 1828–1928: Four Accounts of Moravian Mission Work on the Eastern Cape Frontier*, Paarl Print, Paarl, 2004, cited in Jensz, *Influential Strangers*: 155.
35 Jensz, *Influential Strangers*: 146.
36 Jensz, *Influential Strangers*: 150.
37 Jensz, *Influential Strangers*: 154.
38 For example, Felicity Jensz cites the case of the Ebenezer missionary Kramer, who in 1877 requested that a copy of the 1869 Act be made available to the local Dimboola police station. See *Influential Strangers*: 195.

was located in eastern Gippsland on a picturesque site separated by 2 kilometres of water from Lakes Entrance, and was built on the traditional lands of the Krowathunkooloong clan of the Gunai Kurnai nation. Despite starting out with lower numbers than the Moravian missions, by 1886 Lake Tyers had grown to be the largest. John Bulmer, the mission manager from its establishment until his death in 1913, came from a Methodist background and has been characterised by historian Peter Carolane as 'a hard worker with a quiet temperament and a strong humanitarian and Evangelical dedication'. Carolane claims that Bulmer's almost uniquely uncontroversial status amongst the missionaries of colonial Victoria was due to his 'ability to work around social, political and ecclesiastical changes', which was also 'the reason he was able to last so long as a missionary'.[39]

Framlingham Aboriginal Station, located on the traditional lands of the Girai wurrung, was first gazetted as a reserve in 1861; however, by 1865 virtually no infrastructure had been developed to support an Aboriginal station. Consequently the BPA agreed to the Church of England Mission establishing a station and allowed a grant of stores and supplies to facilitate this. This too failed and within a year the administration of Framlingham was again in the hands of the BPA after apparent poor attendance from Aboriginal people. Only a year later the BPA decided the station was to be closed and the residents were to relocate to Lake Tyers. The Framlingham residents resisted the closure and only a few were relocated to Lake Tyers, some of whom soon returned to Framlingham. The Framlingham mission officially reopened in 1869 with William Goodall in place as manager. Determined to give the residents more autonomy and freedom Goodall allowed them to play in the local football league and to take absences from the mission to travel. Framlingham, more than any other of the Victorian missions or reserves, had always existed under the threat of closure by the BPA, and its survival owed more to the persistence of its Aboriginal residents than it did to any official desire to keep it running.[40]

Of the missions and reserves under discussion here, Lake Condah – located on the traditional lands of the Gunditjmara – was the last to be founded. Although frequently described as a government reserve, Lake Condah Mission was staffed by the Church of England Mission Committee, and the salaries of its station managers paid by them.[41] This power-sharing arrangement between the Mission

---

39 Peter Carolane, 'Parallel fantasies: tourism and Aboriginal mission at Lake Tyers in the late nineteenth century', in Amanda Barry, Joanna Cruickshank, Andrew Brown-May and Patricia Grimshaw (eds), *Evangelists of Empire?: Missionaries in Colonial History*, eScholarship Research Centre in collaboration with the School of Historical Studies, Melbourne, 2008: 162.
40 Mary Tomsic, 'Disparate voices: Framlingham as a site of resistance', in Julie Evans and Tracey Banivanua-Mar (eds), *Writing Colonial Histories: Comparative Perspectives*, RMIT Publishing, Melbourne, 2002: 39–55.
41 Barwick, *Rebellion at Coranderrk*: 92; Critchett, 'A history of Framlingham and Lake Condah': 60. There is some confusion in the literature as to Lake Condah's precise status as a mission or a government reserve. Jan Critchett characterises it a 'Mission station' which was favoured over the 'Board station' Framlingham (p. 81), Richard Broome calls it a government reserve and does not mention that managers' wages were paid

Committee and the Board was not always conducive to a stable management regime. The mission was established jointly by the Mission Committee and the BPA in 1867, and in its first few years was managed by a succession of Church of England missionaries – Job Francis (1867–1868), Joseph Shaw (1868–1873) and Amos Brazier (1873–1875), before the ex-Moravian minister Heinrich Stähle (formerly of Coranderrk) took over.[42] Stähle, whose approach to mission management has been described by several historians as 'authoritarian',[43] managed the station until its closure in 1913.

Space and time on the mission

On all of these missions and stations, the lives of Aboriginal people were controlled and constructed in particular by the regulation of space and time. Bain Attwood has shown in his study of Ramahyuck how carefully laid-out spatial plans ensured buildings and dwellings were linear in configuration and highly structured. Time was moderated by systems of bells and the day was carved into segments for work, prayer, schooling, sleep and so on.[44] These practices, however, varied amongst mission reserves and managers. John Green, for example, chose to live among the Aboriginal people on Coranderrk suggesting an attempt to flatten out the relationship between manager and residents – however, the Board insisted he move into the dormitory buildings.[45]

---

by the Church (Broome, Aboriginal Victorians: 126). See also Jan Critchett, *Untold Stories: Memories and Lives of Victorian Kooris*, Melbourne University Press, Melbourne, 1998, and Robert Lowe, *The Mish*, University of Queensland Press, St Lucia, 2002. Penny van Toorn even claims that wages on Condah were paid by the BPA (van Toorn, 'Hegemony or hidden transcripts? Aboriginal writings from Lake Condah, 1876–1907', *Journal of Australian Studies* 86, 2006: 17; van Toorn, *Writing Never Appears Naked: Early Aboriginal Cultures of Writing in Australia*, Aboriginal Studies Press, Canberra, 2006: 155), yet the accounts of the Victorian BPA do not contain any record of his salary being paid, although they do record the Board's support of a matron on the station from 1883 onwards (see the *Seventh Report of the Board for the Protection of Aborigines in the Colony of Victoria*, John Ferres, Government Printer, Melbourne, 1871, Appendix VI: 25, etc [henceforth, BPA Annual Report]). Contemporary newspaper reports also corroborate the fact that the Anglican Church considered Lake Condah to be one of 'their' missions ('Church of England Mission to the Aborigines', *The Argus*, 24 July 1869: 6). This said, BPA funding for Lake Condah was certainly more extensive than that provided by the Church. In 1869, for example, the Church of England Mission Committee spent 151 pounds 13s 4d on the mission, whereas the BPA spent £529 5s 8d during the same period (Seventh BPA Annual Report (1871), 25). In 1870, the Mission Committee spent £210 11s 10d on Lake Condah; the BPA spend £382 0s 7d ('Mission to the Aborigines', *The Argus*, 30 May 1871: 7; Eighth BPA Annual Report (1872): 26). It should be noted, however, that the amounts spent by the BPA on Lake Condah were generally less than those spent on Coranderrk and Framlingham, the two exclusively government-funded reserves during this period.

42   For a discussion of disputes between the BPA and the Anglican Church Mission Committee over the management style of Joseph Shaw, see Barwick, *Rebellion at Coranderrk*: 93.

43   Robert Kenny, 'Stähle, Johann Heinrich (1840–1915)', *Australian Dictionary of Biography*, National Centre of Biography, The Australian National University, http://adb.anu.edu.au/biography/stahle-johann-heinrich-13204/text23905, accessed 14 December 2012; Critchett, *Our Land Till We Die*: 25.

44   Bain Attwood, 'Space and time at Ramahyuck, Victoria, 1863–85', in Peter Read (ed.), *Settlement: A History of Australian Indigenous Housing*, Aboriginal Studies Press, Canberra, 2000: 52.

45   Barwick, *Rebellion at Coranderrk*: 118.

In this sense, the regulation of the residents' daily activities as well as the spatial layout of the reserves was part of both the colonising process and its idiosyncratic local expressions. Contestations over space amplified tensions both between Aboriginal people and their managers, and between settlers themselves. Giordano Nanni has observed that the control of Aboriginal people was paramount to the government and missionaries alike. He notes, however, that ironically 'this vision of order and regularity that was viewed with satisfaction' was understood as the success of colonial management 'rather than the productivity of Indigenous labour itself'.[46]

Space and time were not the only aspects of Aboriginal lives that were carefully regulated. By restricting access to resources, missionaries and reserve managers exerted control over the lives of Aboriginal people. Even before the 1869 Act, the distribution of food, clothing and other resources was closely rationed.[47] As noted before, many Aboriginal people did not live on the reserves and missions, and the practice of distributing rations to Aboriginal people through the system of local guardians that had emerged during the reserve system's infancy continued throughout the 1860s and 1870s. However, at least some of the mission and reserve managers saw an opportunity here to consolidate their position as the primary mediators of government benevolence. In 1868, John Green suggested to the Board that rations no longer be issued through local correspondents but be available only through the six stations it administered. This would force or at least encourage Aboriginal people to relocate to the stations where they could be controlled. He wrote: 'They would all very soon make to one or another of the stations, when they found that they could not get supplies elsewhere.'[48] With the 1869 Act, Green's vision became a reality, and as missionaries and reserve managers gained control over government resources, including food depots, it became increasingly difficult for Aboriginal people to survive away from missions and reserves.[49] This incident is an interesting example of how even 'humanitarian' reserve managers like Green, often characterised as the 'only friend' of the Kulin people, used and even pre-empted the legislative rulings necessary to pursue their own goals.

The 1869 Act gave the BPA control over where Aboriginal people should reside, and by extension their freedom of movement. Yet the extent to which missionaries and reserve managers applied these powers varied from station to station. Indeed, according to Diane Barwick: 'The power to prescribe an individual's residence by Order-in-Council was not used until 1872, and

---

46 Giordano Nanni, 'Time, empire and resistance in colonial Victoria', *Time and Society* 20(1), 2011: 14.
47 See, for example, Seventh BPA Annual Report (1871), Appendix 1: 5 (Lake Condah); Seventh BPA Annual Report (1871), Appendix 2: 9 (Coranderrk); Ninth BPA Annual Report (1873): 5 (Lake Hindmarsh).
48 Marguerita Stephens, 'White Without Soap: Philanthropy, Caste and Exclusion in *Colonial Victoria 1835–1888: A Political Economy of Race*', unpublished Phd thesis, University of Melbourne, 2003: 194.
49 Attwood, *The Making of the Aborigines*: 2.

then primarily to force Europeans to release children and young girls, but occasionally to control men who resisted station discipline.'[50] Of the 25 orders made from 1875 to 1883, for example, nine were used to restrain adults from leaving their stations, and most of the rest were used to force Europeans to give up Aboriginal children and women 'living in unsavoury circumstances'.[51] At Lake Condah Stähle strictly controlled movement on and off the station, a policy which brought him into conflict with Goodall, the manager of nearby Framlingham. Stähle sought back up from the Board to force inmates to remain on the mission. Goodall, however, was not opposed to the residents coming and going as they pleased. Jan Critchett writes that the policy of segregation was not as rigidly enforced as contemporary reports implied, especially in the case of Goodall at Framlingham, who 'believed there was no point in keeping Aboriginal people against their will'.[52]

Economic and spiritual life

After the 1869 Act, the Board's (and subsequently the reserve and mission managers') responsibility for distributing governmental expenditure on Aboriginal people, including food rations, was legislatively codified. The ways in which rations were handed out varied amongst the missions and stations, but the quantity and quality of food received seems to have been an almost constant source of contention for Aboriginal people. On some missions, such as Ramahyuck and later Lake Tyers, communal resources were monitored through the positioning of storehouses close to the mission house, so that missionaries could keep a close watch on food supplies.[53]

So too, the Act stipulated that the wages of individual Aboriginal people should be shared amongst the larger group. This was controversial, not only amongst Aboriginal people but also amongst many of the missionaries and reserve managers. Hagenauer, for example, 'took particular objection to this Section of the Act, as he, like many other nineteenth-century missionaries, believed in the "dignity of labour"' – that is, the principle that an individual should receive individual remuneration for his or her work.[54] However, despite Hagenauer's objections, the Act ensured that the control of Aboriginal bodies was effected by the regulation of their labour. In essence they were not 'free', as Coranderrk superintendent Hugh Halliday demonstrated in 1876 when he expelled one young resident as a disciplinary measure and 'licensed [him] out … with a view

---

50 Barwick, *Rebellion at Coranderrk*: 89.
51 Barwick, *Rebellion at Coranderrk*: 90, ftn 12.
52 Critchett, 'A history of Framlingham and Lake Condah': 69–74.
53 Attwood, *The Making of the Aborigines*: 12.
54 Jensz, *Influential Strangers*: 193.

to forming associations for him with the white population'.⁵⁵ The 'freedom' to contract with settlers, whilst seemingly prohibited by the Act, could also function as a disciplinary measure itself.⁵⁶

Labour and its economic benefits became an even more important element of the disciplinary regime of the BPA after 1871; the 1871 *Regulations and Orders made under the Act* gave the BPA (and through them the mission and reserve managers) the authority to regulate which Aboriginal people were permitted to undertake private employment. Without a valid work certificate, Indigenous workers could be fined or imprisoned.⁵⁷ Lake Condah, where in the 1880s Indigenous residents were refused work certificates and were therefore unable to work for private authorities off the reserve, is a good example of the power mission managers wielded in these circumstances. Freedom and restraint on labour were, for Aboriginal people, domains already codified by the BPA and the decision about which domain they operated in was made by managers and missionaries.⁵⁸

Missionaries and reserve managers also attempted to transform Aboriginal people through the regulation and control of their spiritual lives. By restricting traditional spiritual practices and instead encouraging the shared experience of Christianity, they hoped to instigate a wholesale change in Aboriginal peoples' spiritual, emotional and behavioural worlds. This was much more focused on the Church-run missions, though it varied across the colony and through time. On the government-controlled reserves the focus was less on conversion and more on education and acculturation. Nonetheless, it is evident that the limits placed on mission residents' traditional spiritual practices, and their long-term exposure to Christian ideas, was a key way that missionaries and reserve managers attempted to (and indeed did) transform the lives of Aboriginal people.

Diane Barwick writes that, after John Green's departure, the Kulin families of Coranderrk (all of whom had lost one or more family member) missed not only Green's medical care, but also 'the familiar Presbyterian rituals with which he had comforted the sick and mourners'.⁵⁹ Even grief and succour could function as a mechanism to draw Aboriginal people into the influence of missionaries – here, perhaps most clearly, unfolded the battle for the habits of 'heart and mind' that Stoler describes.⁶⁰

---

55   BPA Minutes, 25 April 1876, 3 May 1876, quoted in Stephens, 'White Without Soap': 208.
56   On the production of liberal subjects in this regard, see Boucher, in this collection.
57   *Aborigines Protection Act 1869*: 112–113, cited in Andrew Gunstone, 'Indigenous peoples and stolen wages in Victoria, 1869–1957', in Natasha Fijn, Ian Keen, Christopher Lloyd and Michael Pickering (eds), *Indigenous Participation in Australian Economies II*, ANU E Press, Canberra, 2011.
58   Jan Critchett, *Untold Stories: Memories and Lives of Victorian Kooris*, Melbourne University Press, Carlton, 1998: 151–152.
59   Barwick, *Rebellion at Coranderrk*: 116.
60   Stoler, *Haunted by Empire*: 2.

For Moravian missionaries Hagenauer and Spieseke, internal spiritual transformation was more important than external transformation, although emphasis was certainly also placed on the latter.[61] In 1865, 750 religious services were held on Ramahyuck – approximately two per day and 300 more than had been held on Ebenezer in 1870.[62] While there were many who resisted the unrelenting schedule of church services and prayer meetings, for some Aboriginal residents the community experienced in religious services provided a common experience that bound missionaries and Aboriginal people together.[63]

At Lake Condah, the mission manager Reverend Stähle heavily emphasised religious instruction, with prayers conducted every morning and evening and divine service on Sunday. Sunday school was provided for the children. Similarly, Bulmer at Lake Tyers placed much importance on regular church gatherings, the application of the Christian message to both Aboriginal men and women,[64] the distribution of church responsibility amongst the congregation (including its Aboriginal members), and encouraged a nineteenth-century Christian European model of marriage. At Framlingham, although William Goodall was himself a Christian, he did not emphasise religious practice during his years as manager there, and only Sunday service and one weekday prayer meeting were offered.[65] However, for a brief period while Reverend Thwaites was the manager (between July 1882 and August 1885), religion played a more important role.[66]

Sexuality, family and children

Regulating the sexual and intimate life of the residents was another preoccupation of the managers of colonial Victorian Aboriginal missions and reserves. Segregation of unmarried men and women was common. At Ramahyuck, the architecture of the Aboriginal cottages relegated sexual relations to the bedroom, and the separation of children in the boarding house was justified on the assumption that 'a married couple could not live with their children in

---

61   Jensz, *Influential Strangers*: 179.
62   Jensz, *Influential Strangers*: 173.
63   Attwood, *The Making of the Aborigines*: 16.
64   Carolane, 'Reading colonial mission photographs: viewing John Bulmer's photographs of nineteenth century mission life at Lake Tyers Aboriginal Mission Station through an Evangelical lens', in Penelope Edmonds and Samuel Furphy (eds), *Rethinking Colonial Histories: New and Alternative Approaches*, RMIT Publishing, Melbourne, 2006: 116.
65   Critchett, *Our Land Till We Die*: 27.
66   Critchett, *Our Land Till We Die*: 27.

"a right and comfortable way'".[67] In stark contrast to traditional sexual and marriage practices, missionaries often sought to create a 'sense of guilt' about sexual morality, especially in Aboriginal women.[68]

On Coranderrk, the sexuality of teenage girls was a subject of particular concern, as is demonstrated by testimony given by the schoolteacher, Mr Deans, to the 1877 Royal Commission:

> The girls are very strictly watched by the matron Mrs. Halliday ... When she is away I think the place is locked up. They are secure, as there is no way of their getting out, except the few who are at work doing their various domestic work. Mr. Halliday has one key and I have the other.[69]

Another means of controlling the intimate and sexual life of the residents was to ensure that Aboriginal people were dressed in western clothes. On Ramahyuck, as on the other Victorian missions and reserves, clothes were 'held to be integral to the civilizing process', and residents' appearances were closely monitored.[70] In addition, bathing, spitting, urination and defecation were all objects of control, with the provision of toilets identified as a 'civilising agent' by the BPA in the 1870s.[71]

It was not only the sexual behaviour of the Aboriginal women that concerned station managers. As Liz Reed noted, in the early 1860s at Coranderrk, a local 'white girl' Selina Johnson and an Aboriginal man known only as 'Davy', had conducted a secret love affair for over eighteen months resulting in the birth of their child. Tragically, the child died just two weeks after his birth in August 1861. Selina and Davy expressed the desire to be permitted to marry, which was rejected by her family and subsequently became the subject of concern for the Board.[72] There is ample evidence that other residents, too, resisted these attempts to control their intimate lives and clandestine sexual relations were not uncommon. As Richard Broome has argued, the reserve system 'which aimed to order and control' every aspect of Aboriginal lives was only ever partially

---

67 Attwood, *The Making of the Aborigines*: 21.
68 On missionaries and guilt, see Jessie Mitchell, 'Corrupt desires and the wages of sin: Indigenous people, missionaries and male sexuality, 1830–1850', in Ingereth Macfarlane and Mark Hannah (eds), *Transgressions: Critical Australian Indigenous Histories*, Aboriginal History Inc. and ANU E Press, Canberra, 2005: 238.
69 Victoria, Royal Commission on the Aborigines (1877), 'Report of the Commissioners Appointed to Inquire into the Present Condition of the Aborigines of this colony, and to Advise as to the Best Means of Caring for, and Dealing with Them, in the Future, Together with Minutes of Evidence and Appendices', *Papers Presented to Both House of Parliament, Victoria*, Session 1877–78, Vol III, Minutes of Evidence: 91.
70 Attwood, *The Making of the Aborigines*: 20.
71 Attwood, *The Making of the Aborigines*: 21.
72 Liz Reed, 'White girl gone bush with the blacks', *Hecate* 28(1), 2002: 9–22.

realised.[73] Yet, the lengths to which Aboriginal people had to go in order to gain even a modicum of emotional and sexual autonomy suggest how far-reaching its effects and affects could be.

While the adult residents' sexual and intimate lives were the subject of scrutiny, for children the focus was on education and discipline. At Ramahyuck, Coranderrk and later Lake Tyers, the boarding houses that confined the children were kept fenced off from the rest of the mission, and visiting parents required the permission of the missionaries, who 'fought strenuously' over their control.[74] At Coranderrk, children were 'subjected to a program of continuous discipline and training' and were kept 'under close observation all day'.[75]

The Moravian missionaries at Ramahyuck were proud of their education standards. In 1872, the pupils' examination results (100 per cent) were celebrated as the best in the colony, and this high standard continued throughout the 1870s.[76] While the Ramahyuck school's outstanding results were 'a source of pride within religious circles',[77] the BPA interpreted it, and similarly impressive results at Lake Tyers and Lake Condah, as a result of these schools 'being under the inspection of the Education Department', and expressed its 'wish to carry out this system wherever possible'.[78] Once more, the ostensibly disparate actions of the missionaries could be smoothly subsumed into a narrative of legislative and bureaucratic success.

In the Moravian-run boarding schools at Ramahyuck and Ebenezer, Aboriginal children were provided with 'an alternative reality' to the traditional lifestyles that shaped many of their parents' childhoods.[79] As Felicity Jensz has observed, 'the missionaries actively tried to provide what they saw as the necessities for raising children in a Christian way, much like the choir systems at Herrnhut, yet without regard for Indigenous customs.' While 'sensitive to the parents' wishes', they believed in the superiority of their institutions and actively encouraged parents to place their children in the boarding house.[80]

In 1871, the first school was built at Lake Condah Mission and a teacher appointed. Framlingham, on the other hand, did not gain a teacher until 1878.[81]

---

73   Broome, *Aboriginal Victorians*: 130.
74   See, for example, Attwood, *The Making of the Aborigines*, 18; Stephens, 'White Without Soap': 191.
75   Stephens, 'White Without Soap': 191. The quote is from *The Argus*, 9 September 1876: 9.
76   Amanda Barry, '"A matter of primary importance": Comparing the colonial education of Indigenous children', in Penelope Edmonds and Samuel Furphy (eds), *Rethinking Colonial Histories*, University of Melbourne History Department, Melbourne, 2006: 173.
77   Jensz, '"In future, only female teachers": staffing the Ramahyuck Mission school in the nineteenth century', *Provenance: The Journal of Public Record Office Victoria* 11, 2012.
78   Twelfth BPA Annual Report (1876): 4.
79   Jensz, *Influential Strangers*: 177.
80   Jensz, *Influential Strangers*: 178.
81   Critchett, *Our Land Till We Die*: 27.

Furthermore, in at least one case colonial legislation on education was used by mission managers not just to exert control over Aboriginal people, but also over the teachers who taught in their schools. In a recent article, Felicity Jensz has built on Amanda Barry's work to show that Hagenauer

> wished the Ramahyuck school to be brought under the control of the Department of Education to ensure regular inspections and also to ensure that teachers would 'look out to do [their] duty'.[82]

Children's lives were now strictly controlled and the special provisions in the 1869 Act gave the Board pervasive new powers over them. At Coranderrk, Richard Broome writes that the child removal policy was 'practised fairly benignly by Green'.[83] In contrast Marguerita Stephens' study of Coranderrk, 'White Without Soap', argues that:

> While John Green publicly denied that force was used when collecting children for the asylum, Board records, including his own reports, indicate that pressures of various sorts, from bribery, to the withholding of rations, to direct police intervention, were regularly employed to persuade Aborigines to relinquish their children.[84]

Stephens details many instances of Green coercing people to stay on the stations, especially young women and girls. By 1875, Green had, according to Stephens' reckoning, 'relocated some 80 Aboriginal children to the Board's stations, in addition to those who relocated with their families'.[85] It is important to note, however, that Stephens, like Broome, also acknowledges that some Aboriginal people actively sought education for their children and approached Green themselves.[86]

Disciplinary practices

When the effectiveness and affectiveness of interventions in the spatial, temporal, economic, intimate and family lives of Aboriginal residents were undermined, missionaries and station managers used a variety of disciplinary tactics. Whilst the paternalism that Broome and others have described certainly created some possibilities for Aboriginal people to exert influence over their everyday lives,

---

82   Jensz, 'In future, only female teachers'. The quote is from Hagenauer, examined 23 May 1877, Royal Commission on the Aborigines, *Victorian Parliamentary Papers* 1877, Minutes of Evidence: 36, quoted in Amanda Barry, 'Broken Promises: Aboriginal Education in South-Eastern Australia, 1837–1937', unpublished PhD thesis, School of Historical Studies, University of Melbourne, 2008: 111.
83   Broome, *Aboriginal Victorians*: 134.
84   Stephens, 'White Without Soap': 183–184.
85   Stephens, 'White Without Soap': 201.
86   Stephens, 'White Without Soap': 194.

the blunt instruments of coercion and discipline haunted the peripheries of this apparently humanitarian system. Whilst Broome has characterised the contestations between missionaries, reserve managers and Aboriginal peoples as negotiations,[87] incarceration and physical punishment could be wielded by missionary managers to sway these engagements. Legislative authority could be employed for profound disciplinary effect, and part of the power in this threat lay in its apparently inconsistent deployment.[88] At Ramahyuck, Hagenauer believed in the 'reformative capacity of carceration'.[89] So too at Ebenezer and later Lake Condah Stähle was a strict disciplinarian. As early as 1876, at Lake Condah a resident charged him with assault; after the charge was dismissed Stähle then sought more authorised power to discipline his charges.[90] The history of violence at Lake Condah, however, predated Stähle; in 1871, several Aboriginal residents there had made complaints about his predecessor Mr Shaw, that he 'had shot their fowls, and that he had whipped one of them with his riding whip'.[91] Acknowledging both these actions, Shaw responded that he had struck the man with his whip because he had refused to do the work set out for him, and gave 'some insolence' on being challenged about this matter. John Green, who visited the mission in his capacity as Inspector for the Board, wrote in the Annual Report that he had managed to convince the Aboriginal people involved to forgive Shaw 'for all past things', and to 'go on the same as though nothing had happened'; for Green, it seems, the 'satisfactory' progress that Shaw was making in other aspects of mission management was enough for him to overlook this relatively minor problem.[92]

For the most part, missionaries aspired to manage Aboriginal people through their own personal authority, and not through the hard power of legislation. Nonetheless, as Bain Attwood observes, 'physical coercion, legal action and government regulation were the ultimate sources of their authority'.[93] In contrast to Attwood's contention that it was 'the less powerful missionary managers' that most often 'turned to these temporal sanctions', the material examined in this paper (as well as Attwood's own analysis of Hagenauer's involvement in the framing of the 1886 Act, and his high level of involvement in colonial politics) suggests that the more personally powerful missionaries also appreciated the need for legislative and political support, and that those who refused to engage in politicking were less likely to meet with success.[94]

---

87   Broome, *Aboriginal Victorians*: 128–129.
88   In a subtle, but nonetheless significant difference in terminology, Attwood characterised these engagements as 'battles'. Attwood, *The Making of the Aborigines*: 34.
89   Attwood, *The Making of the Aborigines*: 8.
90   Kenny, 'Johann Heinrich Stähle'.
91   Seventh BPA Annual Report (1871), Appendix 1: 6.
92   Seventh BPA Annual Report (1871), Appendix 1: 6.
93   Attwood, *The Making of the Aborigines*: 28.
94   See, for example, Jensz's discussion of Spieseke's failure to engage with colonial politics. Jensz, *Influential Strangers*: 195.

Conclusion

Confinement, discipline and intimate intervention meant that time and time again it was made clear to Aboriginal people in colonial Victoria that missions and reserves were not their 'homes'. They had no guaranteed rights of residence, limited freedom of movement both on and off the missions, and faced a range of measures designed to coercively control and regulate their lives. If British notions of paternalism sustained the authority of the head of the household to determine the 'best interests' of those who lived within it, then this right of rule took on remarkable regulatory consequences in the reserve system without the tempering influences of familial obligation. In the words of Alan Lester and Fae Dussart, although '[a] man's conduct towards all of his dependants was to be respectful and kind, as well as authoritative and instructive … the reality of conforming to this specific mandate for masculinity was ambivalently pressured in ways that became acute in certain contexts, such as on the colonial frontier'.[95]

The paternalism that prevailed on missions and reserves was thus a specific mobilisation of some of the elements of paternal power in service of certain articulations of settler colonialism: the power to control movement operationalised to segregate, concentrate, and create assimilable populations/peoples; the regulation of sexuality operationalised to assimilate both socially and biologically; the power to manage household finances operationalised to limit Aboriginal people's financial independence and social mobility. The male missionary's position as father of the mission residents was both an effect of, and produced, settler colonialism in Victoria 'between the Acts'. And this was the case because the domestic everyday was a location of government, a location that should be thought of as different to that of police and formal judicial regulation, but not as fundamentally distinct. Violence and paternalism were, as Eugene Genovese has observed for the context of North American slave plantations, two sides of the same coin.

After 1869, as Boucher has noted elsewhere, the limitations on Aboriginal rights seemed to turn Aboriginal subjects into the Board's legal children; for these 'children', however, there would be no passage into the civil or personal rights of adulthood. Instead these were endlessly deferred, with missionaries and station managers standing in as both paternal protectors from, and arbiters of, settler colonial governmental power. In this context, the 'homes' that provided one of the few spaces for communities to remake their lives only offered the emotional nourishments of family and community because Aboriginal people struggled hard to forge them.

---

95   Lester and Dussart, 'Masculinity, "race", and family': 64.

Table 1: Numbers of Aboriginal residents at the six missions and reserves, 1868–1886.

Mission	1868[96]	1871[97]	1872	1876[98]	1877[99]	1878[100]	1879[101]
Coranderrk	76	107	111–128[102]	137	145	148	113
Ebenezer	57–95[103]	80	100+[104]	67	65	70	91
Lake Tyers	23	87	60[105]	63	63	88	88
Ramahyuck	69	74	76[106]	81	86	87	83
Lake Condah	80	81	70[107]	89	85	83	81
Framlingham	N/A[108]	63	58[109]	63	59	70	67

Mission (cont)	1880[110]	1881[111]	1882	1883[112]	1885[113]	1886[114]
Coranderrk	105	93	101	112	107	98
Ebenezer	78	81	85	76	78	73
Lake Tyers	90	112	112	112	110	101
Ramahyuck	81	76	80	83	83	83
Lake Condah	92	100	105	89	112	110
Framlingham	75	75	83	96	104	91

---

96   Sixth CBPA Anuual Report (1869).
97   Seventh BPA Annual Report (1871), 3.
98   Twelfth BPA Annual Report (1876): 3.
99   Thirteenth BPA Annual Report (1877): 3.
100 Fourteenth BPA Annual Report (1878): 3.
101 Fifteenth BPA Annual Report (1879): 3.
102 The higher number comes from Dr J Gibson's report from 30 March 1872; the lower is the daily average as estimated by the manager John Green. Eighth BPA Annual Report (1872), Appendix IV: 12; Appendix VIII: 17.
103 Bill Edwards, 'Ebenezer through Ernabella Eyes': 13. Edwards does not specify where his numbers come from.
104 Bill Edwards, 'Ebenezer through Ernabella Eyes': 13.
105 Numbers taken from Dr James Jamieson's report from 8 May 1872 in the Eighth BPA Annual Report (1872), Appendix V: 14–15.
106 Average of daily attendance at Ramahyuck between January–December 1871, Eighth BPA Annual Report (1872), Appendix VIII: 19.
107 Average of daily attendance at Lake Condah between January–December 1871, Eighth BPA Annual Report (1872), Appendix VIII: 20.
108 As the status of Framlingham was uncertain in 1867–68, it was not included in the 1868 Sixth CBPA Anuual Report (1869).
109 Average of daily attendance at Framlingham between January–December 1871, Eighth BPA Annual Report (1872), Appendix VIII: 22.
110 Sixteenth BPA Annual Report (1880): 3.
111 Seventeenth BPA Annual Report (1881): 3.
112 Nineteenth BPA Annual Report (1884): 3.
113 Twenty-first BPA Annual Report (1885): 3.
114 Twenty Second BPA Annual Report (1886): 3.

6. Photography, authenticity and Victoria's *Aborigines Protection Act* (1886)

Jane Lydon

As Darwinism took hold among the global scientific community during the 1860s and 1870s, visitors to Australia such as the Darwinist Enrico Giglioli (in 1867) and Anatole von Hügel (in 1874) followed a well-beaten path around Victoria. Under the auspices of colonial officials such as Robert Brough Smyth and Ferdinand von Mueller, they pursued authentic Indigeneity and Aboriginal 'data' including photographs, which subsequently played an important role within their arguments about Aboriginal identity and capacity. This paper examines how photographs became a powerful form of evidence for Aboriginal people, in turn shaping global debates about human history and what Tony Bennett has termed the 'archaeological gaze' that characterised a new scientific world view.[1] In addition, given the dual interests of many colonial figures both in administering Aboriginal policy and in recording Indigenous culture, local applications of such ideas were influential in debates about managing Koories across the Victorian reserve system. In particular, emergent theories and their visualisation shaped policies, management procedures and legislation such as the *Aborigines Protection Act 1886* (Vic).

In this chapter I make two related arguments: I show first how the experience of visiting scientists to Victoria during the late nineteenth century, especially at Coranderrk Aboriginal Station, shaped and was shaped by their view of Indigenous Australians and racial difference. Such experiences, and the visual records they produced, in turn affected larger schemes of human origins and progress. Second, I explore how such imagery in turn reinforced hardening notions of biological race, and assisted local administrators such as the Board for the Protection of the Aborigines in arguing for specific notions of Aboriginality, eventually expressed in the 1886 'Half-Caste Act'.

These issues are exemplified by the work of German-born photographer Fred Kruger, who worked in Victoria over the second half of the nineteenth century, and that of the Italian Darwinist Enrico Giglioli, who visited Australia in 1867. Giglioli subsequently wrote two books about Australian Aboriginal people, and his work demonstrates both the impact of the theory of natural selection outside Britain and the global importance of Australian data – particularly imagery – in establishing the evolutionist schema.[2]

---

1   Tony Bennett, *Pasts Beyond Memory: Evolution, Museums, Colonialism*, Routledge, London, 2004: 39.
2   For a comprehensive overview of Kruger's life and works, see Isobel Crombie, *Fred Kruger: Intimate Landscapes, Photographs 1860s – 1880s*, National Gallery of Victoria, Melbourne, 2011. For detailed consideration of Giglioli's career and impact see Jane Lydon, '"Veritable Apollos": Aesthetics, evolution, and Enrico Giglioli's photographs of

Australian Aboriginal people had played a significant role in Western conceptions of progress and civilisation since first contact with Europeans. Following publication of Charles Darwin's *The Origin of Species by Means of Natural Selection* in 1859, such ideas only strengthened. By the early 1860s, scientific observers believed that the pace of extinction had accelerated and that several races, such as the Tasmanian Aboriginal people, were on the verge of disappearance. Scientific interest in Australian Aboriginal people stemmed from the view that living Indigenous societies provided evidence for prehistoric human life, and that Australians were survivors from humankind's earliest stages. Thomas Henry Huxley was the first to draw this ethnographic parallel in his 1863 exploration of 'man's place in nature', one of the first applications of Darwinism to humankind.

Figures such as Huxley, and archaeologists John Lubbock and Augustus Henry Lane Fox Pitt Rivers, were central to the emergence of a new scientific world view based on limitless 'vistas of time'. This new, shared understanding across archaeology and other disciplines (geology, palaeontology, anthropology) of a 'continuous unfolding of the past into the present' called forth intellectual procedures such as retrospective deduction.[3] Crucial in this shift was the development of a systematic method for reading the past on the basis of the physical qualities of the artefact – what became known as the typological or comparative method – providing a new 'grammar for spatialising and temporalising the past'.[4]

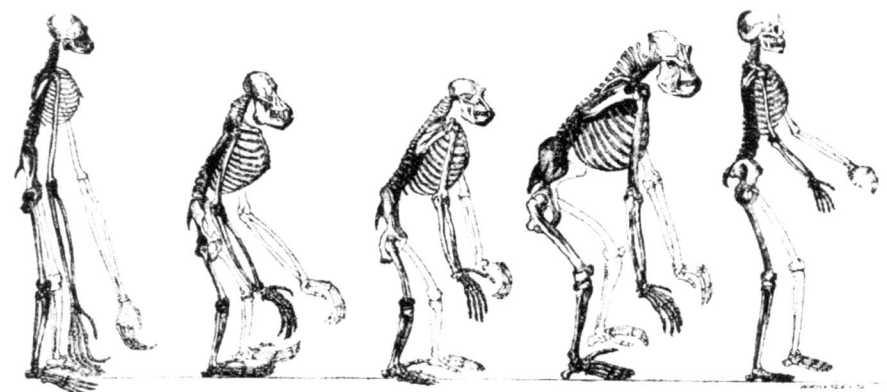

Figure 1: 'Skeletons of the Gibbon. Orang. Chimpanzee. Gorilla. Man.' TH Huxley.

Source: TH Huxley, *On the Relations of Man to the Lower Animals*, 1909: 50.

Indigenous Australians 1867–78', *Interventions: International Journal of Postcolonial Studies*, 2013: 72–96.
3   Bennett, *Pasts Beyond Memory*: 39.
4   Bennett, *Pasts Beyond Memory*: 43.

An important dimension of this approach was the development of a distinctive visual rhetoric by influential figures such as Huxley and Pitt Rivers, which became the basic structure of natural history displays, showing successive linear transformation into increasing larger, more developed forms. Within this schema, the abstract concept of a human 'racial type' came to be seen as having concrete form, and although its definition was in fact highly subjective, anatomical measurement, especially of skulls, was seen as an objective means of classification and comparison. Increasingly, scientists across a range of disciplines advocated the application of the comparative method to humankind using the photographic 'portrait type', which made an abstract sense of human variation observable and real.[5]

Exchange between European theorists and colonial correspondents centred upon the procurement of Indigenous bodies and the interpretation of their supposed racial characteristics, and there was widespread agreement that Aboriginal bodies would provide evidence for 'ancestral relations between races that over time had come to exhibit morphologically distinct physical and psychological characteristics'.[6] By the 1860s, technological developments within photography made portraits of Indigenous people available in the form of *cartes de visite*, produced by professional photographers as well as amateur practitioners. This availability contrasted strongly with the rarity of Australian artefacts and anatomical specimens. By 1870 Museum Godeffroy curator Schmeltz noted that skulls and skeletons from Australia were some of the rarest objects in Europe.[7]

Enrico Hillyer Giglioli (1845–1909) was a zoologist and anthropologist who is remembered as a founding figure of Italian science, as an early scientific observer, and as an avid institutional collector. His research regarding marine vertebrates and invertebrates, and to a lesser extent, birds, continues to be cited in these

---

5   Elizabeth Edwards, 'Evolving images: photography, race and popular Darwinism', in Diana Donald and Jane Munro (eds), *Endless Forms: Charles Darwin, Natural Science and the Visual Arts*, Fitzwilliam Museum, and Yale Center for British Art, Cambridge, 2009: 169.
6   Paul Turnbull, 'British anthropological thought in colonial practice: the appropriation of Indigenous Australian bodies, 1860–1880,' in Bronwyn Douglas and Chris Ballard (eds), *Foreign Bodies: Oceania and the Science of Race 1750–1940*, ANU E Press, Canberra, 2008: 212.
7   Thomas Theye, '"... ein Blick für alles Bemerkenswerthe ..." – einige wissenschaftsgeschichtliche Aspekte der Queensland-Photographien Amalie Dietrichs in der anthropologischen Sammlung des Museums Godeffroy', *Jahrbuch des Museums für Völkerkunde zu Leipzig*, Bd. 42, 2004, S. 161–280. Mit 46 Abbildungs-Tafeln.

fields.⁸ Scholars have also noted his legacy in the form of extensive natural history and ethnographic collections in Florence and Rome, as well as the objects he gave in exchange, now housed within institutions around the world.⁹

Figure 2: Enrico Hillyer Giglioli. [19--] photograph: b&w; 10.7 x 8.2 cm. Part of GM Mathews collection of portraits of ornithologists [picture], 1900–1949.

Source: National Library of Australia.

---

8   For example, Hitoshi Ida, Makoto Okamoto and Jiro Sakaue, '*Epigonus cavaticus* (Teleostei: Perciformes), a new epigonid fish from Palau, western Central Pacific', *Ichthyological Research* 54(2), 2007: 131–136; G Bearzi, RR Reeves, G Notarbartolo-di Sciara, E Politi, N Cañadas, A Frantzis and B Mussi, 'Ecology, status and conservation of short-beaked common dolphins *Delphinus delphis* in the Mediterranean Sea', *Mammal Review* 33(3), 2003: 224–252.

9   For example, BJ Gill, 'The Cheeseman-Giglioli correspondence, and museum exchanges between Auckland and Florence, 1877–1904', *Archives of Natural History* 37(1), 2010: 131–149; ES Tiberini, 'Plains Indians artifacts in the E. H. Giglioli Collection of the Pigorini Museum in Rome', *European Review of Native American Studies* 4(2), 1990: 41–44.

His documentation of the Florence collection of artefacts collected on Cook's voyages also continues to be cited.[10] However, in sharp contrast to the work of many nineteenth-century British scientists, Giglioli's accounts of Australian Aboriginal people, comprising two books illustrated with engravings, and associated archival and photographic documentation, have not been closely examined by Anglophone historians.

Giglioli attended the National College and Technical Institute in Pavia, and the Royal School of Mines in London at age 16, where he pursued his studies in natural science with Charles Lyell, Richard Owen and Thomas Henry Huxley between 1861 and 1863. As well as these links with British science, he was closely integrated into Italian networks, his father holding the first Italian Chair of Anthropology, instituted at the University of Pavia in 1860.

Returning to Italy in 1864, he attended lectures by Filippo De Filippi (1814–1867), who introduced Darwin's *Origin of Species* to Italy in that year, and established a department of comparative anatomy at Turin, perhaps the first in the new Kingdom of Italy to embrace the theory of evolution. Darwinism was rapidly taken up by Italian naturalists, and was widely influential across a range of disciplines. In 1865, De Filippi invited his student to accompany him on a proposed trip to circumnavigate the world, the 1865–1868 diplomatic and naturalists' expedition of the Italian warship, *Magenta*. However, Giglioli was forced to take over from his teacher when De Filippi died in Hong Kong in 1867.

Giglioli arrived in Melbourne in May 1867 and set out in search of 'authentic' Indigenous Australians. He visited Parliament and then the Mines Office, where he met its Chief Secretary and keen ethnologist, Robert Brough Smyth: 'He told me that the aborigines, of whom I had seen only a couple of miserable individuals in the streets of Melbourne, had almost disappeared from the neighbourhood of the city and the other centres of settlement', and advised him to visit the Coranderrk Aboriginal station, and then to go to Geelong, or Echuca on the River Murray, where Aboriginal people might be seen 'still in an almost independent state'.[11] He followed this advice, but was disappointed to encounter in the streets of Echuca 'troops of Aborigines', poorly dressed and intoxicated, who had gathered for the distribution of blankets.

---

10   See, for example, Adrienne L Kaeppler (ed.), *Cook Voyage Artifacts in Leningrad, Berne, and Florence Museums*, Bishop Museum Press, Honolulu, Hawaii, 1978.
11   Enrico Hillyer Giglioli, *Viaggio intorno al globo della r. pirocorvetta italiana Magenta negli anni 1865-66-67-68*, Maisner, Milano, 1875: 750.

He had greater success in Jaengenya, west of Echuca, and then Moama, where he 'had the pleasure on my walk of running into a family of aborigines who had kept their native appearance rather more', who were going from Lake Moira to Echuca. He described the scene and their camp, including their spears, skin cloaks and gunyahs, concluding that 'the scene was highly typical and amply rewarded me for my long journey'.[12]

Indigeni dei dintorni del lago Moira, New South Wales. — (Da fotografie.)

Figure 3: Engravings 'Indigeni dei dintorni del lago Moira, New South Wales. – (Da fotografie.)' [Aborigines from the environs of Lake Moira, NSW (From a photograph).]

Source: EH Giglioli, *Viaggio intorno al globo della r. pirocorvetta italiana Magenta negli anni 1865-66-67-68*, Maisner, Milano, 1875: 772.

Excited and impressed by his first bona fide encounter with Indigenous people, Giglioli obtained a series of *cartes de visite* by Melbourne-based travelling photographer Thomas Jetson Washbourne (some via the Italian Consul, Cavalière Giuseppe Biagi), that were the basis for some of his published engravings.[13]

---

12 Giglioli, *Viaggia intorno al globo*: 773–774.
13 These are held in the Pigorini, Rome, accession 4161. For identification as Dhudhuroa I thank Indigenous Elder Gary Murray for his advice.

Figure 4: 'Australiani della tribu di Moama & Echuca sul fiume Murray. Dono del comm. G. Biagi 1872 ed acq. a Melbourne Maggio 1867. Enrico H Giglioli.' (Australians of the Moama and Echuca tribes, on the river Murray. Donated by Consul G. Biagi 1872, acquired in Melbourne May 1867).

Source: National Museum of Prehistory and Ethnography 'Luigi Pigorini', Rome.

These are held in the Pigorini, Rome. While this would make the subjects Yorta Yorta people, the woman is identified in Australian collections such as the State Library of Victoria as belonging to the 'Barwidgee Tribe', and so is rather affiliated with the Dhudhuroa. Following a well-beaten path, Giglioli took botanist Baron Ferdinand von Mueller's advice and went to Coranderrk, only 41 miles from the city, then numbering around 100 residents, of whom he noted: 'They occupied one good house (for young adolescents) and fairly well-maintained shacks, the inside walls of which were in most cases papered with cuttings from English and Australian illustrated journals, and photographs, greatly prized by these people.'[14]

He made his own photographic portraits of six of the residents. These included Derrimut (or Derremart or Terrimoot) (c.1810 – 28 May 1864), who was a headman or *arweet* of the Boonwurrung people. He fought in the late 1850s and early 1860s to protect Boonwurrung rights to live on their land at Mordialloc reserve. When the reserve was closed in July 1863, his people were forced to unite with the remnants of Woiwurrung and other Victorian Aboriginal communities and to settle at Coranderrk. Derrimut became very disillusioned and died in a Benevolent Asylum at about 54 years of age in 1864.

Giglioli noted that: 'Later I received from Dr Mueller an almost complete collection of photographic portraits of the aborigines and halfbloods living at Coranderrk which has been very useful to me in recalling my impressions.' This well-known series, originally comprising 104 portraits, was produced by botanical collector and photographer Charles Walter in 1865 in preparation for the 1867 Paris International Exposition.[15] Although lacking scientific utility, these Victorian portraits were the foundation of Giglioli's collection of Australian photographic 'types', as I explore further.

On his return to Florence, Giglioli wrote up the zoology of the voyage of the *Magenta*, and in 1869 began to lecture in this field. Giglioli was to enjoy a long and distinguished academic career, becoming director of the Royal Zoological Museum in Florence in 1876. Like his mentor, Thomas Henry Huxley, marine vertebrates and invertebrates were his central research interest, but he was also a noted amateur ornithologist and photographer, and continued his research in the developing discipline of anthropology. In 1892, Frederick Starr of the University of Chicago surveyed the international anthropological scene and singled out Mantegazza and Giglioli as the two foremost Italian anthropologists of the day.

14 Giglioli, *Viaggia intorno al globo*: 773.
15 Jane Lydon, Eye Contact: *Photographing Indigenous Australians*, Duke University Press, Durham, 2005.

6. Photography, authenticity and Victoria's *Aborigines Protection Act* (1886)

Figure 5: 'Australiani della Victoria, tribu Yarra-Yarra. Acq. A Melbourne 1867. Enrico H Giglioli.' (Australians of Victoria, of the Yarra-Yarra tribe. Acquired in Melbourne 1867).

Source: National Museum of Prehistory and Ethnography 'Luigi Pigorini', Rome.

Figure 6: 'Portraits of Aboriginal Natives Settled at Coranderrk, near Healesville; about 42 miles from Melbourne. Upper Yarra. Also Views of the Station & Lubras Basket-Making.' Charles Walter, Panel, 1866.

Source: State Library of Victoria.

Two books remain the major sources for Giglioli's Australian experiences and research: *I Tasmaniani: Cenni storici ed etnologici di un popolo estinto* (*The Tasmanians: The History and Ethnology of an Extinct People*) published in 1874,[16] and the following year *Viaggio intorno al globo della r. pirocorvetta italiana Magenta negli anni 1865–66–67–68* (*Voyage Around the Globe on the* Magenta), with an ethnological introduction by the 'founder' of Italian anthropology, Paolo Mantegazza. These works express his profound engagement with European debates about race and humankind and the work of prominent scientists who had theorised about Australian data, as well as revealing an extensive knowledge of the Australian literature. As a zoologist, Giglioli's research relied upon the comparative method, an investigative philosophy that was well-established by the early nineteenth century, and which was an important plank underpinning Darwin's theory of evolution.

What was distinctive about Giglioli's account of mainland Aboriginal people in *Voyage Around the Globe* was his innovative use of photographic imagery

---

16 This book was based on a lengthy article he had contributed to the first volume of the *Archivio per l'Antropologia e la Etnologia* in 1871, the journal of the new Società Italiana di Antropologia e di Etnologia.

to argue against more senior colleagues such as French anthropologist Paul Topinard. His early application of the comparative method to the new medium argued for homogeneity within the Australian mainland population, as well as its distinctiveness, on the basis of photographic portraits. Giglioli's primary aim was to demonstrate sameness, or the 'ethnic unity', of Indigenous Australians, and to this end Giglioli drew upon his extensive scientific networks in assembling a collection of photographs of Aboriginal people from across Australia. As an evolutionist, for Giglioli, variations between the 'various strains of Australian Aborigines [*genti*]' were determined by adaptation to environment – for example suggesting that good nourishment produced a fairer skin.[17]

Giglioli's research was influential in disseminating ideas across Italy about social Darwinism and human adaptation to environment. He closely engaged with British theories and the growing perception at this time that Indigenous Australians were an important element in the story of human origins. The 1860s was a decade of great visual ferment and photography was used to great effect in catering to European popular and scientific demand for Indigenous 'data' from the expanding frontier. Photography was a means of naturalising ideas about race and culture as Darwinism became scientific orthodoxy over the following decades. However, understanding the thought of scientists such as Giglioli works to undermine modernist scientific concepts of race by tracing the concept's normalisation and the ambivalence of visual meaning during the mid-nineteenth century, with the effect of revealing the contingency of racial categories in the present.

Fred Kruger at Coranderrk

My second example is the work of a German-born photographer, Johan Friedrich Carl Kruger, who went to Coranderrk during the 1870s and 1880s. During this decade, ideas about race began to narrow and harden, a transition traced by Friederich Kruger's more than 160 photographs of Coranderrk spanning almost two decades, which circulated as newspaper engravings, official and commercial albums, and as anthropological data, generating a wide range of sometimes competing meanings. This was an intensely political decade, and contradictory ideas about Aboriginality focused public attention on Coranderrk as a test case for Aboriginal policy – the humanitarian reformists supported the residents and their demands, opposing those seeking to close the station and resume its valuable farm lands.

---

17   Giglioli, *Viaggia intorno al globo*: 796.

Settler Colonial Governance

Kruger's first photographs of Coranderrk appeared in the colonial illustrated newspapers, showing Aboriginal people undergoing cultural transformation – scenes of hop pickers, a fishing holiday or cricket. What is remarkable about these images and distinguishes them particularly from contemporary representations of a 'doomed race' is that they show Aboriginal survival. Gurindji photographer Brenda Croft, for example, sees them as reflecting Kruger's personal interest in and sympathy for the residents' situation, and she considers that 'he was closest to honestly depicting a rapidly changing lifestyle, and Aboriginal peoples' adaptation to those changes'.[18] They reveal Aboriginal industry and vitality; change here could be understood as progress, with the implication of a hopeful future.

Aboriginal idylls

Kruger's picturesque views of Coranderrk stressed harmony, productivity and peace, assuring viewers of the residents' appropriation of a rural peasant lifestyle – as in one of Kruger's best-known images, the idyllic 'Fishing scene at Badger's Creek'. Engraved versions of this photograph appeared at least twice in early 1878, titled 'The Hop Paddock, Coranderrk, Victoria, from Badger Creek', and accompanied by an optimistic account of the Station, as an attempt 'to prevent the extinction of the aboriginal race', and teach 'habits of order and industry'.

Figure 7: 'Badger's Creek at Coranderrk Aboriginal Station, c.1870–78', Fred Kruger.

Source: Museum Victoria XP 1934.

---

18 Brenda L Croft, 'Laying ghosts to rest', *Portraits of Oceania*, The Art Gallery of New South Wales, Sydney, 1997: 13.

6. Photography, authenticity and Victoria's *Aborigines Protection Act* (1886)

Figure 8: 'The Hop Paddock, Coranderrk, Victoria, from Badger Creek', *Illustrated Australian News*, **January 1878, front page.**

Source: National Library of Australia.

While stressing progress towards civilisation and discipline, almost despite itself the text dwells upon the Arcadian quality of this moment, describing how the Aboriginal workforce

> are allowed occasional holidays, one of which they are enjoying as presented to our view. On such occasions there is no issue of rations, but that is immaterial, as the creek abounds with fish, and the aboriginals are expert anglers, and find no difficulty in supplying themselves with an ample quantity of food in a short time.[19]

Kruger was drawn to 'thoroughly domesticated' landscapes, unlike contemporaries such as Nicholas Caire and JW Lindt, who sought out scenes of picturesque wilderness such as the giant tree ferns and ash forests of the Dandenongs. Like 'Coast scene, Mordialloc Creek, Cheltenham', the Coranderrk 'fishing scene' is a gentle, lyrical celebration of Australian leisure.[20] 'Fishing scene' signals the advent of Aboriginal people enjoying an ideally tranquil, harmonious relationship with each other and with the landscape, yet clearly

---

19   *Illustrated Australian News*, 1 January 1878: 10.
20   Isobel Crombie, *Victorian Views: Photographs of the Landscape 1850s–1920s*, National Gallery of Victoria, Melbourne, 1995: 4.

not leading a 'traditional', pre-colonial way of life. Their closeness to nature was emphasised, but at the same time, the fishing 'holiday' encouraged the 'sable labourers to persevere in habits of order and industry': the subjects' 'civilisation', marked, for example, by their European dress and their diligence, is the framing trope of the text.

In April, the *Illustrated Australian News* featured two scenes from Coranderrk's new hop industry based on Kruger photographs, titled 'The Hop kilns, Coranderrk' and 'The Hop grounds – Dinner Hour'.[21]

Hop cultivation became a particularly appealing theme at this time, representing an archetype of rural picturesqueness, and evoking a sense of nostalgia for the pre-industrial, European lifestyle it recalled. Scenes of hop-picking remained a popular subject in the colony's illustrated newspapers and tourist guides throughout the century. As one Melbourne writer mused,

> the mere association of ideas recalls the charming fields of Kent and the pleasant scenes of harvest time … It is the season of rejoicing. Bustle and animation is discernible on every hand. Nature never looks so beautiful and benignant. She pours forth with unstinted hand her barn of plenty, and all the land smiles like a garden full of the choicest products.[22]

Figure 9: 'Hop Gardens at Coranderrk Aboriginal Station, c.1870s', Fred Kruger.

Source: Museum Victoria XP 1933.

---

21 *Illustrated Australian News*, 18 April 1876: 52. See also MV XP 1932 which shows 'Hop Gardens at Coranderrk', a similar scene to XP 1933.
22 *Illustrated Australian News*, 31 March 1886.

6. Photography, authenticity and Victoria's *Aborigines Protection Act* (1886)

To homesick immigrant eyes, hop-picking seemed the archetypal scene of European plenty. Settlers' nostalgia for home, combined with their own experience of the colony's rapid growth, gave a particular local inflection and poignancy to a larger modernist consciousness of loss amid a fast-changing world. This nostalgic sensibility, often couched in older, pastoral, terms, was a defining characteristic of Western responses to the effects of industrial capitalism from the early nineteenth century, as observers lamented the destruction of the natural environment and the rustic order.[23] For colonists, Melbourne's astonishing growth, particularly following the discovery of gold in the early 1850s, invoked a sense of dizzying change, as industry and progress flourished in what some colonists still remembered to have been a pristine wilderness peopled by 'savages'. It was an 'instant city' whose swelling population threatened to outrun government control, and many feared that the forces of chaos and anarchy would prevail.[24]

A vision of agrarian stability was advanced against the uncertainty and fluctuations of gold-seeking, praising the moral value of the small farmer embedded in a fixed social hierarchy.[25] The increasingly urban population found refreshment in the picturesque Gippsland lakes, and the rainforests of the Dandenongs, and especially enjoyed arcadian scenes of 'pioneer' farmers leading productive lives of simplicity and contentment.[26]

For a moment, in Kruger's picturesque views, a vision of Aboriginal arcadia flickered into existence, impelled perhaps by local humanitarians' hopes for their future, but also underwritten by an older European aesthetic. The notion of Aboriginal villages – combining European agrarian ideal with traditional skills such as fishing, involving above all a closeness to nature, assumed the form of an idyll, a charming scene of rural peace.

---

23   Christopher Wood, *Paradise Lost: Paintings of English Country Life and Landscape 1850–1914*, Barrie & Jenkins, London, 1988; Christiana Payne, *Toil and Plenty: Images of the Agricultural Landscape in England, 1780–1890*, Yale University Press, New Haven and London, 1993: 27–28.
24   David Goodman, 'Making an edgier history of gold', in Iain McCalman and Andrew Reeves (eds), *Tailings: Forgotten Histories and Lost Artefacts of Australian Gold*, Cambridge University Press, Melbourne, 2001: 23–36; Graeme Davison, 'Gold-Rush Melbourne', in *Tailings: Forgotten Histories and Lost Artefacts of Australian Gold*, 2001; Graeme Davison, *The Rise and Fall of Marvellous Melbourne*, Melbourne University Press, Carlton, 1978.
25   Goodman, *Gold Seeking*: 105–148.
26   See for example Tanjil, *Our Trip to Gippsland Lakes and Rivers, with new tourist's map, in colour*, ML Hutchinson, Melbourne, 1882.

However, as critics of the rustic idyll have often pointed out, its apparent peace and plenty were a fantasy of the disenchanted modern viewer, signifying a rural stability which had in fact long been disrupted by urbanisation and industrialisation.[27] British observers pointed out that the apparent harmony of hop-picking, in particular, masked its use of itinerant urban labour and its associations with vagrancy, promoting the old myths of rural happiness despite prevailing circumstances of social unrest and poverty.[28]

Kruger's tranquil Aboriginal arcadias also worked to disguise the dispossession of the Indigenous people, expressing the humanitarians' vision of Coranderrk as idyll, in which the residents would lead productive Christian lives as the colony's rural peasantry. But peaceful scenes of hop-picking were misleading as evidence for the community's stability, as I discuss further.

For example, although a commercial success, the demands of the hop-field and the constant attempts of the Board to hire European labour became a problem for the Aboriginal residents and their supporters, forcing them to work for profit rather than their own subsistence. More importantly, Kruger's views appealed to a yearning for return to a lost world of peace and harmony with nature, excluding as they do any reference to everyday modernity as experienced by the urban readers of Melbourne's newspapers. They constructed a fantasy which located the Aboriginal subjects in a country retreat, secluded from the present and its conflicts, denying their battle for autonomy.

Visual movement, a temporal narrative

Images such as 'fishing scene' also work in specifically photographic ways to affect the viewer. Kruger's views embody photography's mimetic impulse, creating an embodied sense of movement to embrace the object of vision, and constructing an intimate, domestic relationship with their subjects. The remarkable depth of field evident in many of Kruger's 'views', and notably in 'Badgers Creek, Fishing Scene', prompts a similar engagement with the image, a sense of movement beyond the picture's surface, into its heart. Kruger created this effect using a small aperture and short focal length, as well as the large plate format available by this time.

---

27 As early as 1856, George Eliot noted that 'idyllic literature' had always 'expressed the imagination of the cultivated and town-bred, rather than the truth of rustic life'. George Eliot, 'The natural history of German life', *Westminster Review*, 1856, reprinted in T Pinney (ed.), *Essays of George Eliot*, London, 1963; Raymond Williams, *The Country and the City*, Chatto and Windus, London, 1973: 30–71.

28 See, for example, Payne, *Toil and Plenty*; Anne Janowitz, 'The Chartist picturesque', in S Copley and P Garside (eds), *The Politics of the Picturesque: Literature, Landscape and Aesthetics since 1770*, Cambridge University Press, Cambridge, 1994: 261–281.

6. Photography, authenticity and Victoria's *Aborigines Protection Act* (1886)

When we look at nineteenth-century photographs we should remember that what appears to be a flattened space stripped of perspectival depth was in fact often intended to be viewed stereoscopically, and even in the process of consuming still photographs, the 1870s viewer would willingly have succumbed to the magic of verisimilitude. Rosalind Krauss argues that the sensation of refocusing the eyes within the image, re-coordinating the eyes to fix on different points, is a 'kinesthetic counterpart to the sheerly optical illusion of the stereograph … [a] physio-optical traversal of the stereo field';[29] like cinema, the isolated viewer is transported optically by a sensation of physical movement, travelling into the image.

As the viewer gazes, time passes almost imperceptibly, and the many complex elements of place, action and character begin to suggest a story.[30] Poring over a photograph is like diagnosing an illness, trying to understand the hidden story concealed by its surface. The spatio-temporal dimension opened up tells us of the people, their association and purpose, their relationship to the landscape. It tells a story of domestication, its Aboriginal fishers living in natural harmony with the landscape and each other. Although drawing the Aboriginal subjects into an intimate and familiar relationship with the viewer, this took a fundamentally paternal form, prompting a narrative which linked humanitarian hopes for an Aboriginal future to a nostalgic return to a European past.

Photographing Coranderrk's rebellion

However, in the context of local debates about the station's management, which prompted Aboriginal protest, government intervention, and widespread public interest, Kruger's views also participated in increasingly contested narratives about Coranderrk; on the one hand, that Aboriginal people were becoming successful peasant farmers, or alternatively that they were helpless children who needed to be controlled and disciplined, yet whose impurity rendered them unworthy of protection. This local conflict effectively ensured the destruction of the Aboriginal idyll, and in the eyes of their white audience, the residents' fall from grace.

Coranderrk's rebellion came to public attention in early 1876, when a headline in *The Age*, 'Coranderrk Hop Farm: Mr Green and Mr R. Brough Smyth', told a fascinated public about the authoritarian and unjust treatment of the residents, and their much-loved manager Green, by the Board. This was particularly

---

29   Rosalind Krauss, 'Photography's discursive spaces', in *The Originality of the Avant-Garde and Other Modernist Myths*, MIT Press, Cambridge, Massachusetts, 1985: 133, 136–137.
30   R Barthes, *Camera Lucida: Reflections of Photography*, Vintage, London, 1993: 99.

newsworthy because only weeks before, the Board's secretary, Brough Smyth, had been suspended from his position as head of the mining department for his bizarrely dictatorial work practices.

However, this was just the first shot in the battle over the station's future; although hop cultivation had been a commercial success under the management of John Green and the Kulin, it became a problem in diverting resources away from basic subsistence and maintenance of the settlement, and to improve profits the Board sought to hire white labour. When the hop income was diverted to central revenue, the Board lost any incentive to support the station, and began to push to close it down.

Residents allied with humanitarian supporters (such as the Reverend Hamilton and wealthy philanthropist Anne Bon), agitated to work their lands without outside interference, and to protect their home. In the developing conflict between the Board and residents, personal links with the major newspapers – the reformist *Age* as well as the conservative *Argus* – in turn allied to opposed political factions, saw their arguments translated into polemical feature articles, attracting a wide readership and articulating different ideas about Aboriginality.[31] A pro-Green view emerges strongly from an April 1876 review of the hops industry, giving him credit for its success, referring sympathetically to Green 'himself having been discharged under what many may hold to be rather harsh circumstances'.[32] Kruger's images expressed the humanitarian vision of a hard-working agrarian community, domesticating their industrious, orderly Aboriginal subjects and incorporating the settlement into a stable colonial hierarchy.

Before and after: Board commission 1877–78

Perhaps it was the domestic quality Of Kruger's first photographs from Coranderrk that prompted the Board to employ Kruger at a key political moment, as the residents' opposition to the Board and its goal of closing the station reached a climax. Between mid-1877 and mid-1878, Kruger was commissioned to produce a series of Coranderrk portraits.

---

31   Elizabeth Morrison, 'Black Wednesday 1878 and "the manufacture of public opinion" in pre-Federation Victoria', in A Curthoys and J Schultz (eds), *Journalism: Print, Politics and Popular Culture*, University of Queensland Press, St Lucia, 1999: 36–55.
32   *Illustrated Australian News*, 18 April 1876: 52.

The residents' political campaign ranged from strikes and disputes within the station, to writing letters and petitions and even sending deputations walking 41 miles down to Melbourne to speak directly to Chief Secretary Graham Berry. As a result, in early 1877, a Royal Commission was appointed. It focused on future policy for the so-called 'half-castes' amid widespread criticism of the humanitarian segregationist position, and demands for assimilation. The Royal Commission endorsed the view of the Board at this time, that the so-called 'half-castes' lacked the capability to live independently of the stations, largely because of white prejudice. It recommended retention of the station.[33]

So at this crucial moment, in response to public criticism and accusations of poor management, the Board mounted its own public relations campaign, aware of the need to represent itself in a positive light. It introduced a system of Visitors Books,[34] and commissioned a series of 36 photographs of the model Ramahyuck mission, in Gippsland.[35] Kruger's Coranderrk commission must have been conceived as part of this propaganda-gathering exercise, intended to lend weight to Board arguments regarding its effective management. Unlike the exemplary Ramahyuck, Coranderrk's appearance had by this time begun to attract criticism,[36] so instead of showing the settlement itself, Kruger recorded the progress the Aboriginal subjects had made, producing a sequence of portraits of 'civilised', well-cared-for residents.

But in this series Kruger created a structural relationship between individuals dressed in simulated 'traditional' garb, and those showing the same person in 'modern', European dress, prompting a narrative of evolutionary change. They suggest the effectiveness of the work of civilising through the juxtaposition of these opposed material and visual signs. While we do not know the original sequence of the images, this pairing is particularly consistent with respect to the adult women, such as Annie Reece. Annie Reece is also shown seated in an indoor studio setting, with her children and her husband James Reece, in a typical studio portrait pose.

---

33 Victoria, Royal Commission on the Aborigines (1877). 'Report of the Commissioners … together with Minutes of Evidence': xii.
34 'expecting these to be useful propaganda in reflecting the views of observers who already had a kindly interest in the welfare of Aboriginal people'. Board for the Protection of the Aborigines Minute Book, 4 September 1878, National Australian Archives (NAA), Series B314, Item 3.
35 Coral Dow, '"In search of the picturesque": Aborigines and tourists in nineteenth century Gippsland', *Journal of Tourism, Culture and Communication* 2, 2000: 111–122.
36 The 1877 inquiry concluded that 'Greater attention might not improperly be paid to the appearance of the area surrounding the settlement – no effort has as yet been made in this direction. The effect of tidiness, and *per contra* of untidiness, on the Aboriginal mind is most important; the inculcation of tidiness forms part of civilization as well as discipline.' Royal Commission on the Aborigines (1877): x–xi.

Figure 10: 'Annie Rees and child at Coranderrk Aboriginal Station, c.1875–76', Fred Kruger.

Source: Museum Victoria XP 1788.

6. Photography, authenticity and Victoria's *Aborigines Protection Act* (1886)

Figure 11: 'Annie Rees with her children, Maryann and Charlotte, at Coranderrk Aboriginal Station, c.1876–77', Fred Kruger.

Source: Museum Victoria XP 1787.

Others make the same transition. In all, there are 26 such pairings which conform to this formulation, and as a result, viewing the series prompts a narrative movement, as a specific, oppositional relationship is created between the uncivilised 'native', on the one hand, and the docile subject making satisfactory progress towards a European lifestyle on the other. Overall, however, a majority of portraits show the subjects in European dress. Of course by this time none of the residents would willingly have removed their clothes, being well aware of how they were viewed by whites.[37] The residents' concern to present a reputable appearance in this case coincided with the Board's.

---

37   In 1870 Robert Brough Smyth had refused TH Huxley's request for anthropometric data, stating that the Victorian Aboriginal people were 'not sufficiently enlightened to submit themselves in a state of nudity for portraiture in order to assist the advancement of Science. Indeed, they are careful in the matter of clothing, and if I empowered a photographer to visit the stations and take photographs with Professor Huxley's instructions in his hand, he would I am sure offend the Aborigines and meet with little success.' Letter from R Brough Smyth to the Chief Secretary, 17 May 1870, Office of the Central Board for Aborigines, Melbourne. Government House Adelaide, Huxley Papers, Imperial College London, Vol. XVI. Notes and Correspondence. Anthropology. Vol. 1. f. 117.

Settler Colonial Governance

Figure 12: 'Sambo and Mooney at Coranderrk Aboriginal Station, c.1875', Fred Kruger.

Source: Museum Victoria XP 1803.

Men such as Edward Mooney, appearing in one portrait with Matilda and their son, are also shown in traditional dress. The emphasis on weapons and fighting as exemplified by outdoor views of staged opponents holding clubs and boomerangs underlines the theme of savagery in these 'before' shots. However, there are a large number of exceptions to this evolutionary formulation. Portraits of men are not as consistently organised as those of women: men tend rather to be shown in *either* traditional *or* European dress, as if they had not bothered to change their clothes for Kruger. Tommy Avoca, for example, photographed 'indoors' in a suit, as well as in traditional attire outside, holds a boomerang in both. Yet various contestations should be seen in the context of the political activism of the people of Coranderrk, which was producing political results at precisely this time.

'Real natives': Board commission 1883

Their campaign was successful in prompting another, parliamentary, inquiry into Coranderrk's management in mid-1881, reflecting the great interest the case aroused among the general public. Ominously however, the commissioners focused particularly upon the status of the so-called 'half-castes', perceived by some since the mid-1870s to be basically different from so-called 'full-blood' Aboriginal people.

Despite the 1877 Royal Commission's decision not to send 'half-castes' out to work, Board officials began to push for this policy, and it was provisionally adopted – for boys – in January 1879.[38] Yet even while the parliamentary inquiry was underway in late 1881, the Board fiercely debated this issue, its annual report arguing that 'half-castes' while 'sharp and cunning enough in small matters' would be unable to compete within settler society.[39] At this time, many observers noted that Coranderrk had a large 'half-caste' population, and critics attributed the unrest at the station to their influence; it became increasingly common to argue that the 'full-bloods' alone had a claim to government support, even by humanitarian supporters.

The inquiry criticised Board management of the station and recommended its retention. However, it also recommended that while the 'full-bloods' should be supported at the station, the 'halfcastes and quadroons' should be encouraged to leave to seek work as servants and labourers. This policy would subsidise Aboriginal support, and address the colony's labour shortage – but crucially, assimilation of the 'half-castes' into the white population would also solve the Board's problems in controlling these rebellious people.[40] Under strong official pressure the Board immediately began to formalise this policy.[41]

---

38 Diane Barwick, *Rebellion at Coranderrk*, Laura E Barwick and Richard E Barwick (eds), Aboriginal History Inc., Canberra, 1998: 166.
39 *Board for the Protection of the Aborigines, Seventeenth Report*; July 1881 Board for the Protection of the Aborigines, 'Minutes', 6 July 1881, NAA Series B 315, Box 1, Item 1.
40 Michael Christie, *Aborigines in Colonial Victoria, 1835–86*, University of Sydney Press, Sydney, 1979: 194–98, 199–201.
41 The Chief Secretary, writing in December 1882 to the Board, directed them to reconsider their opposition to hiring out young 'half-caste' women, noting that '[t]he Chief Secretary desires the Board will be so good as to again consider the matter, more especially in regard to the half-castes and guardians of both sexes.' 15 December 1882, NAA, B 313, Item 201. A conference in August 1882 aimed to formulate such a policy: Report of the Managers' Conference, 18 August 1882, NAA, Series B313, Box 13, item 229.

The highly gendered nature of arguments about assimilation emerges from contemporary debates; it is evident that a profound fear of miscegenation underlies popular and official arguments, focusing on the Aboriginal women. The press consistently commented on the 'white' appearance of some residents as evidence for racial mixing, and deplored the creation of a pauper under-class.[42] The accusation that the Aboriginal women were 'unchaste' was hinted at slyly or rejected with embarrassment by a society that did not openly acknowledge sexual exchange between black and white. While these slurs on the residents' morals caused some annoyance to the Board, it too saw the 'half-castes' as less authentic, and less deserving of support.

Again, at this key moment, the Board decided to obtain visual proof of the difference between the 'full-bloods' and 'half-castes'. In July 1883, Captain Page, Secretary of the Board, commissioned Kruger to make another series at the station.[43] Kruger was enthusiastic about this project, writing 'I think it is a capital suggestion of yours to have a Panorama view',[44] and 'I ... will agree to make you 12 or 15 large views of Station ... & *groups of the real natives*'.[45] Kruger's 'groups of the real natives' show people still living in mia-mias, using traditional artefacts, in strong contrast to his earlier portraits. 'Group of Different Tribes', for example, suggested that these people were still leading a hunter-gatherer lifestyle, and located the 'full-blooded' residents in the past.

There are eight views of this kind, establishing a temporal relationship with the altered, potentially civilised subjects of the earlier portraits. It is important to remember, however, that in the context of the entire Board series, this group provided a counterpoint to the dominant theme of civilisation, a contrast which served to underline the overall progress made under Board supervision. This correspondence participated in constructing the contradictory formulation of Aboriginality – still powerful today – whereby 'real Aborigines' are located in the remote past, leaving no room for change.[46]

---

42 For example, Undated [c.March 1883], unsourced newspaper clipping, NAA, Series B313, Item 204.
43 Prompted in the first instance by Chief Secretary Graham Berry's desire to be represented at the 1883 Calcutta Exhibition. PROV, VPRS 3991, Chief Secretary, Inward Registered Correspondence, Part II, item Z4777.
44 'which I am confident I can obtain from one of the hills near the School, in eather [sic] 3 or 4 parts'. NAA, B313/1, Item 207.
45 Headed 'Geelong July 24. 83': NAA, B313/1, Item 207 (original emphasis).
46 Jeremy Beckett, 'The past in the present; the present in the past: constructing a national Aboriginality', in J Beckett (ed.), *Past and Present: The Construction of Aboriginality*, Aboriginal Studies Press for the Australian Institute of Aboriginal Studies, Canberra, 1988: 191.

6. Photography, authenticity and Victoria's *Aborigines Protection Act* (1886)

Figure 13: 'Group of Aboriginal people from Different Tribes at Coranderrk Aboriginal Station, c.1870', Fred Kruger.

Source: Museum Victoria XP 1929.

Figure 14: 'Group portrait outside a dwelling at Coranderrk Aboriginal Station, c.1870', Fred Kruger.

Source: Museum Victoria XP 1926.

These images provided visual evidence for the different appearance and capabilities of 'half-castes' and 'full-bloods', underpinning arguments about their differential treatment. The following year, 1884, the Board formally adopted a policy of 'absorption' or assimilation. The final blow came in 1886 when the Aborigines Protection Law Amendment Bill was passed, stating that only 'full-bloods' and 'half-castes' over the age of 34 years were entitled to remain on the station.[47] Among the punitive clauses the Board had originally proposed was a provision empowering magistrates to decide 'on their own view and judgement' whether a person was Aboriginal or 'half-caste', suggesting that in the Board's opinion, this distinction was clearly visible to the eye.[48] The amended Act redefined Aborigines as 'full-bloods', 'half-castes' over 34 years old, female 'half-castes' married to 'Aborigines', the infants of 'Aborigines', and any 'half-caste' licensed to remain on a station.[49]

This divisive move weakened the Aboriginal campaign, in part because the wider public now believed in a basic difference between the 'full-bloods' and 'half-castes', readily discernible on the basis of appearance. Kruger's 'real natives' participated in this work of documenting and defining Aboriginal people through the clarity and objectivity of photography. Sympathy for the residents as a dispossessed people fighting for their heritage, represented in a picturesque pastoral aesthetic, was undermined by a perception that they were in fact divided by an essential biological difference, in turn grounded in miscegenation. As demonstrated by Kruger's portraits which revealed their visibly different skin colour, their fall from grace marred the Aboriginal idyll, and the 'half-castes' were expelled from their Arcadia. As colonial attitudes respecting race became more rigid, images such as Kruger's were appropriated by contemporary scientific and popular notions of race, disseminating ideas about biological difference, and creating fixed visual types which stood for a race. These stereotypical meanings were to become the dominant way of understanding Aboriginal people over the following decades.

---

47 For discussion see John Chesterman and Brian Galligan, *Citizens Without Rights: Aborigines and Australian Citizenship*, Cambridge University Press, New York, 1997.
48 *An Act to provide for the Protection and Management of the Aboriginal Natives of Victoria 1869* (Vic), section 8; VPD, Legislative Assembly, vol 53, 15 December 1886: 2913.
49 50 Victoriae, no. 907 (1886), cited in Christie, *Aborigines in Colonial Victoria*: 197.

7. Women, authority and power on Ramahyuck Mission, Victoria, 1880–1910

Joanna Cruickshank and Patricia Grimshaw

By the late nineteenth century, Christian missions in the Colony of Victoria, as in many other settler colonies, had become central to the governance of Indigenous people. While missionaries generally saw their aims as distinct from those of the settler administration, in practice missions provided a focus for colonial efforts to control and assimilate Aboriginal people. Missions are thus central to the task of understanding colonial governance and its impact on Indigenous people in Australia. Voluminous mission and bureaucratic archives, containing records produced by missionaries, colonial administrators and Aboriginal mission residents, provide rich sources for analysing how colonial policies towards Indigenous people were implemented and experienced 'on the ground'.

These sources make clear that while missions became locations where the authority of the settler colonial state was extended over the country, bodies and families of Indigenous people, they were also sites of intimate relationships, shifting power balances and complex interdependencies. For both ideological and practical reasons, missionaries were rarely willing or able to act simply as extensions of state power. Their role within the colonial bureaucracy also varied over time and from place to place. For their part, Aboriginal people negotiated a tangled and often oppressive web of colonial regulations, mission politics and personal loyalties to maintain themselves and their families.

This chapter explores this complex situation through the lives of four women who lived on Victorian missions in the late nineteenth and early twentieth centuries. It considers how colonial authority was wielded on the mission and how power was experienced in people's lives. We focus particularly on women, both Indigenous and non-Indigenous, because they had little official authority within the structures of the colonial state or missionary organisations and their voices are rarely heard in official mission records. Nonetheless, they were not without influence.

Postcolonial and feminist scholarship has given us a language for talking about the choices and experiences of those who are oppressed by colonialism and by patriarchy. Terms such as 'agency', 'resistance' and 'negotiation', combined with the method of reading historical sources 'against the grain' have helped us to understand and express how people preserved the capacity to make some choices while experiencing oppressions that severely curtailed their liberties. This chapter stands within this tradition of scholarship.[1] However, valuable as such approaches are, we would argue that they can result in the interpretation of all experiences, actions and relationships purely in terms of a hierarchy of oppressive power relations. For all the power of colonialism in people's lives, their lives were not simply about colonialism. This is, of course, particularly true of Indigenous people, whose stories have so often been distorted and ignored by the records of the colonial state. In this chapter we adopt in part a biographical approach because narratives of lives help us to see the other powerful realities in people's lives – such as family, friendship and spirituality – as well as the interactions between the mechanisms of settler colonialism and these other aspects of life.

In this chapter we tell the stories of two Indigenous women – Emily Milton Stephen and her daughter Maud Stephen Mullett, who lived for many years at Ramahyuck Mission – and two non-Indigenous women – Louise Hagenauer, wife of the missionary manager at Ramahyuck, and her daughter, Ellie Hagenauer Le Souëf. The Stephen and Hagenauer families spent much of their lives at the Ramahyuck Mission on Gunai country in south-eastern Victoria. The mission was established in 1862 by German Moravian missionaries, Friedrich and Louise Hagenauer, with the support of the Presbyterian Church of Victoria. For many years, Ramahyuck was the largest mission in Victoria and its manager, Friedrich Hagenauer, became accepted as an expert on Indigenous matters within the colonial bureaucracy. He supported the implementation of the *Aborigines Protection Act 1886* (Vic) (the infamous 'Half-Caste Act') and was appointed secretary of the Board for Protection of Aborigines (BPA) in 1889. He also advised on the development of missions in other Australian colonies, particularly the north Queensland missions of Mapoon and Aurukun.

Not surprisingly, then, Ramahyuck Mission has received attention from historians. Ramahyuck provides the central case study for Bain Attwood's discussion of the role of missions in his influential book, *The Making of the Aborigines*.[2] Felicity Jensz has provided a detailed study of the role of German Moravians, including the Hagenauers, in establishing missions in Victoria.[3] She has also analysed issues relating to the education of children at Ramahyuck, through a study of the colonial education department archives.[4] Robert Kenny's

---

1   For example, Ann Laura Stoler, *Carnal Knowledge and Imperial Power: Race and the Intimate in Colonial Rule*, University of California Press, Berkeley and Los Angeles, 2002; Anne McClintock, *Imperial Leather: Race, Gender and Sexuality in the Colonial Context*, Routledge, New York, 1995.
2   Bain Attwood, *The Making of the Aborigines*, Allen & Unwin, Sydney, 1989.
3   Felicity Jensz, *Moravian Missionaries in the British Colony of Victoria, Australia, 1848–1908: Strangers in a Strange Land*, Studies in Christian Missions, 38, Brill, Leiden, 2010.
4   Felicity Jensz, '"In future only female teachers": staffing the Ramahyuck Mission school in the nineteenth century', Provenance: The Journal of Public Record Office Victoria 11, 2012. http://prov.vic.gov.au/publications/provenance/in-future-only-female-teachers.

award-winning book on the Aboriginal convert Nathaniel Pepper, *The Lamb Enters the Dreaming*, though it deals primarily with the period before the establishment of Ramahyuck, pays close attention to Pepper's relationship with Hagenauer.[5] John Harris and Aldo Massola also discuss Ramahyuck in their more general overviews of mission history.[6]

These accounts of the mission tend to rely heavily on archival sources authored by Friedrich Hagenauer, or by other settler officials and missionaries. Ramahyuck was a Presbyterian Church mission, run by German Moravian missionaries and receiving funds from the colonial government. Hagenauer thus had to report to three bodies – the Presbyterian Church of Victoria, the Moravian bishops in Germany and the BPA. Many of his reports and official correspondence have been preserved.[7] Other sources provide a more personal perspective on the mission, from both an Indigenous and non-Indigenous perspective. These include published sources, such as the accounts of Ramahyuck history given by Aboriginal elder, Phillip Pepper, and the letters of Aboriginal women at Ramahyuck to the BPA.[8] They also include a wealth of unpublished material in the papers of Ellie Hagenauer Le Souëf, consisting of her diaries and correspondence written during and after her years at Ramahyuck.[9] Through this diversity of sources it is possible to reconstruct a more nuanced picture of the experiences of those who lived at Ramahyuck, particularly the stories of the women who are being considered in this chapter. We focus particularly on their experiences at Ramahyuck until its closure in 1909, but we also examine their lives after leaving Ramahyuck as reflected in these sources.

Louise Hagenauer, the oldest of the four, was born Christiana Louise Knobloch in Saxony in March 1834. In a letter written towards the end of her life, she recounted how she had joined the Moravian movement at the age of 12. After overcoming some resistance from her parents, she moved to the Moravian

---

5 Robert Kenny, *The Lamb Enters the Dreaming: Nathanael Pepper and the Ruptured World*, Scribe, Melbourne, 2007.
6 John Harris, *One Blood: 200 Years of Aboriginal Encounter with Christianity, A Story of Hope*, Albatross Books, Sutherland, NSW, 1990; Aldo Massola, *Aboriginal Mission Stations in Victoria*, Hawthorn Press, Melbourne, 1970.
7 Key collections of this material include 'Letterbooks of R. A. Hagenauer, 1865–1885', MS 3343, National Library of Australia, Canberra (henceforth, 'Letterbooks', NLA); 'Moravian Mission Papers' MF 163–179, Australian Institute of Aboriginal and Torres Strait Islander Studies, Canberra (henceforth, 'Moravian Mission Papers', AIATSIS); and the published Proceedings of the General Assembly of the Presbyterian Church of Victoria, Uniting Church Archives, Melbourne (henceforth, Proceedings of the General Assembly).
8 Phillip Pepper and Tess de Araugo, *The Kurnai of Gippsland*, What Did Happen to the Aborigines of Victoria, vol. 1, Hyland House, Melbourne, 1985; Phillip Pepper, *You Are What You Make Yourself to Be: The Story of a Victorian Aboriginal Family*, Hyland House, Melbourne, 1980; Elizabeth Nelson, Sandra Smith and Patricia Grimshaw (eds), *Letters from Aboriginal Women of Victoria, 1867–1926*, History Department, University of Melbourne, Melbourne, 2002.
9 Ellie Hagenauer Le Souëf's diaries and correspondence are held with the Le Souëf Family Papers, MN 1391, Battye Library, Western Australia (henceforth Le Souëf, WA). Permission to access and quote from the Le Souëf Family Papers has very kindly been given by Marjorie Le Souëf.

community, where she lived like all Moravian children in a dormitory and rarely saw her own parents or siblings.[10] The Moravian movement was characterised by a commitment to missionary work around the world and on reaching adulthood, Louise offered herself for this task. She was chosen by lot to marry Friedrich Hagenauer, who had already left for Australia. She followed him and on 15 June 1861 at St Paul's Church, Melbourne, she married him. The couple had nine children, seven of whom were born at Ramahyuck.

Emily Stephen was a Gunai woman, born Emily Wood around 1860. She was brought to Ramahyuck at the age of nine in circumstances that are unclear.[11] Emily was employed as a nurse to some of the Hagenauer children, including their daughter Ellie. She was educated in the Ramahyuck school and acted for many years as teaching assistant at the school. Emily married another Ramahyuck resident, Harry Stephen, and the couple had 11 children. In later years, she sought a living away from Ramahyuck and also spent time living at Lake Tyers mission.[12]

Ellie Hagenauer was born at Ramahyuck in 1873. She was educated at Ramahyuck for her primary schooling and was then sent to Melbourne to attend the Presbyterian Ladies' College. After finishing high school in 1891, she returned to the mission and assisted her parents. In 1899, she married Ernest Le Souëf, son of Albert Le Souëf, who founded the Melbourne Zoo. She moved with her husband to Perth, where he established a zoo and she became involved in a number of charitable causes. The couple had four children.[13]

Emily's oldest daughter, Maud Stephen, was born at Ramahyuck in 1881. She grew up on the mission and worked for some years in Melbourne caring for the children of the Hagenauers' oldest daughter, Ida. She later married Dave Mullett, who had grown up at the Lake Condah reserve. The couple, who had nine children, lived for some years in the Melbourne suburb of Carlton. Her husband enlisted in the Australian Army during World War I and served in the Middle East. After his return, the family were moved to the Lake Tyers mission.[14]

The writings of these four women allow a closer analysis of their lives on the mission, their relationships with each other and the broader power structures

---

10 Louise Hagenauer to Ellie Le Souëf, 30 June 1914, 4370A 713/9, Le Souëf, WA.
11 Emily Stephen to Louise Hagenauer, nd [c.1908 from internal evidence], 4370A/479, Le Souëf, WA.
12 See Patricia Grimshaw, '"That we may obtain our religious liberty…"': Aboriginal women, faith and rights in early twentieth century Victoria, Australia', *Journal of the Canadian Historical Association / Revue de la Société historique du Canada* 19(2), 2008: 39–40.
13 A brief overview of Ellie's life, with a focus on her years in Perth, is given in Noel Stewart, 'Mrs Ellie Grace Le Souëf (1873–1947): She helped to found a zoo', in *As I Remember Them*, Artlook Books, Perth, 1987: 103–108.
14 See Grimshaw, 'That we may obtain our religious liberty…': 35, 41.

within colonial society. Louise founded the mission with Friedrich, in a situation remote from white settlement. In old age, she wrote to her daughter: 'No need for me to say I felt it hard, especially to be so much alone with the natives, which were very cruel sometimes, but I had a strong nature and not easily frightened.'[15] In addition to giving birth to nine children, she was involved in the establishment and maintenance of the mission, performing domestic labour and training Aboriginal women in European domestic skills. She conducted sewing lessons for the adult women, while school-aged girls were taught 'sewing, washing, mending, housework and ironing etc.'[16] She nursed the Indigenous and non-Indigenous residents in times of sickness and in old age. The mission residents called her *yuccan*, the Gunai word for mother.[17]

Friedrich Hagenauer's reports often describe the responsibility for the mission in the first person plural, commenting, for example, that 'The general oversight is, of course, in *our* own hands.'[18] This may well have reflected a Moravian understanding of mission, in which both men and women were understood to share the missionary task. It was, however, Friedrich who was employed as manager at Ramahyuck and he saw the mission as ultimately his responsibility. When he visited north Queensland in 1885, on a trip to identify locations for a new mission there, he reassured the Presbyterian Missions board:

> The work at Ramahyuck, during my absence, was carried on as usual. Mr Beilby kindly took the services; my eldest son, the farming and station work; my eldest daughter, the Government part; of course, all under the direction of Mrs Hagenauer, so that on my return, I found all in best working order.[19]

Historians have generally followed Friedrich's lead in focusing primarily on his role on the mission. Yet this view can obscure both the complexity of the power dynamics on the mission and the practical realities of mission life.

By the late 1880s, life on the mission had changed. The passing of the 1886 'Half-Caste Act', which removed all younger Indigenous people of mixed descent from the mission, meant that the number of mission residents dropped significantly. In 1889, Friedrich took on the role of Secretary of the BPA and was hardly at the mission during the week. In his absence, Louise undertook most of the day-to-day running of the mission. Friedrich's official reports do not make

---

15 Louise Hagenauer to Ellie Le Souëf, 30 June 1914, 4370A 713/9, Le Souëf, WA.
16 Report on 'Aboriginal Mission Station, Ramah Yuck, Gipps Land', *Proceedings of the General Assembly* (1871): 69.
17 Pepper, *You are What You Make Yourself to Be*: 10.
18 Report on 'Aboriginal Mission Station, Ramah Yuck, Gipps Land', *Proceedings of the General Assembly* (1881): xxiii (emphasis added).
19 Report on 'Aboriginal Mission Station, Ramah Yuck, Gipps Land', *Proceedings of the General Assembly* (1885): xx.

this division of labour clear, but it emerges as a source of significant tension in Ellie's diary. In 1893, she commented: 'I am too sorry for Mother having so much to do … Poor Mother has a very hard life, never gets a grain of credit but is always looked upon as a well I can't say the word, I am so indignant'.[20] Where historians have depicted Friedrich as an autocratic figure, Ellie wrote in 1896: 'I wish Papa were as firm as Mother in keeping his threats, but Papa is soft & can't bear to punish – & so the natives never believe what is said to them.'[21]

As this situation demonstrates, European gender norms meant that while missionary wives were often in the background of mission reports, in practice they could assume substantial responsibility for mission management.[22] Yet the official structures of missions meant that their power in this role was constrained; ultimately, the decision of the husband would be considered final by external authorities. Missionaries and Aboriginal people lived in close proximity, which meant that Aboriginal people were undoubtedly aware of this potential tension and could exploit it. Ellie's diary suggests that during the late 1880s and 1890s, mission residents whom Louise attempted to coerce or punish would wait until Friedrich came home and convince him to overrule Louise's decisions. Ellie noted with frustration in one such situation: 'Mother who manages the station should have her word & authority upheld and not always have the disagreeables.'[23]

Emily, too, had some official authority on the mission during this period. As noted, at times she acted as teaching assistant at the school, making her one of the few Aboriginal people with a formal role in the Ramahyuck hierarchy. Felicity Jensz has traced the history of the school at Ramahyuck, which became a government school in 1871 and received consistently excellent results in the annual inspections by the Department of Education.[24] Emily was assisting at the school during part of this period, but from 1901, after the population of the mission had declined considerably, the school reverted to the control of the mission, and Emily had sole responsibility for educating the children until 1905.[25] Her authority was, of course, profoundly contingent upon the Hagenauers. Her interactions with the Hagenauer women, as described in Ellie's diary, provide evidence of the complicated nature of such relationships between missionaries and Indigenous people whom they perceived as allies.

---

20   4–14 January 1893, Diary of Ellie Hagenauer, 4370A/634, Le Souëf, WA.
21   23 March 1896, Diary of Ellie Hagenauer, 4370A/637, Le Souëf, WA.
22   This was true on other late nineteenth-century missions such as the Manunka mission in South Australia, which was putatively run by Daniel and Janet Mathews, but in practice run almost entirely by Janet. See Patricia Grimshaw, 'Rethinking approaches to women and missions: the case of colonial Australia', *History Australia* 8(3), December 2011: 7–24.
23   27 March 1896, Diary of Ellie Hagenauer, 4370A/637, Le Souëf, WA.
24   Jensz, 'In future only female teachers'.
25   Jensz, 'In future only female teachers': 12.

In 1894, Ellie recorded tension between her parents over the behaviour of her younger brothers, who had committed some unspecified misdemeanour. In the absence of her father in Melbourne, she noted that her mother was working herself to exhaustion and commented: 'Poor Mother is blamed for the misdemeanours of the boys by both Alf [her older brother] and Papa.'[26] Shortly afterwards, she wrote: 'Emily Steven [sic] helped me in the house, she was very good. She and Mother had a long talk over things in general. The things Donald says about the boys are horrible & it troubles Mother.'[27] In this situation, overworked and troubled by criticism of her sons by Donald (Cameron), an Aboriginal mission resident, Louise clearly looked to Emily for both emotional and practical support. This was not without cost to Emily, however. Ellie noted a week later that Emily's children were 'very cross' about Emily helping in the Hagenauer home again.[28]

As this small incident suggests, missionaries relied on trusted mission residents for practical and emotional support within the often conflict-ridden life of the mission. In addition, they depended to some degree on Aboriginal cooperation for their authority within settler society as a whole. Mission managers who completely alienated mission residents could find themselves the focus of external scrutiny and even, in the case of the Coranderrk reserve, an official enquiry.[29] By contrast, missionaries could strengthen their own authority by demonstrating support from mission residents.

In 1892, for example, two new teachers, Miss Vidler and Miss Moss, were appointed to the Ramahyuck school by the Education Department.[30] Conflict quickly developed between the Hagenauers and the teachers, whom Ellie referred to derisively as the 'Pilgrims', apparently because of their sense of religious superiority.[31] According to Ellie, in a series of confrontations with Louise, Emily and Ellie, Vidler and Moss claimed that the mission was no longer a Christian mission: 'it was once a [Christian] mission, but love of money & pride of worldly position came in & took away the love of Christ.'[32] Emily was a central participant in this conflict. She withdrew her children from the school in late February and wrote to the teachers to defend her decision. 'I don't think it right or just to say to the children that Mr Hagenauer is a wicked man', she wrote,

---

26 11 February 1894, Diary of Ellie Hagenauer, 4370A/635, Le Souëf, WA.
27 5 March 1894, Diary of Ellie Hagenauer, 4370A/635, Le Souëf, WA.
28 12 March 1894, Diary of Ellie Hagenauer, 4370A/635, Le Souëf, WA.
29 For the Coranderrk inquiry see Diane Barwick, Rebellion at Coranderrk, Laura E. Barwick and Richard E. Barwick (eds), Aboriginal History Inc, Canberra, 1998.
30 Jensz has given a brief account of this affair from the perspective of the Education Department records in 'In the future only female teachers': 8–9.
31 See entries for February–March 1892, Diary of Ellie Hagenauer, 4370A/633, Le Souëf, WA. It seems likely that they were members of the Salvation Army, as Ellie mentions that she offended them by laughing about the Salvation Army.
32 8 March 1892, Diary of Ellie Hagenauer, 4370A/633, Le Souëf, WA.

'what is between you & him has nothing to do with the children.'[33] When the teachers accused the Hagenauers of mistreating Aboriginal children and misusing government funds, Emily wrote to local pastoralists to defend the Hagenauers against these charges.[34] After the mission, children had been withdrawn from the school by their mothers, Hagenauer wrote to the Secretary of the Education Department to request that the teachers be replaced. He enclosed a petition from the mothers and the letter that Emily had written to the teachers. These documents, as evidence of the mission residents' wishes, were clearly intended to give authority to his own request that the teachers be removed. On 14 March, Ellie wrote in her diary: 'The Pilgrims left amidst loud hurrays & flying flags 9 in all. Bessie rang the ration bell & all the natives shouted for joy.'[35]

The joint effort between the Hagenauers and the mission residents to remove Vidler and Moss is an example of the complicated alliance between the missionaries and the Aboriginal people on the mission. The mothers at the mission apparently withdrew their children from the school partly out of loyalty to the Hagenauers, whom the teachers had criticised. But according to the petition signed by the mothers, the teachers had also insulted the children as 'horrible nasty creatures'.[36] Emily wrote that by insulting the Hagenauers and 'all the people', the teachers had made the older children 'disobedient & defiant'. She was withdrawing her children, she wrote, because she wished them 'to respect both Mr & Mrs Hagenauer & myself'.[37] This letter suggests that within the structures of the mission, Emily saw her own authority bound up with the Hagenauers, just as their authority was in part tied to her cooperation.

All this is not to suggest that the relationship between Emily and the Hagenauers was equitable. When describing the conflict with the teachers, Ellie noted that a non-Indigenous friend of hers, Colina, had accompanied Emily in her confrontations with the teachers: 'if Col had not been there Emily would have been bamboozled, the things were twisted round so very cleverly'.[38] The assumption that Emily required a white 'witness' in order to stop her from being 'bamboozled' communicates very clearly the condescension that shaped many of the Hagenauers' interactions with mission residents.

---

33 Emily Stephen to Miss Vidler and Miss Moss, 25 February 1892, Item 1892/8131, VPRS 640/PO Central Inward Primary Schools Correspondence, Unit 657 School No. 1088, Public Records Office Victoria (henceforth, PROV).
34 Entries for March 1892, Diary of Ellie Hagenauer, 4370A/633, Le Souëf, WA.
35 14 March 1892, Diary of Ellie Hagenauer, 4370A/633, Le Souëf, WA.
36 Petition signed by Bessy Cameron, Florance Moffat, Mary Scott, Emily M Stephen, Lulu Darby to J Brodruble Esq, 27 February 1892, Item 1892/8131, VPRS 640/PO Central Inward Primary Schools Correspondence, Unit 657 School No. 1088, PROV.
37 Emily Stephen to Miss Vidler and Miss Moss, 25 February 1892, Item 1892/8131, VPRS 640/PO Central Inward Primary Schools Correspondence, Unit 657 School No. 1088, PROV.
38 9 March 1892, Diary of Ellie Hagenauer, 4370A/633, Le Souëf, WA.

Ellie herself had no official authority at Ramahyuck, but while living at the mission after her return from school in Melbourne, she helped her mother with the housework and care of the sick, taught Sunday school and music to the children. On the rare occasion that her mother went on holiday, she would take on many of her roles, in particular supervision of the teenage girls, whose conduct was of concern to the missionaries. 'The girls are rather provoking', she wrote in April 1894, 'I must watch so constantly that they do not make love to the boys.'[39] The following year she lamented 'I hate to act "policeman" yet it is so necessary with the blacks. When Mother is away I dread the responsibilities, but if Mother knew my feelings she would never go & so I can say nothing to her.'[40] If her father was also absent, she could take on herself more substantial authority. In December 1894, for example, she 'lectured the natives for not coming to prayers – they must attend to the rules on the place'.[41] In 1897, she noted that she 'spoke to' one of the Aboriginal men because he had beaten his wife and he had written to her promising not to do so in future.[42] Ellie was a single woman in her early 20s, but she clearly understood herself as having the right to police (however reluctantly) Indigenous young women, 'lecture' Indigenous people much older than her and intervene in Indigenous marriages. Her behaviour demonstrates clearly how racial hierarchies structured the mission. Her power was, in some ways, limited. When, in her father's absence, two young Aboriginal people ran away from the mission together, she sent a telegram to her father to ask for advice. He responded that 'nothing could be done'.[43] Nonetheless, as representative of her parents, who in turn represented the colonial state, she acted in deeply paternalistic ways.

The power structures on the mission can be seen even more clearly in the experience of Maud Stephen. During the 1890s, Maud was one of the teenage girls whose sexuality so concerned the missionaries and over whom Ellie felt she had to 'act policeman'. In August 1895, Ellie noted that her mother was investigating 'all sorts of love affairs' on the mission. 'Maud is a naughty child', she continued, 'at 14 she commenced a matrimonial correspondence with Walter McCreedie.'[44] The following year, while Emily was away from the mission, Louise intercepted a letter that Maud had written to her mother. '[I]t was an impertinent letter, Maud is a little hypocrite … Papa read Maud's letter to her, Louise Conolly & Mother, & Maud was shown herself in her true light.'[45]

---

39   13 April 1894, Diary of Ellie Hagenauer, 4370A/635, Le Souëf, WA.
40   19 June 1895, Diary of Ellie Hagenauer, 4370A/635, Le Souëf, WA.
41   1 December 1894, Diary of Ellie Hagenauer, 4370A/635, Le Souëf, WA.
42   30 September 1897, Diary of Ellie Hagenauer, 4370A/636, Le Souëf, WA.
43   21 October 1892, Diary of Ellie Hagenauer, 4370A/633, Le Souëf, WA.
44   23 August 1895, Diary of Ellie Hagenauer, 4370A/636, Le Souëf, WA.
45   6–7 April 1896, Diary of Ellie Hagenauer, 4370A/637, Le Souëf, WA.

This scrutiny of Maud's correspondence – and the attempt to shame her in front of Louise Hagenauer and Louise Conolly (an older Indigenous resident) – is evidence of how intrusive the Hagenauers could be. In particular, in both these instances they saw it as their right to scrutinise and discipline Maud, rather than leave the matter to her parents, even though both Emily and Harry Stephen were mission residents. In the same month that Maud's letter was intercepted, Ellie wrote that the Hagenauers had read a letter from Emily to another woman on the mission in which Emily had apparently been critical of the Hagenauers. '[W]e found out again how very two-faced she is; Really it is difficult to manage a Station, here we do our best for the natives & yet we know that they think anything but pleasantly of us.'[46] On an earlier occasion, Ellie had defended Emily against what she saw as 'unjust' accusations that her mother had made against Emily, but her primary loyalty was clearly with her family.[47] While there might be a kind of intimacy and a level of interdependency, as well as affection, between these two pairs of mothers and daughters, there was also underlying resentment which at times boiled over into open hostility.

Small encounters between the four women, such as those considered above, are evidence of the complicated nature of their relationships with each other and their power – or lack of it – within the mission. Can such seemingly insignificant details shed light on broader questions of colonial governance and Indigenous people? For this, it is helpful to consider the longer story of these women's relationships, and their lives, which lasted beyond their years at Ramahyuck. In the remainder of the chapter we focus particularly on Emily Stephen, who maintained relationships with all three of the other women considered here, and whose voice and experience appears in unusual detail in the colonial archive.

By the late 1890s, numbers at Ramahyuck had declined steeply and many of the original mission residents had died or moved elsewhere. In 1899, Ellie Hagenauer married Ernest Le Souëf and left Ramahyuck for Perth. Maud Stephen asked Ellie if she could accompany them and work as their domestic servant. Ellie's discussion of this request in her letters to Ernest displays their shared anxiety about Aboriginal women's sexuality. He wrote that he had heard that in Western Australia 'half-caste' girls all 'go wrong' when grown up and Ellie responded that she would need to be very strict with Maud to stop her going astray.[48] Ultimately, Maud went to work for Ellie's sister in Melbourne instead, but the following year Emily wrote to Ellie to say that Maud still 'had it in her head' to join Ellie if possible.[49] In the five years following Ellie's departure, Emily

---

46 29 April 1896, Diary of Ellie Hagenauer, 4370A/637, Le Souëf, WA.
47 28 November 1894, Diary of Ellie Hagenauer, 4370A/635, Le Souëf, WA. According to this entry, Louise had 'words' with Emily for visiting a local settler who was critical of the Hagenauers.
48 See Ernest Le Souëf to Ellie Hagenauer, 2 December 1898; Ellie Hagenauer to Ernest Le Souëf, 23 December 1898, 4370A/232–239, Le Souëf, WA.
49 Emily Stephen to Ellie Hagenauer Le Souëf, 5 February 1900, 4370A/713/8/11, Le Souëf, WA.

wrote to her regularly. Emily's letters describe life at Ramahyuck in familiar and domestic terms, passing on news about the mission residents and recounting her attendance at social events in the local town, Sale. She noted that around 72 Aboriginal people had attended the Sale Show in 1903, exclaiming 'don't you think that was a great gathering of coloured folk? I for my part enjoyed it very much, especially the flowers, some were just perfection … the Scones home made, I pride myself I could have made better.'[50] During these years, Emily wrote often of her affection for and gratitude to Ellie and her family, referring to her former role as Ellie's nurse. When Ellie had her first child, Emily wrote to her:

> And darling you have a dear little baby boy of your own I'm so happy I told mamma the other day that that was my little grannie also. I hope by now that you will be getting strong again, take care of yourself dear kiss your dear little baby for me. I would just love to see it & hold it in my arms God bless & keep you both darling you must excuse me how I call you but I do love you so much & am always thinking of you.[51]

However, alongside such expressions of affection and accounts of social occasions, trips to camp in the bush and the progress of her garden was evidence of the many restrictions placed on her and other Aboriginal mission residents. All journeys away from Ramahyuck, even day trips, required the permission of Friedrich Hagenauer, as did visits from family members classified as 'half-castes' under the 1886 Act.

It was during these years between 1901 and 1904 that Emily was given the role of sole teacher at the school at Ramahyuck. In 1904, however, the school was closed and Emily left the mission with her younger children. The sequence of events that led to her leaving is unclear, but it appears that she left early in the year after conflict with the Hagenauers and with the intention of living outside of the mission system. In June of that year, however, she wrote to the vice-chairman of the BPA, requesting that she and her children be allowed to return to Ramahyuck and occupy the cottage where they had lived previously. She was writing from Gippsland Hospital, where she had been for six weeks with tuberculosis, unable to work to support her children.[52] The vice-chairman, Mr Ditchburn, responded that by 'leaving Ramahyuck in the manner you did you forfeited all your claims'. Nonetheless, he conceded, he was sure she would be given her old privileges, 'provided you act and live differently than when you were previously at the station'.[53]

---

50   Emily Stephen to Ellie Hagenauer Le Souëf, 14 November 1903, 4370A/713/8/13, Le Souëf, WA.
51   Emily Stephen to Ellie Hagenauer Le Souëf, 5 February 1900, 4370A/713/8/11, Le Souëf, WA.
52   Emily Stephen, Gippsland Hospital, Sale, to Vice Chairman, BPA, 23 June 1904, *Letters from Aboriginal Women of Victoria*: 130.
53   Mr Ditchburn to Emily Stephen, nd, quoted in *Letters from Aboriginal Women of Victoria*: 130–131.

While Emily returned to Ramahyuck briefly, in 1905 she was transferred to Lake Tyers, along with most of the remaining residents at Ramahyuck. Whatever the tensions that had existed in her relationship with the Hagenauers, the connection was a significant one for both her and Louise. In 1909, Friedrich Hagenauer died and Emily wrote a letter of sympathy to Louise:

> My heart is with you dear, dear Yackan, oh you do not know how I feel. I loved my dear Mongan as though he was my own father. Both you and him have been to me as my own parents, since I came to the Mission a little child only 9 years old. You will have thought that when I came down here I had quite forgotten about you, but it was never so, I could not write because I only would have fretted to go back. As it is I am always thinking of you. I do not talk much about it, but I truly feel a great longing for you it is too sore to talk about ... All your goodness & kindness is always before me for which I thank you most sincerely.[54]

Emily added, with reference to Ellie, who was visiting from Perth: 'My dearest love to my darling & her dear little children if they are with her.' If the relationship between Louise and Emily had not been mended before this, Emily's letter appears to have brought about a reconciliation. In the letter, Emily begged to be able to visit 'even if I had to walk ... just to press your dear hands to show my love & sympathy to you'.[55] Shortly afterwards, Emily was given permission to travel to Ramahyuck, where Louise was still living, to provide her with emotional and practical support. The two women spent a number of weeks together and Louise gave Emily furniture and other goods from the Hagenauers' house.[56] In this period of crisis, there is again evidence that on both sides of the relationship, for all its tensions and inequity, there appears to have been real affection.

For Emily, the visit to Ramahyuck appears to have been the catalyst for significant conflict between Emily and the BPA-appointed manager at Lake Tyers, Captain Howe. Howe had recently replaced John and Caroline Bulmer, the Church of England missionaries who had established the mission. When Emily extended her visit to Ramahyuck beyond the permitted two weeks, Captain Howe threatened to have her summoned if she did not return immediately.[57] On her eventual return, tensions continued, playing out within the complicated web of relationships at Lake Tyers. Patricia Grimshaw has described elsewhere how Emily had allied herself with the Bulmers, who continued to live at the

---

54   Emily Stephen to Louise Hagenauer, nd [c.1909], 4370A/479, Le Souëf, WA.
55   Emily Stephen to Louise Hagenauer, nd [c.1909], 4370A/479, Le Souëf, WA.
56   Emily Stephen to Mr Watts, MP, 16 March 1910, *Letters from Aboriginal Women of Victoria*: 162–163.
57   Stephen to Watts, 16 March 1910.

mission, providing an alternative source of authority to the Howes.[58] Emily's youngest daughter, Blanche, worked for the elderly Caroline Bulmer, and when Captain Howe insisted that Blanche should work for his wife instead, Emily wrote repeatedly to members of the BPA to complain. Captain Howe was furious, writing to the BPA: 'Emily Stephen is detrimental to the good order & discipline of this station … she practically defies me but in such a manner that I can only make a general complaint, and she goes round all the blacks and the Bulmers telling them that she has the "Board" on her side.'[59] He claimed she had threatened that she would bring about an enquiry into his management and have him removed, a likely reference to the earlier enquiry into Coranderrk reserve, which had resulted in very public criticism of the reserve manager. Emily's use of letter-writing and awareness of the mechanisms of settler society outraged Captain Howe, who fumed 'that is what education has done for her'.[60]

At this stage, the members of the BPA refused to agree to Howe's request to transfer Emily, noting that this could not be done where no specific transgression could be proved. However, Howe continued to complain about Emily's defiance and, in June 1911, the BPA received a petition from 22 of the residents at Lake Tyers, asking that Emily be removed from the mission. Emily defended herself, arguing that many of those who signed had no idea what they were signing. Her letter made clear, however, that there were significant tensions between the Aboriginal people who had been moved to Lake Tyers from Ramahyuck and those who had lived there for many years.[61] Unsurprisingly, forcibly combining these two communities, each drawn in large part from different Aboriginal tribal groups, had created friction. In October 1911, the BPA forced Emily to move again, this time to the Moravian-run mission at Lake Condah, where she was refused permission to return to Lake Tyers to see her children.

In 1914, Emily wrote to the BPA once again, this time from Lake Condah, requesting that she be allowed to move off the mission for good. Though, on her arrival at Lake Condah, she had apparently formed a good relationship with Reverend Stähle, the Moravian missionary manager, Stähle had recently been replaced by a BPA-appointed manager.[62] By this time, all of Emily's children had reached adulthood. She assured the Board that one of her sons had permanent

---

58   Patricia Grimshaw, 'Colonising motherhood: evangelical reformers and Koorie women in Victoria, Australia, 1880s to the early 1900s', Women's History Review 8(2), 1999: 329–346.
59   R Howe, manager, Lake Tyers, to Mr Ditchburn, 3 April 1911, Letters from Aboriginal Women of Victoria: 167–168.
60   Captain Howe, Lake Tyers, to Mr Callaway, Vice President, BPA, 9 August 1911, Letters from Aboriginal Women of Victoria: 172.
61   Emily Stephen, Lake Tyers, to Mr Callaway, Vice President, BPA, 26 June 1911, Letters from Aboriginal Women of Victoria: 170–171.
62   The Rev. Stähle wrote repeatedly to the BPA supporting her requests to see her children, but these requests were denied. See Letters from Aboriginal Women of Victoria: 172–173.

work and two of her other children would be able to get employment shortly. The Board revoked the order requiring her to live at Lake Condah, with the proviso that she would no longer receive any financial support.[63]

In the same year that Emily left Lake Condah, Louise Hagenauer reflected on her role at Ramahyuck. Challenged by a sermon on God's guidance, she wrote a brief account of her life in a letter to Ellie. After describing her childhood commitment to the Moravians, the process by which she came to Ramahyuck and her early years there, Louise concluded:

> I know the Lord called me, had led & guided me all my life, saved me from all troubles in many ways – but the Lord who called me expects fruit from my labour – but alas! I have only emptiness & sin to bring, I have no fruit – I left the great commandment Love out of my labour & without love you cannot do any good – I only worked & worked & left love behind – Oh pray for me dear Ellie that in my last days I may be able to love & do some good.[64]

In 1917, three years after writing this letter, Louise died. In the same year, Emily's youngest son Gilbert enlisted in the Australian army and departed for England. He became seriously ill during training and shortly after his return to Australia, he too died.[65] This was one of many hardships that Emily was to experience during the years that followed. In spite of her continual efforts to earn a living, she was forced to write to the BPA on multiple occasions to request temporary rations.

Like her mother, Maud spent much of this period living outside the mission system. Letters that Maud wrote in 1913 show that she and her husband, David Mullett, a former resident of the Coranderrk reserve, were travelling around Victoria for work. Their lives were, however, still restricted by the controls of the BPA, as they had to request permission to visit their relatives at Coranderrk, Lake Condah and Lake Tyers, and at times asked for rations to supplement their earnings.[66] In 1915, David enlisted in the Australian Imperial Force (AIF) and was not discharged until 1920.[67] In his absence, Maud initially remained in the Melbourne suburb of Carlton where the couple had been living with their four children. Here she became involved with a Pentecostal religious group, meeting

---

63 Emily Stephen to Secretary, BPA, 21 March 1914, and Emily Stephen to Captain Crawford, manager, Lake Condah, 10 September 1914, *Letters from Aboriginal Women of Victoria*: 174.
64 Louise Hagenauer to Ellie Hagenauer Le Souëf, 30 April 1914, 4370A/713/9/4, Le Souëf, WA.
65 Emily Stephen, Dartmoor, to Mr Parker, Secretary, BPA, 24 May 1920, *Letters from Aboriginal Women of Victoria*: 134–135.
66 Maud Mullett to Mr John Murray, Chief Secretary, 17 June 1913, *Letters from Aboriginal Women of Victoria*: 290.
67 National Archives of Australia, Canberra, Australian Imperial Force, Base Records Office, Series no. B2455, First Australian Imperial Force Personal Dossier, 1914–1920.

at the Good News Hall in North Melbourne. As Patricia Grimshaw has described elsewhere, in 1916 Maud began visiting the Coranderrk reserve, along with women evangelists from the Good News Hall. She encouraged residents of the Coranderrk reserve to visit the Good News Hall, and then suggested holding Pentecostal meetings at the reserve itself. Coranderrk, like most of the other Victorian missions, was by this time no longer run by Christian missionaries, and the manager was horrified by the prospect of such 'disturbing' influences on the reserve. He complained to the BPA after one of Maud's visits: 'Her influence over the natives is very undesirable … After her departure last night a meeting was again held in one of the cottages and the screams and wails even heard at a great distance.'[68] Maud persisted with her visits, in spite of the manager's disapproval, until in October the BPA responded to his concerns by revoking her permission to visit Coranderrk.

During David Mullett's military service, the BPA had determined that Maud would no longer be eligible for support from the BPA, as she could live off her husband's military pay.[69] Like other Aboriginal people, however, the Mulletts discovered that the equal opportunities apparently offered by service in the AIF were often illusory. The AIF cancelled Maud's allotment, arguing that she should be supported by the BPA. Maud wrote desperately to the BPA, arguing: 'David never inlisted [sic] from the mission[;] we were out earning our living like white people and Sir we have troubled the Government for very little help … I have been out earning my living ever since I was 19 years of age.'[70] The BPA replied that this was a matter for the Department of Defence and they could not intervene. Facing such inequities, on David's return from service in the Middle East, the Mulletts returned to living at Lake Tyers.[71]

Emily, however, remained determined to maintain some degree of independence, in spite of the difficulty that she and her family had in finding permanent work. She was forced repeatedly to request rations and other supplies from the BPA. Perhaps as a result, in 1918, the BPA offered her and her family the opportunity to move to Lake Tyers. Emily replied on behalf of herself and those of her family who lived with her. After 'thinking very deeply over it', she wrote, they had decided that they 'would all rather battle on out among white people'.[72] While she expressed gratitude for the offer, she stated that it 'was much better to be

---

68   Mr Robarts, manager, Coranderrk, to Mr Ditchburn, Secretary, BPA, 17 July 1916, *Letters from Aboriginal Women of Victoria*: 230.
69   Mr Robarts, manager, Coranderrk, to Mr Ditchburn, Secretary, BPA, 20 November 1915, *Letters from Aboriginal Women of Victoria*: 291.
70   Maud Mullett, Hamilton, to Mr Parker, Secretary, BPA, 22 May 1919, *Letters from Aboriginal Women of Victoria*: 291.
71   Albert Mullett, interview by Lou Bennett, 'Mission Voices', http://www.abc.net.au/ missionvoices.laketyers/voices of lake tyers/default.htm, accessed 20 January 2013.
72   Emily Stephen, Clark St, Hamilton, to Mr Parker, BPA, 23 May 1918, *Letters from Aboriginal Women of Victoria*: 131.

on your own, than among a crowd, especially your own people, further away so much the better'.[73] The family planned to purchase a cheap block of land in Hamilton, erect a house, grow vegetables and find work in the local area. The BPA commended this desire for independence and continued to send her occasional rations, sometimes unasked, in the years that followed.[74]

As a result of Gilbert's death, the Stephen family were eligible to claim various payments from the Department of Defence. Emily's attempts to claim this money reveal something of the nature of her relationship with her husband, Harry Stephen, who is barely mentioned in any of her other correspondence to the Hagenauers or to the BPA. She informed the BPA that she had not lived with Harry since 1914 and that she had never relied on him for financial support, as 'what ever he earned he drank & gambled & was so often in Gaol'.[75] Harry was living at Lake Tyers, Emily wrote, where he was cared for and restricted from drinking. She urged the BPA to prevent him from receiving any money from the Department of Defence, as 'he will only squander & gamble it'.[76] She was living in the Hamilton region, where her family had nearly finished building their new house. Though she was repeatedly unwell, she wrote of her delight in the location: 'it is lovely out here in the bush[;] we are very lucky to have beautiful fresh water to drink & use[;] in fact it is spring water clear as crystal & cool on the hottest day.'[77]

Emily was not able to enjoy her new house for many years. After a long stay in hospital, she died in November 1926. A notice in the local newspaper, inserted by her family, thanked the staff at the hospital for 'their kindness, care and attention' and the Christian Endeavour Society and all other friends 'who in any way helped to cheer her during her long stay in the hospital'.[78]

In the 1930s, Maud and David Mullett were moved off the Lake Tyers mission, along with all those Aboriginal people who were judged not to be 'full-blood'. They lived on the fringes of the Lake and travelled around the state attempting to find work. Maud's grandson remembered that in the late 1930s he had visited Melbourne with his grandparents, staying with other Aboriginal people surviving on the fringes of the city.

> I remember that quite well – my grandfather carrying me on his shoulder, and down to all these little tin humpies over there near the Westgate

---

73 Emily Stephen to Mr Parker, 23 May 1918.
74 See *Letters from Aboriginal Women of Victoria*: 131–135.
75 Emily Stephen, Dartmoor, to Mr Parker, BPA, 24 May 1920, *Letters from Aboriginal Women of Victoria*: 134–135.
76 Emily Stephen to Mr Parker, 24 May 1920.
77 Emily Stephen, Dartmoor, to Mr Parker, BPA, 9 February 1920, *Letters from Aboriginal Women of Victoria*: 133.
78 *Portland Guardian*, 15 November 1926: 2.

Bridge. And there was Koories and non-Koories and I remember walking over the sand hills and the fires were going and I remember that really well.[79]

Though there is no record of any correspondence between Ellie and Emily after 1904, Ellie kept Emily's earlier letters, together with her own diaries from the years at Ramahyuck, suggesting that her connection to Ramahyuck remained an important aspect of her identity. Ellie became a prominent member of Perth society, actively promoting multiple charities while her husband established the Perth Zoo. When she died in 1947, aged 74, notices appeared in newspapers in most of the major state capitals. In Melbourne, the notice in *The Argus*, inserted by her brothers, described her simply as 'youngest daughter of the late Rev. FA and Mrs Hagenauer, of Ramahyuck Mission Station, Gippsland'.[80]

In conclusion, though Ramahyuck Mission was closed in 1908, it shaped the lives of these four women in significant ways. The mission was a profoundly inequitable environment, in which non-Indigenous missionaries wielded the power of the colonial state over Indigenous residents. Emily and Maud were subject to conditions of surveillance and restriction, which aimed to control every aspect of their lives. Louise and Ellie were active in enforcing these conditions, while showing little awareness of the profound injustice and loss that Indigenous people had experienced and continued to experience through colonisation. It is not at all surprising that resentment and conflict were an ongoing part of the interactions between the four women. Yet the situation at Ramahyuck produced a degree of intimacy and inter-dependence between the two mothers and daughters. Louise relied on Emily for both emotional and practical support and Ellie grew up with Emily as her nursemaid. Louise tirelessly nursed the sick and elderly at Ramahyuck, including Emily's family. Ellie wrote of Emily's kindness to her mother and when Friedrich Hagenauer died, Louise sought Emily's support. Emily's letters, written in the familial and religious language that the women shared, speak of affection and intimacy. While her connection to Louise and Ellie undoubtedly offered Emily practical benefits, it would be simplistic to conclude that her motivations were simply strategic. As in many human relationships, real affection could exist alongside condescension, resentment, deception and open conflict.

Emily's and Maud's experiences after their departure from Ramahyuck suggest that these personal relationships continued to influence their engagement with the colonial state. This is particularly true for Emily, whose ongoing connection with the older missionary families proved a source of conflict with the BPA-

---

79   Albert Mullett, interview by Lou Bennett, 'Mission Voices', http://www.abc.net.au/missionvoices.lake tyers/voices of lake tyers/default.htm, accessed 20 January 2013.
80   *The Argus*, 7 August 1947: 9.

appointed manager at Lake Tyers. Her relationships with these families were also, however, an alternative source of support in the early years of her long battle to gain self-sufficiency and hold her family together. Maud's conflict with the management at Coranderrk demonstrated a similar confidence to oppose the representatives of the colonial state and ability to form connections with non-Indigenous religious activists. Both women used their knowledge of the colonial bureaucracy and the tool of letter-writing, which they had learned at Ramahyuck, to negotiate with the state.

Louise and Ellie, through their roles at Ramahyuck, promoted Christian faith, hard work, self-discipline and self-sufficiency. Though Louise later reflected that her emphasis on work had distracted her from a greater good, Emily and Maud both expressed their strong desire for independence and their conviction that work was the key to this independence. It is ironic that this appears to have been in part a result of their desire to escape the restrictive and conflict-ridden environment of the mission system. Their experience demonstrates how late nineteenth-century policies, enacted through missions, which split Indigenous families, forced diverse communities to live at close quarters, replaced long-term missionaries with a constant series of managers and deprived people of their connections and rights to country, disrupted the possibility of stable communities which could support self-sufficiency. Off the missions, in spite of Emily's and Maud's hard work, perseverance and courage, the broader inequities of settler society made it virtually impossible for them to sustain their independence. The stark contrast between their experience of life after Ramahyuck and that of Ellie Le Souëf is evidence of how colonial governance of Indigenous people undermined the very qualities that it claimed to promote.

8. How different was Victoria? Aboriginal 'protection' in a comparative context

Jessie Mitchell and Ann Curthoys

Scholars of settler colonial governance in Victoria have tended to characterise the colony as distinctive. It was, most agree, shaped by unusually intensive efforts to govern, survey, 'civilise' and control Aboriginal people, rather than to destroy or simply neglect them, although the latter certainly occurred too.[1] Here, we wish to scrutinise the idea of Victorian exceptionalism, focusing on the late 1850s and early 1860s, the years shortly after the achievement of responsible government in 1856. With responsible government, Britain lost control over Aboriginal policy, and, just as importantly, British humanitarian societies lost their lines of direct influence on policy. In this period, then, we can trace the beginnings of Aboriginal policy as colonial politicians devised it under the new system of responsible government.

This era provides an especially interesting opportunity to consider how different Victoria really was in relation to Aboriginal affairs. One distinctive aspect of Victoria's history in the late 1850s and early 1860s was a series of significant reports and policies produced concerning Aboriginal 'protection'. While several scholars have considered them,[2] they rarely note that at the same time South Australia, New South Wales and the new colony of Queensland were also conducting inquiries into matters of Aboriginal policy. The reports emanating from these four colonies were markedly different from each other in purpose, tone, content and findings. Although prompted by specific local incidents and concerns, it is striking that they appeared at about the same time – during the first few years of responsible settler government and after a common neglect within the colonies of Aboriginal affairs for most of the 1850s as political structures were refashioned. All were marked in different ways by the legacies of dispossession and the frontier, and all addressed colonists' capacity and responsibility to govern – or control – native peoples in this new self-governing era. This chapter discusses these reports in a comparative context, asking how and why they differed, and what they had in common. It also looks at the

---

1   On physical destruction, see Lyndall Ryan, 'Settler massacres on the Port Phillip frontier, 1836–1851', Journal of Australian Studies 34(3), 2010: 257–273.
2   For example, Bain Attwood, *Rights for Aborigines*, Allen & Unwin, Sydney, 2003; Diane Barwick, *Rebellion at Coranderrk*, Laura E Barwick and Richard E Barwick (eds), Aboriginal History Inc., Canberra 1998; Richard Broome, *Aboriginal Victorians: A History Since 1800*, Allen & Unwin, Sydney, 2005.

remaining two Australian colonies – Tasmania and Western Australia – asking why there were no similar formal reviews of Aboriginal policy in those two colonies at this time, and how they, too, resembled or differed from the situation in Victoria.

Victoria

By the end of the 1850s, most Victorian colonists no longer faced any real threat to their lives or property from Aboriginal people. The rapid seizure of land, the successful bid for government separate from New South Wales, the massive influx of wealth and migration during the gold rush, the acquisition of responsible government, and the comparatively small size of the colony, all meant that by the late 1850s it was relatively easy for colonists to put Aboriginal dispossession behind them. Indeed, thanks to the district's rapid population change, most Victorians had never personally experienced the struggles over Aboriginal land. The Aboriginal population was a little over 2,000, a rapid decline from an estimated population of between 10,000 and 15,000 in 1835.[3] The old Protectorate, established on instructions from the British government in 1839, had been finally disbanded in 1849, though William Thomas remained as Guardian for Aborigines from 1850 until his death in 1867.[4] A subsequent attempt to set up a Moravian mission was also set aside, though a second attempt would begin in 1859.[5]

Nonetheless, a certain inclination towards philanthropy did exist. This was partly a legacy of the old Protectorate and the small efforts of Moravian missionaries in the 1850s. It was also a product of the significant changes in the cultural and social climate in the colony. The new prosperity and mass migration had led to the growth of networks of educated men in Victoria, who aspired to promote cultural progress and scientific enlightenment. The era saw the establishment of scientific societies, plans for a university and a public library, and the rise of public intellectuals such as Ferdinand von Mueller and *The Argus* editor Edward Wilson.[6] In a newly prosperous colony where settlers were used to asserting

---

[3] See Len R Smith, 1980, *The Aboriginal Population of Australia*, Australian National University Press, Canberra, 1980, cited by the Australian Bureau of Statistics (ABS), cat.no. 3105.0.65.001, Australian Historical Population Statistics, Table 8, Minimum estimates of the Indigenous population, states and territories, 1788–1971.
[4] Liz Reed, 'Rethinking William Thomas, "friend" of the Aborigines', *Aboriginal History* 28, 2004: 87.
[5] Jane Lydon, *Fantastic Dreaming: The Archaeology of an Aboriginal Mission*, Altamira, New York, 2009; Robert Kenny, *The Lamb Enters the Dreaming: Nathanael Pepper and the Ruptured World*, Scribe, Melbourne, 2007.
[6] Don Garden, *Victoria: A History*, Nelson, Melbourne, 1984: 98; Linden Gillbank, 'A paradox of purposes: Acclimatization origins of the Melbourne Zoo', in RJ Hoage and William A Deiss (eds), *New Worlds, New*

themselves as successful, free entrepreneurs, proud of their achievements and confident to govern themselves, the idea of a more charitable Aboriginal policy began to gather support.

One of the key movers for a new approach was Thomas McCombie, a writer, merchant and member of the Legislative Council. In 1858, McCombie released *The History of the Colony of Victoria*, where he acknowledged the violence of early colonisation but depicted it as securely in the past, while praising the colonising zeal of what he termed the Anglo-Saxon race. At the antipodes, McCombie said, colonists would build 'a second happy England'.[7] While researching his book, however, McCombie became concerned about Aboriginal circumstances, and in October 1858, he succeeded in setting up a select committee in the Legislative Council to investigate the condition of Aboriginal people in the colony. His initiative was vital to the formation and conduct of the committee – according to Diane Barwick, McCombie was the only committee member who attended all the hearings and a key figure in drafting the final report.[8] The committee investigated Aboriginal numbers, ages, health, education and access to land and resources, as well as including lengthy ethnographic material about linguistics, craniology, diet, dress, ceremonies, funerals and marriage. The report also included questions about Indigenous people's own forms of government, asking whether authority was monarchical, democratic or priestly, how it was conferred, whether a class system existed, and how laws and punishments were enforced.[9]

The emphasis on ethnography – with questions adapted from the British Association for the Promotion of Science and the Ethnographical Society of Paris – pointed towards the kind of governance of Aboriginal people that some Victorian colonists hoped to develop. This body of Victoria's leading settlers, reporting back to parliament and the public, sought to construct themselves as an educated, cosmopolitan community, linked to European scientific trends and safely separate from and superior to the people they documented. The report did not acknowledge directly any Indigenous witnesses, and despite the committee's concern for Indigenous people, there was something ominous about its eagerness to build its own expertise. Echoing sentiments expressed by the British Association, the writers remarked upon:

Animals: From Menagerie to Zoological Park in the Nineteenth Century, John Hopkins University Press, Baltimore, 1996: 74; Christopher Lever, *They Dined on Eland: The Story of the Acclimatisation Society*, Quiller Press, London, 1992: 107.
7   Thomas McCombie, *The History of the Colony of Victoria, from its settlement to the death of Sir Charles Hotham*, Sands and Kenny, Melbourne, 1858: 41. Also Fergus Farrow, 'McCombie, Thomas (1819–1869)', *Australian Dictionary of Biography*, Melbourne University Press, Carlton, 1974: 14–17, 40, 132–133.
8   Barwick, *Rebellion at Coranderrk*: 37–38.
9   Report of the Select Committee of the Legislative Council on the Aborigines, Together with the Proceedings of Committee, Minutes of Evidence, and Appendices', Votes and Proceedings of the Legislative Council of Victoria, Session 1858–59, Vol I.

> the irretrievable loss which science must sustain if so large a portion of the human race ... is suffered to perish before many interesting questions of a psychological, physiological, and philological character ... have been investigated.[10]

The idea that Indigenous people were doomed to extinction underlay the committee's whole enterprise. Indeed, McCombie himself had written 14 years earlier that 'within a century the race will be nearly extinct. This seems almost their inevitable fate, and we cannot but deplore it.'[11]

Perhaps the 'almost' in McCombie's earlier work was significant, for the Select Committee's report that McCombie presented to the Legislative Council in January 1859 demonstrated not only a scientific imperative but also a genuine humanitarian concern. It provided shocking evidence of Indigenous depopulation, and accused the government of neglecting Aboriginal people, abandoning them to poverty, illness, alcoholism and the violence and vices of Europeans.[12] It recommended greater government intervention, including new reserves for agriculture, pastoralism and missionary work. The result was the establishment the following year of the Central Board Appointed to Watch over the Interests of the Aborigines. It was the first of its kind in the Australian colonies, and there was nothing very similar in Britain's other settler colonies with Aboriginal minorities, in North America and New Zealand. In its early years, the Board focused on rations, clothing, medicine, missionary schooling and agricultural training. Its first two reports acknowledged that colonists had a duty to protect Aboriginal people 'and to a certain extent maintain them', having taken their country.[13] In 1869, the *Aborigines Protection Act 1869* (Vic) extended the system and replaced the Central Board with the more powerful Board for the Protection of Aborigines. There was nothing similar in the other colonies until the 1880s; for at least two decades, Victoria had both the smallest Aboriginal population of any mainland colony and the most comprehensive reserve system.[14]

---

10 'Report of the Select Committee of the Legislative Council on the Aborigines' (1858–59): 25.
11 Thomas McCombie, 'Adventures of a Colonies, or Godfrey Arabin the Settler', a digital text sponsored by the Australian Cooperative Digitisation Project 1840–1845, prepared from the print edition published by John and Daniel A Darling, London, 1845, no page number.
12 *The Argus*, 27 January 1859: 7; 'Report of the Select Committee of the Legislative Council on the Aborigines' (1858–59): iii–iv.
13 *First Report of the Central Board Appointed to Watch Over the Interests of the Aborigines in the Colony of Victoria*, John Ferres, Melbourne, 1861: 5, 11; *Second Report of the Central Board Appointed to Watch Over the Interests of the Aborigines in the Colony of Victoria*, John Ferres, Melbourne, 1862: 15 (SLV).
14 Richard Broome, *Aboriginal Victorians: A History Since 1800*, Allen & Unwin, Sydney, 2005: 126.

South Australia

Victoria was beginning to shape a policy of protection and control in a clearly post-invasion context. However, in the other mainland colonies dispossession and frontier violence were ongoing processes. South Australia shared with Victoria a history of missionary and protectorate work amongst Aboriginal people, and indeed a claim to exceptionalism in its relative caring and humanitarian treatment of Aboriginal people. As Robert Foster and Amanda Nettelbeck have shown, this claim was part of South Australia's oft-made portrayal of itself as having an exceptionally civilised character.[15] South Australians often spoke of their progressive, respectable heritage, reflected in their relatively calm local politics, the absence of a convict system in their region, and their liberal franchise. As in Victoria, there was a perception of a need to govern, as opposed to simply displace and ignore, Indigenous people, but in contrast to Victoria, South Australia still had a large, moving rural frontier and a significant body of pastoralists who sought or depended on Aboriginal labour. Indeed, the colony was perhaps most striking for its mixture of accepting the need for 'protection' and education, supporting Aboriginal employment in the pastoral industry, and continuing dispossession by force in marginal 'frontier' areas.

Controversies over Aboriginal policy in both 'settled' and 'frontier' areas led to the establishment in September 1860 of a Select Committee of the Legislative Council. Its task was to enquire into the condition of Aboriginal people, the cost of existing systems of management and control, and to suggest any changes to that system it deemed expedient.[16] Powerful pastoralist, banker and politician, John Baker had originally proposed in the legislature a commission of inquiry, seemingly as part of his dispute with missionary George Taplin over Taplin's siting his mission on Crown land at Point Macleay on the Narrung Peninsula, where Baker had extensive pastoral interests.[17] In the ensuing parliamentary discussion, however, members expressed a variety of views, including Samuel Davenport, the member for Hindmarsh, who aired concerns over Aboriginal wellbeing. The Council agreed that a select committee, which would be necessarily impartial, would be more appropriate.[18] George Hall, a shipping agent and company director chaired the committee; the other members, in

---

15   Amanda Nettelbeck and Robert Foster, 'Commemorating foundation: a study in regional historical memory', *History Australia* 7(3), 2010: 53.1–53.18.
16   Report of the Select Committee of the Legislative Council upon "The Aborigines" together with Minutes of Evidence and Appendix', South Australia, Votes and Proceedings, Legislative Council, WC Cox, Adelaide, 1860.
17   Cameron Raynes, *'A Little Flour and a Few Blankets': An Administrative History of Aboriginal Affairs in South Australia, 1834–2000*, State Records of South Australia (SRSA), Gepps Cross, 2002: 17; *South Australian Advertiser*, 8 June 1859: 3.
18   Lew Chinner, 'Aboriginal Administration and Affairs at the time of the 1860 South Australian Legislative Council Select Committee Report on Aborigines', *Cabbages and Kings: Selected Essays in History and Australian Studies*, vol. 9, 1981: 16–22. http://ura.unisa.edu.au/R/?func=dbin-jump-full&object_id=unisa25975, see p. 19.

addition to Baker and Davenport, were George Fife Angas, a landowner with an interest in Aboriginal improvement, and George Waterhouse, a businessman who would become premier the following year. In other words, it represented a range of views on Aboriginal policy.

The committee's scope was broad, and it examined 19 witnesses, including missionary Taplin, various figures in the Anglican Church, the secretary of the Aborigines Friends' Association that supported Taplin's mission, police, a prison superintendent, and two Aboriginal (both Moorundee) people from Port Lincoln – a man, Panyarra, and a woman, Parako. Its final report represented the diversity of its membership and perhaps the breadth of its inquiries. It recognised that Aboriginal people had had 'an equitable title to the lands they occupied, and of which they are virtually all dispossessed', and concluded that they had lost much and gained little from British rule, suffering as they were from sickness, hunger, disease, alcohol and social breakdown. Harking back to the original instructions to South Australians, and recalling missionary efforts made in the past, the committee agreed that Indigenous people were entitled to compensation for their loss, and called for a new protectorate and wider rationing systems.[19] At the same time, the report also insisted that the costs should be borne by leasing to settlers land originally set aside as reserves for Aboriginal use, asserted they were probably doomed as a race, and concluded with a strong argument for child removal if Aboriginal people were ever to be Christianised.[20]

The report did have some results: the office of Chief Protector, which the newly responsible government in 1856 had abolished, was reinstated in 1861, and the ration system expanded, although not on the Victorian scale.[21] As Robert Foster suggests, the government adopted these measures not only on humanitarian grounds but also as a means to encourage Aboriginal employment, especially in the pastoral industry. Pastoralists had for the first time become aware of the potential of Aboriginal pastoral labour during the preceding decade, when so many European labourers had left for the Victorian gold rushes. As the gold rushes subsided, European labour returned to the settled areas but not to the remote areas in the north and west of the colony where settlers were establishing new pastoral stations. In these areas, with their chronic shortage of European labour, Aboriginal labour became essential. The government had an existing

---

19 On the idea of compensation in humanitarian discourse in the Australian colonies, see Anne O'Brien, 'Humanitarianism and reparation in colonial Australia', *Journal of Colonialism and Colonial History* 12(2), 2011.
20 Graham Jenkin, *Conquest of the Ngarrindjeri*, Rigby, Adelaide, 1979: 84–95; *South Australian Advertiser*, 31 October 1860: 3; 'Report of the Select Committee of the Legislative Council upon "The Aborigines", printed 16 October 1860', in *Proceedings of the Parliament of South Australia: 1860*, vol. 3, Government Printer, Adelaide, 1860: 2.
21 'Report of the Select Committee of the Legislative Council upon "The Aborigines", printed 16 October 1860'; Robert Foster, 'Rations, coexistence, and the colonisation of Aboriginal labour in the South Australian pastoral industry, 1860–1911', *Aboriginal History* 24, 2000: 5.

policy of distributing rations, which had started in the 1840s as a means of humanitarian assistance, a form of compensation for loss of traditional means of subsistence, and a means of exerting control. Now it became, in addition, a means of attracting Aboriginal people to pastoral stations as labourers.[22] In six years, the new Chief Protector, Dr John Walker, increased the number of ration depots from 14 to 58. In the northern and western pastoral districts, rations were issued not by police, as in the south, but by managers of pastoral stations, as recommended by the 1860 Select Committee. Ration-giving would assist the development of a relationship between pastoralists and Aboriginal people, and thus help draw them into the pastoral industry.[23] Rations were not, as in the Victorian case, associated with the development of missions and reserves with a protective and educational mission.

Some of the concerns expressed in this South Australian report, especially those to do with the necessity of assisting the destitute, echoed those in the Victorian report of the previous year. This report, however, differed from the Victorian one in several key ways. It displayed no particular interest in Indigenous cultural life, and the South Australian committee members were not interested in setting themselves up as scientific experts. They were far more preoccupied with how to prevent and manage Aboriginal resistance to the spread of settlement, and their report showed a concern, not evident in Victoria, about the extent and nature of judicial and police powers. The report called for protectors to be given powers to stage summary trials in local districts of Indigenous people accused of non-capital offences. Summary justice – which the committee did not recommend extending to Europeans – would cut down on the cost of sending prisoners long distances and end the practice of capturing Aboriginal witnesses and sending them to the cities in chains.[24] In this context, the report raised the question of whether Indigenous people were British subjects to be treated before the law the same as any other British subject. Crown authorities had always insisted that they were, and settler governments agreed, but the issue had not been resolved in public debate or in local legal practice.[25] The committee hinted that Aboriginal peoples might be recognised as having distinct societies with a degree of internal sovereignty, and commented that 'the strict application of British criminal law to the aborigines of this Colony is not in accordance with the principles of equity and justice'.[26]

---

22 Foster, 'Rations, coexistence, and the colonisation of Aboriginal labour': 2–5.
23 Foster, 'Rations, coexistence, and the colonisation of Aboriginal labour': 11.
24 Jenkin, *Conquest of the Ngarrindjeri*: 84–95; *South Australian Advertiser*, 31 October 1860: 3; 'Report of the Select Committee of the Legislative Council upon "The Aborigines", printed 16 October 1860': 2.
25 See Lisa Ford, *Settler Sovereignty: Jurisdiction and Indigenous People in America and Australia, 1788–1836*, Harvard University Press, Cambridge, MA, 2010.
26 'Report of the Select Committee of the Legislative Council upon "The Aborigines", printed 16 October 1860': 2. There is a considerable literature on the question of the application of British criminal law to

The question of summary justice arose again, with greater urgency, the following year. When some Aboriginal men murdered Mary Rainbird and her two children on a farm near Kapunda, South Australia's largest town outside Adelaide, in March 1861, this excited popular outrage, and four Aboriginal men were hanged for the crime in Adelaide gaol.[27] They were executed there since public hanging had been banned under an *Act to Regulate the Execution of Criminals* three years earlier. Respectable society had come to see public hanging as an offensive practice, encouraging depravity amongst the lower classes.[28] However, in the Rainbird case, local newspapers were angry that the authorities had hanged the convicted men where their countrymen could not see them, and soon after, the legislature amended the Act to enable Aboriginal executions to take place where the crime had been committed.[29] As it turned out, after several public executions in the early 1860s, this law fell into disuse, and the government removed it from the statute books in 1876.[30] This brief reinstatement of public execution for Aboriginal people in South Australia suggests, nevertheless, that Foucault's narrative in *Discipline and Punish* of an historical transition from public execution to private incarceration needs modification in a settler-colonial context. Punishment under colonial conditions did not follow any simple timeline.[31] Orderly and sometimes humanitarian forms of government could and did coexist with the continuing invasion of Aboriginal lands, and with laws and practices that enshrined the values of the frontier.

New South Wales

Policing the frontier was still in the late 1850s of concern in New South Wales, at least in relation to its northern districts that were not separated to form the colony of Queensland until June 1859. In 1857 and 1858, the NSW Assembly held inquiries into the workings of the Native Mounted Police, a paramilitary body first developed in 1839 in Victoria when it was the Port Phillip District

---

Aborigines, especially for inter se crimes; see especially Bruce Buchan, *The Empire of Political Thought: Indigenous Australians and the Language of Colonial Government*, Pickering and Chatto, London, 2008, ch. 4; and Ford, *Settler Sovereignty*.
27 Alex C Castles and Michael C Harris, *Lawmakers and Wayward Whigs: Government and Law in South Australia, 1836–1986*, Wakefield Press, Adelaide, 1987: 22; Peter Liddy, *The Rainbird Murders*, Peacock Publications, Norwood, 1993: 72–83; Cameron Raynes, 'A Little Flour and a Few Blankets': 18; *South Australian Advertiser*, 29 May 1861: 3.
28 Mark Finnane and John Maguire, 'The uses of punishment and exile: Aborigines in colonial Australia', *Punishment and Society* 3(2) April 2001: 279–298.
29 Act to amend Act no. 23 of 22nd Victoria intituled 'An Act to Regulate the Execution of Criminals'. May 1861, repealed 38/1876, s. 3,
30 See also John Maguire, 'Judicial violence and the civilising process', *Australian Historical Studies* 29(111), 1998: 187–209, this material on p. 201.
31 See Amanda Nettelbeck and Robert Foster, 'Colonial Judiciaries, Aboriginal protection and South Australia's policy of punishing "with exemplary severity"', *Australian Historical Studies* 41(3), 2010: 319–336.

within New South Wales, and subsequently used to enforce pastoralists' power in the north of the colony. These inquiries each produced a report containing lengthy findings about the size, style and management of the NMP; the report of the second inquiry, which had been prompted by the murders of the Fraser family at Hornet Bank in 1857 and the subsequent retaliatory settler violence, was especially detailed. In contrast to Victoria and South Australia, where the reports had emanated from the more conservative Legislative Councils, these two reports were generated by enquiries in the democratically elected Assembly. Those prompting the inquiries, however, were pastoralists seeking higher levels of government protection for settlers in frontier districts: Gordon Sandeman, member for Moreton Bay and other northern districts, called for the first NMP inquiry, while Darling Downs squatter, Arthur Hodgson, sought the second. Both reports called for the government to expand the force and govern it through stronger and more systematic processes. The first, recommending the expansion and reorganisation of the force, was adopted in full, with little dissent, and its recommendation quickly put into effect. The second, recommending an increase in the number of white troopers, was rejected, largely on the grounds that the necessary expansion of the force had already taken place.[32]

Ethnography and culture played no significant part in these reports, and they displayed little concern for the treatment, safety and future of Indigenous people.[33] Some northern witnesses took this opportunity to disparage the notion they should be governed from Sydney at all – northern colonists at this time resented southern government and were expressing their desire for independence.[34] In fact, a number of politicians and commentators in the south supported the northern pastoralists and urged the government either to act harshly to suppress Indigenous resistance or let squatters do it themselves. The key message in both north and south was support, with violence if necessary, for the spread of the pastoralist industry through the north. When the Native Police question moved to Queensland, Aboriginal issues virtually disappeared for some years from government policy and parliamentary debate in New South Wales. There were few voices calling for greater protection, assistance, education or control. There was no government funding to support missionary enterprises, and the government had abolished the long-standing grant to the Wellington Valley mission in 1856. In 1859, some consternation arose in the Assembly, when one member asked whether Aboriginal men could vote. No

---

32   *Sydney Morning Herald*, 18 August 1858: 5.
33   *Moreton Bay Courier*, 18 August 1858: 4; New South Wales (NSW) Legislative Assembly, 'Report from the Select Committee on the Native Police Force', 1857: 6, in *Various papers of the government of New South Wales, relative to the Aborigines, 1854–62*, State Library of Victoria (Rare La Trobe collection); NSW Legislative Assembly, 'Report from the Select Committee on Murders by the Aborigines on the Dawson River', 1858, pp. 5–7, in *Various papers of the government of New South Wales, relative to the Aborigines*.
34   J. Mitchell, '"The Gomorrah of the Southern Seas": population, separation and race in early colonial Queensland', *History Australia* 6(3), December 2009: 69.7–69.10.

one knew; Premier Cowper thought they could not, one member said if they could it would be necessary to disqualify them, and the Attorney-General said he would find out, though he never did.[35] In the end, the debate seems to have subsided into indifference, so secure were colonists in their assumption that responsible government was synonymous with white British manhood. There was little scientific interest in Aboriginal societies in New South Wales during this time, although there were a few men interested in collecting information on Aboriginal languages, notably the travelling missionary, William Ridley.[36] Some legal assistance continued, but medical assistance was gradually phased out. Prompted by what was possibly the last exchange on Aboriginal matters between a governor in New South Wales and the Secretary of State for the Colonies in Britain in 1859, the Executive Council commented that previous measures to protect and Christianise Aboriginal people had been unsuccessful and it was clear they would never become civilised.[37] John Robertson, a leading politician and premier during 1860, believed Aboriginal people should be left alone; the colonists had done all they could, to no avail. The only policy was the continuation and expansion of the annual blanket distribution that had operated since the time of Governor Macquarie. Blankets had become essential for many Aboriginal people to survive the winter, but their annual distribution in towns also encouraged contact between Aboriginal people and country police and magistrates, and thus aided population counting and surveillance.

A Victorian-style approach did not come to New South Wales until the early 1880s. It literally crossed the Murray River when Daniel Matthews, a Victorian, established the Maloga mission on the New South Wales side of the river on his private land, selected under the Robertson Land Acts of 1861.[38] When the mission got into financial trouble and needed government assistance from the late 1870s, Matthews found that he had to appeal to an initially very unresponsive New South Wales government, rather than the closer and more familiar Victorian one. From this circumstance, and Matthews's enormous energy, along with that of another Victorian, John Gribble (later to make his mark in Western Australia), came the formation of the Aborigines Protection Society in New South Wales in 1878. Its campaign for a change in policy was ultimately successful.

---

35 Votes and Proceedings, NSW Legislative Assembly, 1858–9, volume 1, entry for 17 February 1859; Anna Doukakis, *The Aboriginal People, Parliament and 'Protection' in New South Wales 1856–1916*, Federation Press, Sydney, 2006: 25.
36 Niel Gunson, 'Ridley, William (1819–1878)', *Australian Dictionary of Biography*, The Australian National University, 1976, http://adb.anu.edu.au/biography/ridley-william-4477.
37 Doukakis, The Aboriginal People: 148.
38 An Act for Regulating the Alienation of Crown Lands, 18 October 1861 (1861 25 Vic. No 1).

Queensland

In Queensland, formed as a separate colony from New South Wales in June 1859, there were two inquiries involving Aboriginal policy during the first two years of responsible government, both primarily to do with the same issues concerning the Native Mounted Police that had preoccupied the two earlier inquiries. From them we gain a strong sense of the depth of pastoralists' concern with the strength of Aboriginal resistance and how to respond to it; we also learn of some competing views and considerations. Both inquiries emanated from and reported to a parliament dominated by pastoralists, distinctly conservative and protective of property rights. The government did not institute universal manhood suffrage for the Assembly until 1872; the first liberal government was elected in 1877.

The first inquiry was a Select Committee to the Legislative Assembly on the Queensland police force, whose report was tabled in parliament in September 1860. The inquiry seems to have been prompted by general debates about recruitments, cohesiveness and dismissals within the police force as a whole, with some specific concerns raised about the costs of running the Native Mounted Police. Frontier violence was never far from the public consciousness, though, particularly following the murder of the crew of the *Sapphire* by Indigenous people in the Torres Strait earlier that year.[39] The resulting report had two parts: one on the administration of the regular police, and the other on the NMP. The latter concluded that the NMP, while costly to operate, remained necessary. The newly responsible government of Queensland reaffirmed its support for this force, while at the same time the language of the report made clear that the NMP were seen as a 'frontier presence', with all the hints of illegality, wildness and distance that this implied. The report recommended that the NMP receive better supplies and clerical assistance, and that the force increase as 'new country becomes occupied', with Aboriginal troopers procured from far away districts, to keep them under the control of their white officers. When the report was tabled in the Legislative Assembly, there appears to have been little debate about it, apart from some disagreement over who should appoint the white officers. The Colonial Secretary remarked with some pride that backing for the NMP would become more efficient now that Queenslanders had their own government, and reiterated the importance of retaining a police force in districts like Gladstone,

---

39   Lesley McGregor, 'The Police Department 1859–1914', in Kay Cohen and Kenneth Wiltshire (eds), *People, Places and Policies: Aspects of Queensland Government Administration 1859–1920*, University of Queensland Press, St Lucia, 1995: 60–69; *Moreton Bay Courier*, 27 March 1860: 2, and 23 June 1860: 2.

where 'the blacks were numerous and daring' and where the government was still selling tens of thousands of pounds worth of land. The Assembly adopted the report without opposition.[40]

Only six months later, the Native Police force was again under parliamentary scrutiny, and this time the accusations were more serious. On 1 May 1861, Robert Mackenzie, a pastoralist and colonial Treasurer, moved in the Assembly for a Select Committee to inquire into the organisation and management of the force. Mackenzie's motion appears to have been prompted, at least in part, by a paid advertisement placed in the *Moreton Bay Courier* by John Mortimer, a squatter relatively sympathetic to Aboriginal people, alleging murderous behaviour by the Native Police on and around his station, Manumbar.[41] At around the same time, Dr Henry Challinor, the coroner investigating the deaths of three Indigenous people on a property at Fassifern, south-west of Brisbane, had reported to the Attorney-General that they had died at the hands of the Native Police, with the pastoralist and local police magistrate clearly implicated. When the Attorney-General refused to lay blame, Challinor, like Mortimer, had given information to the *Courier*.[42] There were, in fact, four separate incidents, including those at Manumbar and Fassifern, for the committee to investigate. The Assembly broadened the committee's terms of reference beyond the NMP, and asked it to inquire into 'how far it may be practicable to ameliorate the present condition of the Aborigines of this Colony'.[43] The committee was controversial from the beginning, composed as it was only of men who supported the Native Police force and opposed attempts to protect and support Aboriginal people.[44] Of the seven members of the committee, five including Mackenzie, the chair, were pastoralists, one was a farmer and station manager, and one had a son in the Native Police. Two members owned stations in the area where the incidents under question had taken place. Significantly, Challinor, a member of parliament, was not included. So weighted was the committee in favour of the Native Police and against Aboriginal interests, that several witnesses in protest refused to appear before it. The committee, however, did interview a variety of

---

40 *Moreton Bay Courier*, 8 September 1860: 3, 6; 'Queensland: Final Report from the Select Committee on Police', 5 September 1860, in *Queensland: Votes and Proceedings of the Legislative Assembly*, TP Pugh, Brisbane, 1860: 534–565.
41 *Moreton Bay Courier*, 16 March 1861: 3; Denis Cryle, *The Press in Colonial Queensland: A Social and Political History, 1845–1875*, University of Queensland Press, St Lucia, 1989: 67–68; Malcolm D Prentis, 'John Mortimer of Manumbar and the 1861 Native Police Inquiry in Queensland', *Journal of the Royal Historical Society of Queensland*, 14, May 1992: 466–480, this point on p. 474.
42 Rosalind Kidd, *The Way We Civilise: Aboriginal Affairs, the Untold Story*, University of Queensland Press, St Lucia, 1997: 13.
43 'Report from the Select Committee on the Native Police Force and the Condition of the Aborigines Generally; together with the proceedings of the committee and the minutes of evidence', ordered to be printed on 17 July 1861, Queensland Votes and Proceedings of the Legislative Assembly, 1861. http://www.nla.gov.au/apps/doview/nla.aus-vn529131-p.pdf.
44 See the report from Brisbane correspondent, *The Argus*, 8 August, 1861: 5, reprinted in the Hobart Mercury, 13 August 1861: 3; Prentis, 'John Mortimer': 474–475.

witnesses, including Challinor, and several others with concerns about Native Police treatment of Aboriginal people, though, as Malcolm Prentis puts it, the chair's questioning of Challinor and Mortimer was 'quite aggressive and pedantic'.[45]

By far the largest part of the report tabled in parliament on 17 July 1861 dealt with the Native Police. It found that some of the allegations of murderous and illegal behaviour by the NMP were justified, but saw these as the actions of a few and not representative of the force as a whole. It recommended some changes to methods of recruitment, management, and discipline. The *Brisbane Courier* (the paper had recently changed its name from the *Moreton Bay Courier*) was appalled at the committee's findings; we should not, it wrote, 'protect aggression, and violence, and murder'.[46]

While the committee focused on the question of the Native Police, it did also address the more general question of the condition of the Aborigines. Its report was harsh indeed on the nature of Aboriginal people and their chances of 'civilisation'. It advised that the evidence taken by the committee 'shews beyond doubt that all attempts to Christianize or educate the aborigines of Australia have hitherto proved abortive', on the grounds that despite education, 'the Natives of both sexes invariably return to their savage habits'. The report went on to say that they were 'addicted to cannibalism', had 'no idea of a future state', and are 'sunk in the lowest depths of barbarism'. Missions and schools in the different colonies had 'but partial success'.[47] Its only recommendation for action to improve their social condition was to establish, on the recommendation of Johann Zillman, former Lutheran missionary and now farmer still actively involved in church activity, a Missionary Cotton Company. The government would supply it land and other assistance, and in return, it would seek to educate the children and employ the parents in cotton growing.[48] There was no recommendation for the formation of the office of Protector on Victorian or South Australian lines, despite Challinor's suggestion in his evidence that they ought to do so, and no suggestion of support for missionary or other educational endeavour. The Assembly adopted the report, though there was no enthusiasm for the suggestion for a Missionary Cotton Company. The question of both child and adult labour was, however, to recur through the following decade; another government inquiry addressed it in 1874, tellingly asked to 'inquire what can be done to ameliorate the condition of aborigines and to make them more useful'.[49]

---

45   Prentis, 'John Mortimer': 475.
46   *Brisbane Courier*, 27 July 1861: 2; Cryle, *The Press in Colonial Queensland*: 67.
47   'Report from the Select Committee on the Native Police Force', 17 July 1861: 4.
48   'Report from the Select Committee on the Native Police Force', 17 July 1861: 5.
49   Kidd, *The Way We Civilise*: 25.

Settler Colonial Governance

It is worth noting, however, that there were dissenting voices against the committee's report. The *Brisbane Courier*, for example, commented angrily on the section dealing with the condition of the Aborigines, suggesting that the committee members were ignorant and might learn from the great orators on the question of African slavery, such as Burke and Wilberforce, before again entering into 'discussions on the nature of the savage, or the means for his civilisation'.[50] Despite this dissent, the government continued to work in the spirit of the report, on the one hand funding and maintaining the NMP, which continued its task of quelling Aboriginal resistance often with little regard for Aboriginal life, and on the other excusing itself from virtually any responsibility for Aboriginal protection and welfare. There was in some areas an annual blanket distribution, and a few pockets of land were reserved for missions in the southern region of the colony, but that was all.[51]

Only three months after the committee tabled its report, reports of the murders by Aboriginal people of 19 members of the Wills party at Cullin-la-Ringo, near Springsure, rocked the colony. As one historian of the Native Police, Jonathon Richards, puts it, 'If the Hornet Bank reprisals were bad, those that followed the Cullin-la-ringo episode were worse'.[52] Despite evidence of provocation by the abduction of two boys, settlers saw Indigenous people as murderous and never to be trusted, and a major killing spree ensued.[53]

Tasmania and Western Australia

For very different reasons, neither Tasmania nor Western Australia at this time produced parliamentary reports on questions of Aboriginal policy. In Tasmania, the most common assumption was that Aboriginal policy would soon be a thing of the past, while in Western Australia there was as yet no parliamentary system. In both colonies, however, governments continued to shape some form of Aboriginal policy.

In Tasmania, the institution of self-government in 1855 meant a slashing of the budget for the remaining Aboriginal population at Oyster Cove.[54] While it continued the annuity awarded to Fanny Cochrane Smith on her marriage to a local colonist, William Smith, the previous year and in 1857 granted her land

---

50   *Brisbane Courier*, 27 July 1861: 2.
51   Kidd, *The Way We Civilise*: 14.
52   Jonathan Richards, *The Secret War: A True History of Queensland's Native Police*, University of Queensland Press, St Lucia, 2008: 23.
53   See also Henry Reynolds, *Frontier: Aborigines, Settlers, and Land*, Allen & Unwin, Sydney: 48–49.
54   Anna Haebich, *Broken Circles: Fragmenting Indigenous Families*, 1800–2000, Fremantle Arts Centre Press, Fremantle, 2000: 124.

at Nicolls Rivulet, near Oyster Cove,[55] the overall picture was extremely dire for Aboriginal people. By 1859, the population at the Aboriginal settlement at Oyster Cove consisted of a mere 14 people. Many colonists were simply waiting for them to die; as senior civil servant Hugh Munro Hull wrote in his well-known almanac in 1859, *The Royal Kalendar and Guide to Tasmania*, 'the race is fast falling away and its utter extinction will be hardly regretted'.[56] There was no call for inquiries or select committees, and the Tasmanian colonial government seems to have effectively abandoned the community.

Over the next two decades, as the remaining population at Oyster Cove died away and no children were born, the idea that Tasmanian Aboriginal people were fast becoming extinct took hold. Nevertheless, a new community was growing in the Furneaux islands of Bass Strait, descended from the Indigenous women and white sealers. The colonial government continued to accept some responsibility for particular women in this community, for example by continuing to pay pensions granted by earlier administrations.[57] The islanders pressed claims for education and secure leases of land that in part rested on their being the descendants of Aboriginal people. In their campaigns, they enlisted the support of clergymen from the Church of England, several of whom became important allies.[58] One of them, the Bishop of Tasmania, Francis Russell Nixon, published his impressions of the islanders in his book, *Cruise of the Beacon* (1857), portraying them as vigorous, intelligent 'half-castes' needing missionary and state intervention.[59]

Nixon's agitation for state support for education of the islanders was, however, unsuccessful, and their campaign continued into the 1860s. Their local member, James Grant, made speeches in parliament criticising government neglect, which was depriving the people of the islands of education and forcing them off their land. In one such speech in October 1861, Grant acknowledged that many of the islanders were 'descendants of the aborigines' who 'had a claim on our sympathies'.[60] Parliament supported his call the following September for an educational fund for the islanders, though only on the condition that

---

55 J Clark, 'Smith, Fanny Cochrane (1834–1905)', *Australian Dictionary of Biography*, The Australian National University, 1988, http://adb.anu.edu.au/biography/smith-fanny-cochrane-8466.
56 Hugh Munro Hull, *The Royal Kalendar and Guide to Tasmania for 1859*, William Fletcher, Hobart Town, 1859: 20. Quoted in Lyndall Ryan, *Tasmanian Aborigines: A History since 1803*, Allen & Unwin, Sydney, 2012: 262.
57 Tasmania, Legislative Council, 'Half-Caste Islanders in Bass's Straits: Report of the Ven. Archdeacon Reibey', printed 26 August 1863, in Journals of the Legislative Council (with papers), vol. IX, James Barnard, Hobart, 1863.
58 James Boyce, *God's Own Country? The Anglican Church and Tasmanian Aborigines*, Anglicare, Hobart, 2001: 50; Lyndall Ryan, *The Aboriginal Tasmanians*, Allen & Unwin, Sydney, 1994: 225.
59 Francis Russell Nixon, *Cruise of the Beacon: A Narrative of a Visit to the Islands in Bass's Straits*, Bell & Daldy, London, 1857: 43–47.
60 *Mercury*, 3 October 1861: 2, 12 October 1861: 3.

an equivalent sum be raised through private charity.⁶¹ In doing so, it was influenced by the prevailing colonial discourse that acknowledged Indigenous dispossession as a debt but not necessarily an injustice, and that could recognise the ancestry but not the ongoing cultural identity of the Bass Strait community. Furthermore, the long-standing reputation of the islands as marginal places populated by supposedly criminal white men and Indigenous women, helped foster a sense that this could be a place for Christian charity. Eventually, in 1871, in response to continuing pressure from the islanders, the government appointed a schoolteacher to Badger Island, offered the residents a block on Cape Barren Island, and gazetted Chappell and Big Dog islands as mutton bird rookeries under the *Game Preservation Act 1871* (Tas).⁶² As a result, the move by the islander mixed-race population onto Cape Barren Island intensified through the 1870s, and in 1881 the government reserved 6,000 acres of land there for their use.⁶³

In Western Australia, the lack of a parliamentary report on Aboriginal matters at this time occurred for very different reasons. In the huge territory to the west, the greater part of which was at this time still occupied by Aboriginal people rather than settlers, responsible government had not yet arrived. Government was through a British-appointed governor responsible to the Colonial Office, supported by appointed officials and a nominated and advisory Legislative Council. The settler population in 1859 was still less than 15,000, not large enough in British eyes to warrant self-government.⁶⁴ Furthermore, Western Australia had begun accepting convicts in 1850, and it was not until convict transportation finally ended in 1868 that it gained, in 1870, a part-nominated, part-elected Legislative Council of the kind the other colonies had had until the mid-1850s. In this situation, then, the select committees that occurred in the self-governing colonies apart from Tasmania could not occur in Western Australia, and there was no major inquiry involving the Legislative Council until 1884. During the 1850s and 1860s, British officials withdrew funding and support for protection policies, and focused on the operations of the law, punishment and imprisonment to manage both frontier conflict and labour relations.⁶⁵

The cause of protection was at a low ebb. When Britain cut off direct funding for the Protector in Western Australia, British officials in the colony did not

---

61 *Mercury*, 19 September 1862: 5; Tasmania, Legislative Council, 'Half-Caste Islanders in Bass's Straits'.
62 Ryan, *The Aboriginal Tasmanians*: 223–227.
63 Kristyn Harman, 'Protecting Tasmanian Aborigines: American and Queensland influences on the Cape Barren Island Reserve Act, 1912', *The Journal of Imperial and Commonwealth History* 41(5): 747; see also *Tasmanian Government Gazette*, 15 March 1881.
64 ABS, *Australian Historical Population Statistics*, Table 1. The Indigenous population was three times this figure, ABS, *Australian Historical Population Statistics*, Table 8.
65 Paul Hasluck, *Black Australians: A Survey of Native Policy in Western Australia 1829–1897*, Melbourne University Press, Melbourne, 1970 [1942]: 79.

arrange for the colony to step in, and the role of Protector was at first combined with other tasks and then in 1857 allowed to lapse altogether.[66] There were no lands reserved for Aboriginal use until 1878.[67]

Missionary and educational activity owed little to government support during the 1850s. George King's Freemantle school closed in 1851, and John Smithies' Methodist institution, established in the early 1840s in Perth, closed in 1855 after two moves westward in an effort to get away from settler influence.[68] The government did support a small school for Aboriginal children in Albany, south of Perth, run by Mrs Camfield, without remuneration, from 1852, its numbers rising to 18 in 1858, but this was small-scale education indeed.[69] Moreover, the government could take little credit for the one successful mission of this period, the Benedictine Catholic mission at New Norcia, 132 kilometres north of Perth. Having begun in 1846 with support from Rome, then been suspended from 1849 to 1853 while its leader, Father Salvado, sought greater financial support in Europe, the mission gained a firmer footing in 1853 when Salvado returned with a further three priests and 37 lay brothers, laying the foundation for its considerable longer-term success. From 1859, the government did support the mission with funding of £100 per year, but the overwhelming picture, nevertheless, is one of little government interest in protection, education, and 'civilisation'. The main measure of control continued to be through the law, punishment, and imprisonment; it is worth noting, though, as Mark Finnane and John Maguire point out, that imprisonment carried with it in the early stages at least some notion of imparting civilisation.[70] Rottnest Island, established as an Aboriginal prison in 1840 but closed in 1849, was re-established in 1855, and became a prime site for Aboriginal punishment for many decades.

Western Australia's difference from the other colonies highlights something a little unexpected; there was more government interest in Aboriginal management and in some cases protection in some of the newly self-governing colonies than in the only one that Britain continued to govern directly. The protectionist impulse of the 1840s survived better in the rapidly expanding colonies of Victoria and South Australia, with their more liberal politics, than in conservative Western Australia with its tiny settler population and exclusive focus on economic development. On the other hand, the difference between Western Australia and Queensland in the management of frontier conflict is striking. Where Queensland relied on the Native Police force to 'disperse' Aboriginal people resisting settlement, with significant injury and loss of life, Western Australia saw the extensive use of the law – arrest, trial and imprisonment – in an attempt

---

66 Hasluck, *Black Australians*: 80.
67 *WA Government Gazette*, 18 June 1878: 145 and 6 August 1878: 6, quoted in Hasluck, *Black Australians*: 114.
68 Hasluck, *Black Australians*: 89–92.
69 Hasluck, *Black Australians*: 93–94.
70 Finnane and Maguire, 'The uses of punishment and exile': 285–286.

to achieve a similar object without loss of life. As settlement spread, however, the use of the law came to be increasingly oppressive, as the government gave pastoralists in the role of magistrates legal powers that they often abused, and Aboriginal people were made to walk vast distances, often connected by chains including neck chains, to places of trial and punishment. Nevertheless, Western Australia did not witness to the same extent the killing fields that characterised large parts of Queensland.

Conclusion

Victoria *was* different. While the first decade of responsible government produced debate about the future of Aboriginal policy in (almost) all the colonies, the focus and tone were distinctive to each one. The debate over how to best defeat Aboriginal resistance that was so important in Queensland, Western Australia and South Australia in the second half of the nineteenth century was no longer relevant in Victoria when McCombie called for his Select Committee. Nor did Victoria share to any great extent those three colonies' concern with the control of Aboriginal labour. On the other hand, the *laissez faire* thinking based on the idea that Aboriginal people were unable to be 'improved' and that they were fast disappearing was less evident in Victoria than in New South Wales and Tasmania. In Victoria more than anywhere else except possibly South Australia, a form of humanitarianism survived that, at one end, was concerned with protection and education and, at the other, with stricter management and control of Aboriginal people within a new colonial order.

There are, we think, several reasons for this distinctiveness. They include the early end of the frontier after the rapid invasion and dispossession of the period from 1835 to 1855, and the lingering influence of the Protectorate of the 1840s. Also important are the rapid rise of a new, scientific, metropolitan culture in the 1850s, and the role of some key figures like Thomas McCombie.

Indigenous agency also played an important part. Loyal addresses and petitions were much more common in Victoria than the other colonies, and although policymakers did not often acknowledge it officially, the propensity of Aboriginal Victorians to place direct pressure on the authorities both helped prompt, and was strengthened by, the Victorian tradition of protection and establishing managed reserves. The Aboriginal men who in their demands for land pressed William Thomas in 1859 and the Central Board in 1860, and who passed on a loyal address to Queen Victoria in 1863, were all helping shape the relationships that emerged in those years. They were not alone in doing so, as the petitions at Flinders Island in the 1840s, and in New South Wales in the 1880s attest, but the tradition was especially strong in Victoria.[71] Perhaps ironically, it would also lead Victorian Indigenous people to voice some particularly passionate criticisms of the 'protection' model, as the many histories of the Coranderrk mission, for example, have traced. The resulting climate of bureaucracy, ethnography and activism produced a history for Indigenous Victorians that was complex, articulate and heavily (if unevenly) documented – a combination that scholars and storytellers continue to find irresistible.

---

71   Ann Curthoys and Jessie Mitchell, '"Bring this Paper to the good Governor": Aboriginal petitioning in Britain's Australian colonies' in Saliha Belmessous (ed.), *Native Claims: Indigenous Law against Empire 1500–1920*, Oxford University Press, New York, 2011: 182–203.

9. The 'Minutes of Evidence' project: Creating collaborative fields of engagement with the past, present and future

Jennifer Balint, Julie Evans, Nesam McMillan, Giordano Nanni and Melodie Reynolds-Diarra

> History for me is best understood when you take the words off the page and voice them. It is a reminder that all people have emotions and desires that drive our actions and words, which in turn creates our history, which in turn we hopefully learn from.
>
> (Melodie Reynolds-Diarra, actor, *Coranderrk: We Will Show The Country*)

The preceding chapters of this collection demonstrate how nuanced and critically informed analyses of historical evidence can deepen and refine our understanding of nineteenth-century Victorian society. In this chapter, we seek a similar outcome; but we shift the focus towards the task of using historical materials to engage a broader public audience. In doing so we consider the potential benefits of expanding the field of engagement with the past through an innovative collaboration which aims to bring Victoria's history 'back to life' through theatre; by (re)citing its historical archive, and taking the words 'off the page' and voicing them out loud, as Wongutha woman and actor Melodie Reynolds-Diarra puts it.

In this chapter, we discuss a recent project – the 'Minutes of Evidence' project[1] – that at once reflects and benefits from the comprehensive considerations and

---

1 The 'Minutes of Evidence project: Promoting new and collaborative ways of understanding Australia's past and engaging with structural justice', is funded by an Australian Research Council Linkage grant, with substantial support from 13 partner organisations. The broader research agenda draws on the 1881 Victorian Parliamentary Inquiry into the Aboriginal Reserve at Coranderrk to encourage greater awareness of the effects of settler colonialism in Victoria's past and present and more open consideration of how to live together justly in the future. It examines how notions of justice have been formulated, invoked and confronted over time and place, and how the enduring legacies of past injustices continue into the present – despite official responses designed to redress them – so as to foster new ways of thinking about structural justice in the present and future. 'Minutes of Evidence' is a collaboration between researchers from the University of Melbourne and La Mama Theatre, ILBIJERRI Theatre Company, Koorie Heritage Trust, Arts Victoria, Regional Arts Victoria, the State Library of Victoria, the Victorian Aboriginal Education Association (VAEAI), the Victorian Department of Education and Early Childhood Development (DEECD) and VicHealth, in association with researchers from Deakin University, the University of Sussex and Royal Holloway, University of London. The project is creating a number of 'meeting points' – in public spaces such as schools, on-Country, in theatres and in universities – to bring together leading Indigenous and non-Indigenous education experts, researchers,

professional skills that academic historians bring to their work. But the 'Minutes of Evidence' project is also a collaborative enterprise that sets out to expand the field of engagement with the notion and practice of history by creating a number of spaces where different ways of understanding Victoria's past and its resonance in the present can interact, and their implications unfold. Its members are Indigenous and non-Indigenous; it is interdisciplinary in its conceptual framing (sharing the insights of researchers in history, cultural geography, criminology, socio-legal studies and law); and cross-sectoral in composition (its partners come from the creative arts, education, major government and public institutions, and universities in Victoria and England).

As previous contributors have foreshadowed, to live in early twenty-first-century Victoria is to live with settler colonialism and, therefore, with the unfinished business between Aboriginal and non-Aboriginal people that was produced by Britain's overarching imperial ambitions and the distinctive modes of settler governance it oversaw in the fledgling state. Accordingly, a key concern of the 'Minutes of Evidence' project is to direct the attention of a range of audiences – academic and non-academic, members of the public, educators and school children – not only to the specific nature of Victoria's foundations but also to the scope and significance of the broader empire in which Victoria was placed. In moving between the local and the global, and the past and the present, the project draws centrally on the concept of structural injustice to raise awareness of the particular historical experiences of Aboriginal and non-Aboriginal peoples post-colonisation and of their enduring ramifications in the present. In so doing, it seeks to foster a more informed understanding of what structural justice might look like in Victoria, and Australia more generally. In reaching beyond Australia, it also opens spaces to consider the importance of accounting for history in justice projects in other contexts, such as post-conflict contexts in which there is a more sustained and holistic engagement with addressing the injustices of the past through so-called 'transitional justice' measures.[2]

At the heart of the project is the wish to extend the field of engagement with history itself. It seeks to draw on, yet move beyond, conventional scholarly ways of knowing; to draw in different perspectives on the meaning and

---

performance artists, community members, government and community organisations to promote new ways of publicly engaging with history and structural injustice through research, education and performance. In highlighting the significance of the 1881 Inquiry, 'Minutes of Evidence' has supported DEECD's production of innovative and collaborative curriculum modules and teaching resources for History and Civics & Citizenship in Victorian secondary schools and also presented a groundbreaking verbatim-theatre play *Coranderrk: We Will Show the Country*, which brings to life the voices of Indigenous and European people who testified at the 1881 Coranderrk Inquiry. The project also supports research training for early-career Indigenous scholars: www.minutesofevidence.com.au.

2 Jennifer Balint, Julie Evans and Nesam McMillan, 'Rethinking transitional justice, redressing Indigenous harm: a new conceptual approach', *International Journal of Transitional Justice* 8(2), 2014: 194–216.

experiences of the past and the present; and to open up new possibilities for a more collaborative future. While the history of Victoria has much to say about the coercive and destructive nature of colonial governance it nevertheless demonstrates, too, that in the past, as much as the present, Aboriginal and non-Aboriginal peoples also shared concerns about justice, despite seemingly overwhelming pressures to consider their welfare and interests as separate. Through the mediums of performance, education and research – all premised on public and community engagement – the 'Minutes of Evidence' project seeks to pursue new ways of connecting the past and the present, as well as connecting contemporary audiences, school children, educators and readers with histories of colonialism and their enduring effects. In so doing, it presents opportunities for these communities to reflect on what justice and redress in such contexts may look like. In the first instance, the project brings together the skills and perspectives of its partners, and the engagement of local Aboriginal peoples and communities, to employ theatre as an initial focal point for engagement. *Coranderrk: We Will Show the Country* is a verbatim theatre performance based on edited primary source materials – principally, the extracts from the official minutes of evidence of a government inquiry into conditions at an Aboriginal reserve near Healesville outside Melbourne that took place in 1881, together with excerpts of petitions, letters and newspaper articles from the time.[3] The project then turns to developing models for community involvement, adapting the play for secondary schools, embedding project themes in resources to support the national curriculum, hosting public seminars and forums, and undertaking interdisciplinary research on the notion and practice of structural justice. As this piece goes to publication, the project is nearing the end of its third and final year of formal operation. Its preparation and development, however, began in 2009 as appropriate partners, models of collaboration, and, of course, avenues for funding were sought and established.[4]

---

3   *Report of the Board Appointed to Enquire into, and Report upon, the Present Condition and Management of the Coranderrk Aboriginal Station, together with the minutes of evidence*, John Ferres, Government Printer, Melbourne, 1882 [henceforth: *Report of the Coranderrk Inquiry*]. The performance history for *Coranderrk: We Will Show the Country* is as follows: initial pilot and workshop, 13–15 August, 2010 (La Mama Courthouse Theatre, Melbourne); community consultation readings, 6 May 2011 (Melba Hall, The University of Melbourne) and 7 May 2011 (Sanctuary House, Healesville); public premiere season, 16–27 November 2011 (La Mama Courthouse Theatre); second season, 11–12 February 2012 (Indigenous Arts Festival, BMW Edge, Federation Square, Melbourne); third season, 28 June – 1 July 2012 (Playhouse Theatre, Sydney Opera House, Sydney). In 2013, the 'Minutes of Evidence' project together with ILBIJERRI Theatre Company developed a new version of the play, entitled *CORANDERRK*, targeted specifically at school audiences. Pilot readings were staged on 15–16 August at the Memorial Hall, Healesville, and at the Open Stage Theatre, The University of Melbourne. An annotated script of the production has now been published by the writers, Nanni, G & James, A, *Coranderrk: We Will Show The Country*, Canberra: Aboriginal Studies Press, 2013.

4   Funding to support the development of the project was kindly received from the following bodies: The University of Melbourne (CCRAG Cultural & Community Grant; School of Social and Political Sciences Seed Grant); The City of Melbourne (Community Services Grant); with contributions from La Mama Theatre, VicHealth (Arts About Us Program) and KereKere. The official 'Minutes of Evidence' project itself was funded under an Australian Research Council Linkage Grant (2011–2014) with funding and support from the following

This chapter focuses on the first phase of the project, which centred on the development and performance of the *Coranderrk: We Will Show the Country* (henceforth *CWWSC*) production. We discuss the role of these performances, and the medium of verbatim theatre more generally in making history accessible to non-academic audiences, and therefore creating new opportunities for bringing history into the present. From our perspective, a key role of these performances is to provide a catalyst for the formation of a number of meeting spaces: firstly, between academic and non-academic audiences, who might share an immediate contact and intimacy with the voices of the archives – the raw materials in the writing and re-telling of history. The production's historical/theatrical method of bringing the past into the present can therefore help to not only spark public interest in the past but also create a shared historical consciousness in Australia. Secondly, *CWWSC* establishes a meeting space between the realms of the spoken and the written word – commonly understood as being the dominant measures of authenticity in Aboriginal and Western cultures, respectively. By honouring and invoking both the oral and written tradition of History, *CWWSC* thus essentially creates an opportunity for a broader, shared space to emerge between Aboriginal and non-Aboriginal audiences. The story that is told takes both the audience and performers on a journey that connects the present to the past through the shared experience of theatre, creating a third meeting space for acknowledgement and possible change. It is through the recognition of the structural injustice of the governance of Aboriginal people in the past, and its echoes into the present, that there may be collaboration on what is needed for structural change in the present and future. The recognition of the injustice heard, and acknowledged, by the inquiry, and the resurrection of this buried legal record through the medium of theatre in the present, may act as a catalyst for new public discussions about structural injustice in Australia – and elsewhere – leading to new conversations about what structural justice may look like and demand.

We begin by outlining the unique and remarkable history on which *CWWSC* is based, a history that highlights the injustice perpetrated against the Coranderrk community, but also its resistance, agency and partnership with non-Aboriginal peoples in its struggle for justice against the settler colonial state. The brief historical introduction which follows does not seek to offer a detailed account of Coranderrk or Victorian history (for this readers may wish to consult preceding chapters of this collection). Rather, it aims to highlight some of the key themes and events that are central to the subsequent discussion concerning the performance and the way in which it capitalises on both the power of theatre and the authenticity of the archive in order to raise awareness of the history

---

partners: The University of Melbourne, La Mama Theatre, ILBIJERRI Theatre Company, The Department of Education and Early Childhood Development, VicHealth, The Koorie Heritage Trust, The Victorian Aboriginal Education Association Inc (VAEAI), Arts Victoria, Regional Arts Victoria and The State Library of Victoria.

of Coranderrk, and colonial Victoria and Australia more generally. The final section concludes by reflecting on the potential contribution of *CWWSC* to bring history into the present.

This piece is a collaborative effort of five professionals associated with the 'Minutes of Evidence' project — four academics from the disciplinary fields of history, socio-legal studies and criminology, and one actor, Melodie Reynolds-Diarra, a Wongi woman from Western Australia who has played the roles of Alice Grant, Caroline Morgan, Eda Brangy and Phinnimore Jackson in *CWWSC*, and whose reflections we draw upon to frame each of the sections of our discussion.[5]

The history of Coranderrk and the 1881 inquiry

The history of Coranderrk provides a window onto the history of colonial dispossession and genocide in settler states more generally. Historian Patrick Wolfe has influentially explained settler colonialism as distinctive from other colonial formations in that colonisers come to stay, claiming the sovereign lands of Indigenous peoples as their own. Within this conceptual framework, settler colonialism is regarded as a continuing 'structure', rather than 'an event' that begins and ends at the point of colonisation.[6] Within Wolfe's framework, settler societies proceed according to a 'logic of elimination' that seeks continually to marginalise the significance of Indigenous sovereignty, thereby explaining enduring state discrimination against Indigenous peoples in contemporary settler states such as Australia, New Zealand, Canada and the United States of America.[7] In the Australian case, the ongoing structure of colonialism is manifest in contemporary society, and stems from dispossession, the attempted destruction of a people and a persistent failure to accord them equal citizenship.

In the south-eastern colonies of Australia, as several of the preceding chapters in this collection have outlined, dispossession was relatively swift and comprehensive. Aboriginal peoples' early modes of resistance were overwhelmed not only by diseases and acts of violence but also by the massive disruption that pastoralism effected to traditional economies. Their communities subsequently 'suffered whiplash' — to borrow Boucher and Russell's words in their introductory chapter — 'as the lethal materialities of settler land hunger

---

5   An early version of this paper was presented at the 2011 Australian and New Zealand Critical Criminology conference: Jennifer Balint, Julie Evans, Nesam McMillan, 'Minutes of Evidence: raising awareness of structural injustice and justice', in *Proceedings of the 5th Annual Australian and New Zealand Critical Criminology Conference*, James Cook University, Townsville, 1(1), 2012.
6   Patrick Wolfe, 'Nation and MiscegeNation: discursive continuinty in the post-Mabo era', *Social Analysis* 36 (1994): 96.
7   Wolfe, 'Nation and MiscegeNation': 93.

were compounded and amplified by the explosive impact of the gold rush'.[8] As a consequence of this, the first three decades of settler colonisation in Victoria saw a serious diminution in the numbers of Aboriginal peoples and widespread interference with their hold on traditional lands and their capacity to maintain cohesive communities and cultures.[9] Meanwhile, although rarely critical of colonialism *per se*, certain individuals amongst the settler population expressed concern about the plight of Indigenous peoples in the Australian colonies and elsewhere. A number of missionary societies became involved in an endeavour to protect, convert and educate Aboriginal peoples, and official 'protectorates' were established in Victoria, South Australia and Western Australia. However, for Aboriginal people, they proved to be little more than short-lived attempts to provide rations and places of refuge; and, in the end, as Leigh Boucher discusses in more detail in Chapter 3, the Port Phillip Protectorate was regarded as a failure.[10]

Aboriginal people in Victoria were not passive spectators in all these events, but rather agents of their own destinies. Whether by forming strategic relationships with settlers and officials, or by way of 'economic entrepreneurialism' and shifting their 'traditional econoscape to accommodate the new resources presented by European colonisation', as Lynette Russell shows in Chapter 1, Aboriginal people adopted, and adapted to, whatever elements they could in the new social order that so irrevocably changed their world. Thus, from the 1840s in Victoria, a new phase of Aboriginal activism emerged. Kulin leaders such as Woiwurrung elder Billibellary, his son Simon Wonga and nephew William Barak, for example, saw the need for the Kulin clans as a whole to adopt a different approach if their peoples were to survive the dramatic consequences of the initial occupation of their lands, which now constituted much of the central regions of the colony. In 1859, Simon Wonga led a delegation of Kulin people to meet with government officials to request a grant of land to settle and farm in Acheron, in the hills beyond Melbourne. Coinciding with a select committee of the Legislative Council of Victoria (discussed by Jessie Mitchell and Ann

---

8   Leigh Boucher and Lynette Russell, 'Introduction: Colonial history, postcolonial theory and the "Aboriginal problem" in colonial Victoria': 1.
9   See Diane Barwick, *Rebellion at Coranderrk*, Laura E Barwick and Richard E Barwick (eds), Aboriginal History Inc., Canberra, 1998; Richard Broome, *Aboriginal Australians: A History Since 1788*, Allen & Unwin, Sydney, 2010: 74–80; Jan Critchett, *A Distant Field of Murder: Western District Frontiers 1834–1848*, Melbourne University Press, Melbourne, 1990; Public Record Office Victoria [PROV] and the Australian Archives, Victorian Regional Office, *'My Heart is Breaking': A Joint Guide to Records about Aboriginal Peoples in the Public Record Office Victoria and the Australian Archives*, Victorian Regional Office Australian Government Publishing Service Canberra, 1993; Elizabeth Nelson, Sandra Smith and Patricia Grimshaw (eds), *Letters from Aboriginal Women of Victoria, 1867–1926*, History Department, University of Melbourne, Melbourne, 2002; Penelope Edmonds, *Urbanizing Frontiers: Indigenous Peoples and Settlers in 19th-Century Pacific Rim Cities*, University of British Columbia Press, Vancouver, 2010.
10 The Port Phillip Protectorate lasted for just 11 years: 1838–49 (see, Michael Christie, *Aborigines in Colonial Victoria, 1835–86*, University of Sydney Press, Sydney, 1979: 81–135, for a general overview) while the protectorates in WA and SA were both wound up by 1857.

Curthoys in Chapter 8) that recommended the creation of reserves in Aboriginal home lands under the supervision of missionaries, the delegation was one of several attempts by Aboriginal leaders in Victoria to establish a permanent and productive stake in the land at sites of their choosing, all of which struggled to succeed in the face of inadequate resources and concerted opposition from hostile settlers and officials.[11]

The Kulin people were soon displaced from the Acheron station, and in 1863 Simon Wonga and William Barak led another deputation that successfully petitioned the government to grant a reserve of 930 hectares (extended to 1,960 hectares in 1866) at a place they called Coranderrk, after the small Christmas Bush that blooms there each December, beside the Yarra River near Healesville. This became one of six reserves that the government eventually established throughout the colony, as Claire McLisky outlines in greater detail in Chapter 5.[12]

The settlement at Coranderrk proved particularly successful with most Kulin people choosing to reside there, along with several Bangerang people who travelled there from the Murray River, together with individuals and families from clans across Victoria who had been similarly displaced. By 1874, despite having no secure title, they had cleared over 1,200 hectares for vegetable, crop and cattle farming, stretched 7 kilometres of fencing, constructed 32 cottages plus outbuildings, raised families and built a thriving community that also made and sold cultural artefacts and mud bricks. The award-winning quality of Coranderrk's hops attracted the highest market prices and by 1875 the settlement was described as being 'virtually self-supporting'.[13] A uniquely respectful relationship had developed between William Barak (Simon Wonga had died in 1874) and John Green who, as well as acting as inspector of stations across Victoria, had also been appointed as manager of Coranderrk, which he had originally founded alongside Barak and Wonga. Green to a relatively large extent supported the continuation of certain Kulin laws and practices, and negotiated community agreement regarding the management of the farm and the punishment of offences.[14]

Yet broader government indifference to the long-term welfare of the Aboriginal population either on or off the six Victorian reserves, along with outright hostility from settlers keen to acquire even more productive land, consistently worked against the achievement of a just settlement between Aboriginal and non-Aboriginal people in the colony. The historian Richard Broome explains

---

11 Barwick, *Rebellion at Coranderrk*: 38, 1–53; Broome, *Aboriginal Australians*: 81–88.
12 These six Victorian reserves were Framlingham and Lake Condah for the Gunditjmara and Kirrae-wurrung clans of the western district; Ebenezer mission at Lake Hindmarsh for the tribes of Wimmera and Lower Murray regions; Ramahyuk and Lake Tyers for the Kurnai tribes of Gippsland; and Coranderrk for the Kulin clans of central Victoria (Barwick, *Rebellion at Coranderrk*: 52).
13 Broome, *Aboriginal Australians*: 84.
14 Broome, *Aboriginal Australians*: 85–86.

that as Aboriginal labour was either unpaid, paid in liquor, or severely underpaid, it was impossible for people to feed their families without seeking additional work, while paternalistic or authoritarian management on reserves led to beatings and withdrawal of rations.[15] As Leigh Boucher illustrates in Chapter 3, Aboriginal people were placed under additional surveillance and control following the *Aborigines Protection Act 1869* (Vic) that established the Board for the Protection of Aborigines (discussed by Samuel Furphy in Chapter 4), which oversaw the movement of people between reserves and the removal of children, and required Aboriginal people to write for official permission to visit family and friends.[16] With respect to Coranderrk in particular, John Green was eventually goaded into resigning his position after several altercations with the Board for the Protection of Aborigines (henceforth, 'the Board'), including over the appropriation of the community's hard-earned profits to supplement state revenue and threats to close Coranderrk and relocate its people to the Murray River region in order to make the land available for private sale.

The Coranderrk community's sustained protests against these developments eventually became known as the Coranderrk 'rebellion', a designation indicating the strength of official fears that Aboriginal quests for self-determination might spread to other reserves. Under the leadership of William Barak, together with his chief aides and 'speakers' Thomas Bamfield (Birdarak), Robert Wandin (Wandon) and Thomas Dunolly, the men and women of Coranderrk mounted a sustained campaign to stay on their country, to maintain their productive self-supporting community there, and to reinstate their friend and ally, John Green, as manager. On numerous occasions they undertook the long walk to Melbourne to talk with government ministers in Spring Street, while also writing petitions, letters and interviews, and recruiting the assistance of influential supporters in the white community such as the redoubtable Scottish woman and friend of Barak and Bamfield, Anne Fraser Bon. The campaign resulted in two official inquiries: a royal commission in 1877 and a parliamentary board of inquiry into the management of Coranderrk in 1881 (the particular focus of this paper and the theatre performance, *CWWSC*).

The 1881 inquiry, and the evidence which it collected from Aboriginal and European witnesses, was unique in many ways. Appointed by Victoria's Chief-Secretary Graham Berry, the nine commissioners sat for two-and-a-half months. They travelled to Coranderrk to hear the views of residents who bravely delivered their testimony before officials despite the overwhelming repression to which their peoples had long been subjected. But unlike many other inquiries into the condition of Indigenous peoples in the British Empire during the nineteenth

---

15 Broome, *Aboriginal Australians*: 92.
16 See Elizabeth Nelson, Sandra Smith and Patricia Grimshaw (eds), *Letters from Aboriginal Women of Victoria, 1867–1926*, History Department, University of Melbourne, 2002.

century, its cause was not the lobbying of British humanitarians (who, by the 1880s, had lost much of their influence in matters of pan-colonial governance), nor solely the work of politicians, missionaries and philanthropists. Rather, the inquiry was in great part a result of the sustained campaign that had been led by the residents of Coranderrk, with support from their friends and allies in the settler community, to appeal for justice and protection from the government against the ongoing effects of settler-colonisation. For although Coranderrk had started off as a refuge, even as a place of incarceration for the Kulin clans of Victoria who had established the station in 1863, it had gradually become a thriving and economically self-sustaining community – one that the Kulin clans were determined to defend. This is evinced by the petition, which the residents presented to the commissioners of the inquiry. Dated 16 November 1881, it was signed by William Barak and 44 men, women and children of Coranderrk. It asked for John Green to return as manager and for the station to be under the Chief Secretary rather than the Board – 'then we will show the country that the station could self support itself.'[17] The inquiry's overall findings rejected the Board for the Protection of the Aborigines' intentions to dispose of Coranderrk; three years later it was gazetted as a 'permanent reservation'.[18] While John Green was not reinstated as manager, his replacement, the reviled Reverend Strickland, was dismissed and – in the short term – conditions improved for Coranderrk's residents.

From a historical perspective, a key feature of the inquiry is the prominent presence of the voices of Aboriginal people involved. Aboriginal people made up almost a third of the 69 witnesses who were examined and their statements are recorded in the official minutes of evidence. Previous commissions of inquiry into the condition and management of the Aboriginal population of Victoria had taken evidence only from a handful of Aboriginal witnesses. The select committee of 1858–59 contains a plenitude of opinions from settlers, missionaries and 'protectors', but no Aboriginal voices; while the 1877 Royal Commission only interviewed four Aboriginal people – cherry-picked witnesses who were counted on to be compliant.[19] The minutes of the Coranderrk inquiry, on the other hand, contain the testimonies of 21 Aboriginal people, including men, women and children, many of whom, in the act of testifying against their overseers and the Board were risking all they had in order to appeal to

---

17   *Report of the Coranderrk Inquiry*, Minutes of Evidence: 98.
18   *Victoria Government Gazette*, No. 119, 10 October 1884: 2867.
19   'Report of the Select Committee of the Legislative Council on the Aborigines, Together with the Proceedings of Committee, Minutes of Evidence, and Appendices', *Votes and Proceedings of the Legislative Council of Victoria*, Session 1858–59, Vol I; Victoria, Royal Commission on the Aborigines, 'Report of the Commissioners Appointed to Inquire into the Present Condition of the Aborigines of this colony, and to Advise as to the Best Means of Caring for, and Dealing with Them, in the Future, Together with Minutes of Evidence and Appendices', *Papers Presented to Both House of Parliament, Victoria*, Session 1877–78, Vol. III. (For these testimonies, see Minutes of Evidence: 26–33).

colonial authorities for the right to remain at Coranderrk. The body of evidence submitted by the Aboriginal people of Coranderrk indeed offers a damning indictment of the governance of Aboriginal people in Victoria. It also represents a valuable early record of the strength, adaptability and sagacity of people such as William Barak, the Wurundjeri leader and spokesperson for the Coranderrk community, who, in the space of a lifetime had experienced a huge cultural shift: from living the pre-colonial ways of life to experiencing firsthand their disruption and destruction at the hand of European invasion; from enduring life on a mission station to witnessing, towards the end of his life, the birth of the Australian nation (Barak was born in the 1820s and died in 1903). The minutes of the Coranderrk inquiry also dispel many prejudices and misconceptions – prevalent then, and unfortunately even now – about how Aboriginal people responded to colonisation. The oral evidence itself demonstrates that, at a time when the dominant view in settler society suggested that Aboriginal people were a 'dying race' – destined to vanish within a short space of time, and incapable of helping themselves – Aboriginal communities remained resilient and strong in their negotiation and contestation of the lived realities of settler colonial rule. Having appropriated and redeployed the settlers' language and literacy in order to write letters, petitions and form deputations to ministers, the Coranderrk community was in fact helping to kick-start the kind of campaigns for justice, self-determination and land rights which would extend into the twentieth and twenty-first centuries.

The body of evidence collected from the European witnesses who testified at the Coranderrk inquiry constitutes another element, which makes this document of particular historical significance. On the one hand, some of the European witnesses (Edward Curr, Captain AMA Page, the Rev. FA Hagenauer, and others) represented the interests of the Board for the Protection of Aborigines and were strongly opposed to the right of Aboriginal people to have a say in the management of their own affairs. But there were other European witnesses (John Green, Thomas Harris, George Alexander Syme) as well as members of the Board of Inquiry itself (such as Anne Bon, Thomas Embling and John Dow), who spoke out in support of the Coranderrk community, often at personal cost. As such, the archive produced by the inquiry provides a rich record of not only Aboriginal voices and activism, and of European injustices, but also of the possibilities for both settlers and Aboriginal people to work as allies on issues of social justice, providing important models and lessons for collaboration in the present and future. The history of Coranderrk highlights that not all Europeans thought about, and behaved towards, Aboriginal people in the same way, challenging the belief that racial intolerance and exploitation of Aboriginal people was simply accepted as the norm in the 1800s.

Thanks to the bureaucratic efficiency of the agents of the British Empire, the minutes of evidence of the Coranderrk inquiry survive to this day in the archives, alongside the volumes of evidence collected and attached to the hundreds of other reports of official commissions during the nineteenth century. As such the document has seldom been visited by anyone other than historians and researchers; and yet these minutes are a record of Aboriginal and non-Aboriginal oral history that provide a valuable and rare insight into a fascinating chapter of Victorian history. When placed in the context of more recent events, and delivered through a publicly engaging medium, this body of evidence can in fact offer an opportunity to broaden the field of engagement with Victoria's history and demonstrate some valuable lessons for the present.

Verbatim theatre, history and re-staging Coranderrk

> I've been acting for over 20 years, primarily in the theatre, and Coranderrk is my first verbatim work. Although many of my plays have been based on events regarding Aboriginal issues, being verbatim, Coranderrk holds the weight of fact, which, through theatre, resonates powerfully. Being given the responsibility of performing these characters differs from past characters I've played because not only did these people exist in time and place, their voice-dialogue holds the truth and fact of that moment.
>
> I love the power of theatre because it takes us out of our analytical mind and into the shared sensorial experience of storytelling. This is exemplified in the verbatim script of Coranderrk where the analytical function is altered because there are few questions to be answered with regard to the truth of the script, in contrast with fictional or interpretive stories where both actors and audience question the truths that are portrayed. This was most apparent during the Q&A sessions after performances. The questions were mainly focused on the personal experiences of the actors in performing this historical play and, how the script came to be put together, not the authenticity of the material.
>
> (Melodie Reynolds-Diarra, actor, *CWWSC*)

Through the re-performance of the actual testimonies that were delivered at the 1881 Coranderrk inquiry, *CWWSC* enables present-day audiences to connect with this remarkable episode in Victorian history. The production, which has been performed On Country and in public, and will be made available to the Victorian secondary school curriculum from early 2015, is thus central to two of the key aims of the 'Minutes of Evidence' project: to raise awareness of historical and structural injustice and to promote new modes of publicly engaging with it. The unique character of *CWWSC* is traceable, as Melodie Reynolds-Diarra suggests above, to its dualistic nature – it is a factual historical piece based on primary source materials, yet it is also a piece of theatre that conjures emotion, activates the senses and enables audiences to connect with and be moved by the history being depicted. It offers audiences an accessible and engaging means of experiencing a personal connection with the voices of the past; allowing those voices to speak again to contemporary Australian audiences, and enabling such audiences to form their own interpretation of the history and voices enacted.

The dualistic nature of *CWWSC* is a function of its status as a verbatim-style theatre production. Verbatim theatre, a form of so-called 'documentary theatre', involves the re-performance of the words used by certain people (as they were recorded in interviews, diaries, legal proceedings or transcripts from an inquiry from a century prior) as a theatrical piece.[20] These testimonies are edited, arranged or re-contextualised to form a dramatic presentation, in which actors play the characters of the actual individuals whose words are being used.[21] In this vein, the *CWWSC* production is an 80-minute theatre performance wholly constructed around the edited testimonies and statements, petitions and letters delivered in the context of the Coranderrk inquiry, as they were recorded in the official minutes of evidence.[22] In total, the script comprises the testimonies of nine Indigenous witnesses and 10 non-Indigenous witnesses and the statements of two of the non-Indigenous commissioners who undertook the questioning at the inquiry.

Reflecting the synthesis between the historical and theatrical worlds that underscores the production, the script was prepared collaboratively, by historian, Giordano Nanni, and Yorta Yorta playwright, Andrea James. First piloted in August 2010 in the form of a rehearsed reading, *CWWSC* has gradually grown into a fully fledged theatrical production that was first presented to the

---

20 See Carol Martin, 'Bodies of Evidence', *TDR: The Drama Review* 50(3), 2006: 8–15; Derek Paget, 'Verbatim theatre: oral history and documentary techniques', *New Theatre Quarterly* 3(12), 1987: 317–336. The production could also be framed as a form of documentary theatre known as 'tribunal theatre'. Indeed, *Coranderrk* represents a blend of both tribunal and verbatim theatre – centred upon the testimonies delivered at a legal inquiry, rather than personal interviews or memoirs (resembling tribunal theatre), yet not striving theatrically to exactly replicate the physical conditions of this inquiry (thus departing from strict tribunal theatre and evincing the artistic license more associated with verbatim theatre). See Alison Forsyth and Chris Megson, 'Introduction', in Alison Forsyth and Chris Megson (eds), *Get Real: Documentary Theatre Past and Present*, Palgrave MacMillan, Houndmills, 2009: 1–5; Derek Paget, 'The "broken tradition" of documentary theatre and its continued powers of endurance', in Alison Forsyth and Chris Megson (eds), *Get Real: Documentary Theatre Past and Present*, Palgrave MacMillan, Houndmills, 2009: 224–238.
21 Will Hammond and Dan Steward, *Verbatim Verbatim: Contemporary Documentary Theatre*, Oberon Books, London, 2011: 1.
22 That is, the testimonies and statements from the inquiry are only supplemented by letters that were also submitted to the inquiry – and some newspaper reports of the testimony/inquiry.

public in November 2011 at the La Mama Courthouse Theatre by the ILBIJERRI Theatre Company in association with the 'Minutes of Evidence' project and its various partners. The pilot production was directed by Rachael Maza (Artistic Director of ILBIJERRI Theatre Company) and developed in collaboration with Liz Jones (La Mama Theatre), with the second stage of *CWWSC*'s development being directed by Isaac Drandic (also of ILBIJERRI Theatre Company). *CWWSC* brings together a cast of four Aboriginal, and five non-Aboriginal actors, who have shifted throughout time, as their availability permits. The production is therefore an inherently collaborative endeavour, which has sought to embody the spirit of Aboriginal and non-Aboriginal collaboration that it depicts.[23]

At a basic level, the performance raises awareness of the history of the Coranderrk Aboriginal station, and of nineteenth-century colonial Victoria more generally, amongst the broader community. Since its pilot phase, *CWWSC* has attracted close to 3,000 audience members, enabling broad public engagement with both the story of Coranderrk and the primary source historical material on which it is based. Moreover, it presents this history in a new and innovative way. It is now widely acknowledged that different fictional and non-fictional representations of suffering and injustice, from memoirs to feature films to documentary films, offer different ways of connecting with such experiences.[24] As Derbyshire and Hodson note,[25] at a time when there is a generalised concern with the 'indifference' or 'compassion fatigue' of global audiences to stories of suffering,[26] mediums such as theatre have the ability to successfully engage spectators on an emotional and affective level. Theatre and performance provide a new way for audiences to relate to events, stories and experiences, one which foregrounds emotion, imagination and affect.[27]

The mode of connection facilitated by *CWWSC* is a function of its character as both a historical work and a piece of theatre. As a piece of verbatim theatre, the production innovatively unites the creative and emotive elements of theatre with the authority and authenticity of the archive.[28] That is, verbatim theatre has an overt claim to truth, positioning itself as an expression, a re-enactment,

---

23 This character of the performance (as collaboration on- and off-stage) was highlighted by its creator, Giordano Nanni, as well as being mentioned in the historical introduction to the initial stagings of the performance delivered by academic Tony Birch.
24 Kay Schaffer and Sidonie Smith, *Human Rights and Narrated Lives: The Ethics of Recognition*, Palgrave MacMillan, New York, 2004; Paola Botham, 'Witnesses in the public sphere: *Bloody Sunday* and the redefinition of political theatre', in Susan C Haedicke, Deirdre Heddom, Avraham Oz and EJ Westlake (eds), *Political Performances: Theory and Practice*, Rodopi, Amsterdam, 2009: 35–55.
25 Harry Derbyshire and Loveday Hodson, 'Performing injustice: Human rights and verbatim theatre', *Law and Humanities* 2(2), 2008: 207.
26 See Susan D Moeller, *Compassion Fatigue: How the Media Sell Disease, Famine, War and Death*, Routledge, New York, 1999; Keith Tester, *Moral Culture*, Sage Publications, London, 1997.
27 Derbyshire and Hodson, 'Performing injustice'.
28 See Botham, 'Witnesses in the public sphere'.

of actual testimonies and events.[29] Importantly, though, the power of verbatim theatre is inseparable from its claim to truth; the power of a performance such as *CWWSC* stems from its self-representation and audience reception as a direct re-performance of the actual words spoken by Aboriginal and non-Aboriginal witnesses in late nineteenth-century Victoria. As Melodie Reynolds-Diarra observes above, 'Coranderrk holds the weight of fact which, through theatre, resonates powerfully'. It is the facticity of the testimonies that – at least, in part – enables them to inspire emotions, such as shock, disavowal and respect, in the audience.

The verbatim nature of the evidence is also crucial in a context such as Australia, where there have been many destructive and divisive debates about the accuracy of 'revisionist' accounts of Aboriginal history and particularly Aboriginal oppression.[30] It acts as an implicit rebuttal to the claims and speakers that seek to downplay the actuality of disadvantage, dispossession and discrimination both historically and in contemporary times. It is the factual basis of this production that also underpins its role as an educational and informative tool.[31] A key contribution of the performance is its capacity to provide audiences with a substantiated picture of particular interactions between Aboriginal and non-Aboriginal communities in nineteenth-century Australia as well as the discriminatory attitudes that prevailed. Leaving, as Melodie Reynolds-Diarra notes, 'few questions to be answered with regard to the truth of the script', *CWWSC* exposes audiences to the history of the Coranderrk station in a way that has the capacity to side-step unproductive debates about the 'reality' of the claims being advanced in order to provide audiences with an opportunity to connect with these historical events and the broader trends of colonial governance that they reflect.

Indeed, *CWWSC* draws attention to various themes that facilitate a more comprehensive understanding of the realities of colonial governance in Victoria. First, the testimonies incorporated into the production provide a snapshot of the prejudice and injustice experienced by Aboriginal peoples and communities. The statements of European witnesses, such as Edward Curr (an influential member of the Board for the Protection of Aborigines), stand as evidence of the racist discourse that prevailed at the time and informed colonial policies.

---

29 See Derbyshire and Hodson, 'Performing injustice'; Botham, 'Witnesses in the public sphere'.
30 Keith Windschuttle, *The Fabrication of Aboriginal History: Van Diemen's Land 1803–1847*, Macleay Press, Sydney, 2002; Stuart Macintyre and Anna Clark, *The History Wars*, Melbourne University Press, Melbourne, 2003; Robert Manne (ed), *Whitewash: On Keith Windschuttle's Fabrication of Aboriginal History*, Black Ink Agenda, Melbourne, 2003.
31 See, more generally, Derbyshire and Hodson, 'Performing injustice'; Paget, 'The "broken tradition" of documentary theatre and its continued powers of endurance'.

9. The 'Minutes of Evidence' project

Through Curr's testimony, it becomes clear how Aboriginal people were seen and treated as 'less than' their European counterparts, as not possessing the capacity for reason and emotion and thus childlike, as in the following excerpts:

Q: I suppose the blacks have the common human affections to places – would not they form an attachment to a place?

A: No, I do not think so.

...

Q: Did you ever consult the blacks about the question [of their removal from Coranderrk]?

A: No.

Q: Do you think that is fair?

A: Most decidedly for their good.

Q: Are they children?

A: Yes.

Q: Are they not men?

A: No, they are children. They have no more self-reliance than children.

Q: If they offend against the law are they punished like children?

A: No, like men.

Q: Is that just?

A: I did not make the laws.[32]

These excerpts also reveal the 'ambivalent' and contradictory character of colonial discourse and its constitutive stereotypes,[33] which rely on the characterisation of Indigenous people as *both* childlike and fully responsible in order to facilitate their oppression. The distinct exploitation characteristic of settler colonialism is also highlighted through a recurring theme throughout the testimonies of the refusal of the Board to fence the land around the Coranderrk station, arguably undermining any community claims to ownership of the land.

---

32 *Report of the Coranderrk Inquiry*, Minutes of Evidence: 121.
33 See Homi Bhabha, *The Location of Culture*, Routledge, London, 1994: 94–95, 118.

As Wolfe has emphasised, such an appropriation of land is key to the settler colonial enterprise, in which the authority and existence of the settler colonial state is – in part – a function of its literal occupation of a certain territory.[34]

Secondly, though, *CWWSC* also testifies to the resistance of Aboriginal people to colonial repression. The words spoken by the Aboriginal witnesses at the inquiry stand as evidence of the continued sense of dignity and agency maintained by Aboriginal peoples and communities in the face of the indignities and exploitation of settler colonial life. Thus, residents of Coranderrk, such as Alice Grant, testify to their refusal to partake in relations of discrimination:

A: I used to do Mrs. Strickland's ironing, but I do not do it now.

Q: Did you refuse to do it?

A: Yes.

Q: Were you receiving wages for doing it?

A: No.

Q: Why did you refuse?

A: Because I did not want to do it.[35]

The resilience of Aboriginal communities, who steadfastly maintained a commitment to self-determination and resisted settler colonial attempts to destroy a sense of their political and social independence, is also well-expressed by the testimony of Coranderrk's acknowledged leader and spokesperson, William Barak. Articulating what it was the Coranderrk residents sought through their deputations to Melbourne and their testimony at the commission of inquiry, Barak explains that they would like it if 'the Government leave us here, give us this ground and let us manage here and get all the money. Why do not the people do it themselves – do what they like, and go on and do the work?'[36]

Thirdly, *CWWSC* also testifies to the collaboration between Aboriginal and non-Aboriginal people. Through the words of Anne Bon and John Green (as well as John Harris and George A Syme) it becomes clear that not all Europeans embraced the racialised and discriminatory discourse and practice of settler colonial life. John Green's testimony, for example, provides a markedly different account of Aboriginal communities than that of Curr and thus a window onto the existence of a different mode of relation. In his testimony, Green states 'I

---

34 Wolfe, 'Nation and MiscegeNation: discursive continuinty in the post-Mabo era'.
35 *Report of the Coranderrk Inquiry*, Minutes of Evidence: 68.
36 *Report of the Coranderrk Inquiry*, Minutes of Evidence: 9.

always treated them as free men, and reasoned with them ... If the Aboriginal is put into the question, he will strive to keep his own law. That is where I consider you have failed.'[37]

This sense of mutual respect and collaboration is also, importantly, expressed through the actions and words of the Aboriginal community at Coranderrk, in their petition to the inquiry, which advances the following demands:

> We want the Board and the Inspector, Captain Page, to be no longer over us. We want only one man here, and that is Mr. John Green, and the station to be under the Chief Secretary; then *we will show the country* that the station could self-support itself.[38]

It is this demand that thus informs the subtitle for the production and positions this re-telling of history as one that seeks to recognise and draw attention to not only Aboriginal exploitation but also the possibility that matters could have been otherwise.

Of course, in drawing attention to these themes, the script and production provide a particular picture of the 1881 inquiry. They are necessarily selective, incorporating some witnesses and some testimony, but not others – the production is not a literal restaging of the entire inquiry. Importantly, the script achieves a balance between Aboriginal and European testimony – a balance that does not reflect the composition of the actual minutes of evidence, which is dominated by European witnesses. In this way, although the translation of the inquiry archives into a shorter, thematic work could be said to qualify the 'truth claim' of verbatim theatre, it is this artistic and historical re-engagement with the primary source documents that contributes to the theatrical power and strength of *CWWSC*. As Martin explains, it is through such choices (in our case, the choice to focus on key themes of colonial governance and collaboration, and to ensure that the voices of the Aboriginal witnesses were heard) that 'the creative work of documentary theatre gets done'.[39]

Moreover, in relying on the actual words that were spoken, and were recorded as being spoken, at the 1881 inquiry, the production still maintains a connection to the 'real' and the 'actual'.[40] These testimonies, despite their arrangement, composition and rendition in the performance, are real; as Melodie Reynolds-Diarra observes of the characters and their testimony, 'not only did these people exist in time and place, their voice-dialogue holds the truth and fact of that

---

37 *Report of the Coranderrk Inquiry*, Minutes of Evidence: 135–136.
38 *Report of the Coranderrk Inquiry*, Minutes of Evidence: 98 (emphasis added).
39 Martin, 'Bodies of evidence': 9. For reflections of the writers on the process of crafting the verbatim script of the play see, Nanni & James, *Coranderrk: We Will Show The Country*: 198–200.
40 See Freddie Rokem, *Performing History: Theatrical Representations of the Past in Contemporary Theatre*, University of Iowa Press, Iowa City, 2000.

moment'. Similarly, writing of another verbatim performance, Simić vividly explains that '[a]lthough a representation of reality and not reality itself, in the performance the audience is reminded that what happened *was a reality*'.[41] In a similar vein, *CWWSC*, although it is a representation of the inquiry and the testimonies delivered there, still gains much of its power from the fact that this inquiry occurred and these testimonies were delivered, speaking to the injustices that occurred, the justice that was sought and the Indigenous and non-Indigenous relations and collaborations that informed such claims.

The contribution of *Coranderrk:* Engendering connections with history for change

> I am passionate about theatre as a medium because it is true to storytelling, where a human being is standing in front of another human being, sharing the air, emotion and wisdom. In Coranderrk, the story that is told takes both the audience and performer on a journey that connects the present to the past, thereby creating a better understanding of our history.
>
> (Melodie Reynolds-Diarra, actor, *CWWSC*)

The *CWWSC* performance highlights the story of Coranderrk as one of historical injustice. In doing so, it has the potential to catalyse public conversations about structural and historical Indigenous injustice in Australia and elsewhere. Audience responses from the performances have been an acknowledgement of the injustices perpetrated and the colonial framework that perpetrated them. The performances have also provided a space for reflection on the continuation of this colonial framework, and the continuities in practices of repression and governance. Such focused engagement can be an important adjunct to the pursuit of more formal legal avenues for redress and reform, effectively supporting the capacity of Australians 'to imagine new paths for moving forward and ... our willingness to overcome any political obstacles'.[42] Verbatim theatre thus functions here as a site and an opportunity for these 'new imaginings', acting as a 'meeting point'. Botham explains how theatre can act as a 'meeting point' for audience members, whilst she and others note the historical role of the theatre (as well as the courtroom, or tribunal venue) as a forum for putting forward claims relating to justice and injustice.[43] In this sense, the audience – who

---

41 Olivera Simić, 'Breathing sense into women's lives shattered by war: Dah Theatre Belgrade', *Law Text Culture* 14(1), 2010: 122.
42 Sean Brennan, Brenda Gunn and George Williams, '"Sovereignty" and its relevance to treaty-making between Indigenous peoples and Australian governments', *Sydney Law Review* 26, 2004: 352.
43 Botham, 'Witnesses in the public sphere': 36. See also Derbyshire and Hodson, 'Performing injustice'.

collectively experience the *CWWSC* performance – is brought together to hear and respond to the claims for justice articulated as part of the 1881 inquiry and the injustices of which they speak.

Through bringing historical figures so powerfully back to life, *CWWSC* re-enacts the past, and thus enables audience members to experience an understanding of the past in the present. This both facilitates a more direct connection between contemporary audiences and historical events, as well as providing ground for links and connections to be drawn between such events and current conditions.[44] In the context of the 'Minutes of Evidence' project, this places past Aboriginal injustice in relation to contemporary Aboriginal disadvantage, acknowledging what Cunneen and Baldry have referred to as the 'unbroken chain'.[45] Such temporal connections have been drawn by people who have seen the production, who have related the *CWWSC* experience to the ongoing Northern Territory Intervention. The Federal government's lack of consultation (despite the explicit recommendations for genuine consultation of the *Little Children Are Sacred* report), and its introduction of degrading income-management policies designed to control the lives of Aboriginal people, reverberates strongly in the paternalistic tone assumed by the Board for the Protection of Aborigines' attempts to control the lives of Aboriginal people at Coranderrk. As Addendum B to the Coranderrk inquiry's report stated, Aboriginal people 'must be, from the nature of the case, the least capable people of all persons in deciding how or by whom the station should be managed'.[46]

The testimony of Edward Curr is particularly significant in terms of highlighting the structural continuities between past and present, given that in recent years his voice has been re-invoked in official settings to justify the continuation of Indigenous dispossession into the twenty-first century. Curr's testimony during the Coranderrk inquiry offers a clear example of colonial governance's refusal to acknowledge Aboriginal rights to self-determination:

Q: Would you think it desirable to send them away from Coranderrk against their own will?

A: Anyone who knows the blacks knows their will is nothing, that they might have a serious objection now which they would not remember three months afterwards. I would suggest that they should be moved for their own benefit. I would not leave them to acquire habits of drink under the mistaken philanthropy of not interfering with them.[47]

---

44 See Rokem, *Performing History*.
45 Eileen Baldry and Chris Cunneen, 'Contemporary Penality in the Shadow of Colonial Patriarchy', *Proceedings of the 5th Annual Australian and New Zealand Critical Criminology Conference*, James Cook University, Townsville, 1(1), 2012.
46 *Report of the Coranderrk Inquiry*, Addendum B: vii.
47 *Report of the Coranderrk Inquiry*, Minutes of Evidence: 20.

As many historians know, in the *Yorta Yorta* native title judgment (1998), Federal Court Justice Olney relied heavily on Edward Curr's memoir, *Recollections of Squatting in Victoria* (published in 1883, just two years after Curr's participation at the Coranderrk inquiry) in formulating his final ruling: that Yorta Yorta title to, and connections with, ancestral lands had been 'washed away' by 'the tide of history' before the end of the nineteenth century.[48] Relying uncritically on Curr's nostalgic memoir, rather than the oral evidence submitted by contemporary Yorta Yorta claimants to demonstrate the continuity of culture from pre-colonial times, Justice Olney claimed that Curr had 'clearly established a degree of rapport with the local Aboriginal people'.[49] Historians have already highlighted Justice Olney's problematic use of Curr's *Recollections of Squatting in Victoria* in the *Yorta Yorta* native title case: Samuel Furphy, for instance, who documents Olney's uncritical elevation of Curr's writings to the status of 'credible primary evidence', advocates 'the need for a critical appraisal of Curr, his life, his biases, his opinions and attitudes to Aboriginal people'.[50] Whilst historians have argued this case in scholarly forums, the general public remains almost entirely unaware of how compromised and ill-judged Olney's reliance on Curr was. But audiences who attended *CWWSC* were able to hear Curr's words and ideas brought back to life; and *they* were left in little doubt as to his actual opinions of and rapport with Aboriginal people.

Redress of structural and historical injustice requires recognition that it occurred. A first step towards redressing structural injustice is heightening public awareness of its existence – a difficult process given the controversy that has often surrounded attempts to acknowledge structural injustice in Australia, such as the apology to Stolen Generations and the ongoing debate about reparations. What this performance seeks to do is to integrate these historical realities back into public discourse, and thus to provide a basis for discussions about the necessity for redress and reform – a new structural justice.

Bringing history back to life

The popularisation of historical stories, through documentaries, films, theatre and other mediums, has the potential to engage broader Australian audiences with the nation's colonial past and its ongoing implications. Yet, in certain

---

48   Wayne Atkinson (Yorta Yorta Native Title Claimant) 2000, '19 Seconds of Dungudja Wala: Reflections Paper on The Yorta Yorta Native Title Judgment', www.kooriweb.org/sljr/dungudjawala.htm, accessed 30 November 2012.
49   The Members of the Yorta Yorta Aboriginal Community v The State of Victoria (1998), Federal Court of Australia, 1606, para. 53.
50   Samuel Furphy, 'Edward Micklethwaite Curr's *Recollections of Squatting*: Biography, history and native title', in Penelope Edmonds and Samuel Furphy (eds), *Rethinking Colonial Histories: New and Alternative Approaches*, History Department, The University of Melbourne, Melbourne, 2006: 39.

circumstances, the imperatives to entertain that shape such public and popular accounts of Australia's past can result in historically inaccurate narratives, in which historical facts are altered or glossed over for dramatic effect. The *CWWSC* production seeks both to facilitate broad public engagement with a unique, yet little known, episode of Victorian colonial history and to do so in a way that is historically and empirically grounded. This is one of the key ways in which the 'Minutes of Evidence' project seeks to expand the field of engagement with the notion and practice of history. To this end, it is crucial that the power of the *CWWSC* production stems from both its theatrical attributes and its historical credentials; through the medium of theatre, *CWWSC* brings audiences into a closer relation with the historical archive and what it reveals about colonial Victoria. The strength of *CWWSC* thus is a function of the remarkable history that it depicts, the theatrical re-enactment of the personal testimonies delivered there and the commitment of all the project's partners to re-perform these testimonies with a sense of loyalty to the history they are portraying and its significance. This sense of loyalty is expressed again by Melodie Reynolds-Diarra who explains the nature of re-performing these historical testimonies in the present as follows:

> The honour of recreating Coranderrk is both nervous and exhilarating knowing that their descendants are in the audience watching. I felt the responsibility to be almost a conduit, where the challenge was to put aside my modern day attitudes and thoughts and let the words tell the story. Doing this, the audience is given the opportunity to form their own impression of the depicted events.

The next stage for the 'Minutes of Evidence' project is already underway. Overseen by DEECD, and in collaboration with VAEAI, Social Education Victoria is making the 1881 Coranderrk Inquiry and its key themes of dispossession, justice and collaboration available to the secondary school curriculum, where it will help to familiarise future generations of Victorians with the history of their own backyard. Students will be exposed to primary historical materials; to the language, ideas, opinions and official government policies that were once commonly adopted towards Aboriginal people to evidence of collaboration between Aboriginal and non-Aboriginal people; and crucially, to the voices of Aboriginal people in the nineteenth century, which are often conspicuously absent from historical records. The project therefore continues to broaden the field of engagement with Victoria's colonial past through engaging students and teachers, including through the power of verbatim theatre, in a way that is entertaining as well as historically rigorous. Alongside this process, researchers are undertaking comparative and interdisciplinary analysis of the overarching project themes of structural justice and injustice. It is in this way that the

'Minutes of Evidence' project seeks to promote a greater public understanding of Australia's past and spark new conversations about the history and legacy of structural injustice and the possibilities of structural justice in the present.

For information about the project's development into the future, readers may wish to visit the website: www.minutesofevidence.com.au.

www.ingramcontent.com/pod-product-compliance
Lightning Source LLC
Chambersburg PA
CBHW060929170426
43192CB00031B/2881